CHINA IN CONVULSION
VOLUME TWO

By ARTHUR H. SMITH

"Not only two of the *very* best books on China, but two of the *very* best books which have ever been published by *any* author on *any* country at *any* time"—*Dr. Talcott Williams.*

Tenth Thousand
Village Life in China
A Study in Sociology, 8vo, fully illustrated, $2.00.

"Arthur H. Smith has added a second to those extraordinary studies of China life, of which he is so easily master. No book like this has been written on China except one, and that is Dr. Smith's 'Chinese Characteristics.' The two books together may fairly be said to give a clearer idea of China as it is than any or all of the 5,000 or 6,000 works published on the Empire during the last century."—*Philadelphia Press.*

A MAGAZINE OF INFORMATION
"He is an acute observer, a discriminating judge of both people and facts, and an entertaining narrator. No one can begin to understand the Chinese until he has read such a work as this."—*New York Observer.*

Fifteenth Thousand
Chinese Characteristics
New Edition. With 20 full-page illustrations and Index, and characteristic decoration for each chapter. 8vo, cloth, $2.00.

"Those best informed call it without exception the best book on the Chinese that is before the public, and a pretty careful survey of it confirms that opinion."—*The Independent.*

"There is all the difference between an intaglio in onyx and a pencil scrawl on paper to be discovered between Mr. Smith's book and the printed prattle of the average globetrotter. Our author's work has been done, as it were, with a chisel and an emery wheel. He goes deeply beneath the surface."—*The Critic.*

A KEEN ANALYSIS OF CHARACTER
"The book is generally accepted by students in the Far East as not only one of the ablest analyses and portrayals of the Chinese character, but, on the whole, one of the most truthful and judicial."—*The Nation.*

FIRST TRAIN PASSING THROUGH THE WALL OF PEKING

China in Convulsion

BY

ARTHUR H. SMITH

Twenty-nine years a Missionary
of the American Board in China

Author of
"*Chinese Characteristics*" and "*Village Life in China*"

With Numerous Illustrations and Maps

IN TWO VOLUMES
VOLUME TWO

NEW YORK   CHICAGO   TORONTO
FLEMING H. REVELL COMPANY
1901

Copyright 1901
by
FLEMING H. REVELL COMPANY
(November)

LIBRARY
FLORIDA STATE UNIVERSITY
TALLAHASSEE, FLORIDA

Press of
Riggs Printing & Publishing Co.
Albany, N. Y.

CONTENTS

VOLUME II

CHAPTER	PAGE
XX. Siege Life	365
XXI. Days of Waiting	383
XXII. Renewal of the Attack	402
XXIII. The Relief	419
XXIV. From Taku to Peking	435
XXV. The Fortifications	462
XXVI. After the Siege	485
XXVII. Hand of God in the Siege	508
XXVIII. Punishment of Peking	517
XXIX. The Capital in Transformation	535
XXX. Ruin of T'ung Chou	555
XXXI. Tientsin after the Siege	571
XXXII. Foreigners in the Interior	594
XXXIII. Notable Experiences	621
XXXIV. The Catastrophe to the Native Church	650
XXXV. Personal Narratives	665
XXXVI. Fire and Sword in Shansi	207
XXXVII. A Twelve-month of Foreign Occupation	713
XXXVIII. The Outlook	733

LIST OF ILLUSTRATIONS

VOLUME II

	FACING PAGE
First Train Passing Through the Wall of Peking	Title
The "International" Gun, "Our Betsey"	373
Fortified Bridge across the Moat near Legation Street	383
British Legation Gate, Fuel Supply Committee	402
Buddhist Temple and Modern Tram Car	416
Water Gate, Peking, through which Allies Entered	416
"Here They Come," General Gaselee on the Right	432
Fraternizing on the Tennis Court	432
Black Fort at Tientsin, Outside View	446
Black Fort at Tientsin, Inside View	446
Wall of Tientsin After Bombardment	452
Gate Through which Allies entered Tientsin	452
Temple of Heaven, British Headquarters	460
Court, Temple of Heaven, British Headquarters	460
Gateway to British Legation, Moat and Barricade	468
The Six "Fighting Parsons" and Sergeant Murphy at Fort Cockburn	474
Group of American Missionaries present during the Siege	494
Ruins of Presbyterian Mission, Peking	498
Ruins of Methodist Mission, Peking	498
British Legation Wall	502
Chinese Gun Platform for Firing on the Legation	502
Coming out of Church, Legation Grounds	508
Railway Station, Peking	518
Police Station, Peking	518
Chien Men Gate, Peking	522
Ruins of Chien Men Gate	522

LIST OF ILLUSTRATIONS

	FACING PAGE
Y. M. C. A. Headquarters, Peking	528
Street Panorama, Peking	528
Coal Hill, Chinese Serving German Officers	532
Summer Palace from the Lake	532
Tartar Wall, Location of Astronomical Observatory	545
Temple of Agriculture, Peking, American Headquarters	548
Entrance Temple of Agriculture, American Headquarters	548
North China College, T'ung Chou	558
American Board Mission, Tientsin	576
American Board Mission, Tientsin, after the Siege	576
Arsenal, Tientsin	586
Ruins of Roman Catholic Cathedral, Tientsin	586
First British-Chinese Regiment, Wei Hai Wei	590
Russian Troops en route to Peking	590
Pei Tai Ho Watering Place, from which Foreigners were rescued by Consul Fowler	604
Corner of City Wall, Pao Ting Fu, destroyed by Allied Troops in Punishment for Massacre	611
Pastor Meng, a Martyr of Pao Ting Fu	680
Miss Gould of Pao Ting Fu and School Girls	682
Manchu Family, some of them Christians	700
Native Christian Refugee	700
Vicinity of Legation Street, Peking	722
Dr. Ament Receiving Village Deputation	730

MAPS

Map showing routes of Relief Forces	438
Plan of British Legation, Peking	480
Map of seat of Boxer Disturbance	620

XX

SIEGE LIFE

THERE is need of a digression at this point, to explain certain phases of the routine of siege life which are otherwise in danger of being overlooked.

The matter of registration labour supply was one of the first importance. No sooner were the foreigners settled in the Legation and the Chinese in the Su Wang Fu, than a systematic census was begun under the Committee on Registration. The list of foreigners was soon complete and required little revision. That of the Chinese proved for a variety of reasons far more difficult.

Two most important and useful officers in the siege were the Superintendent of Labour and the Registrar. Their work to a large extent dovetailed, the former mainly controlling the Protestant labour supply outside the Legation and the latter the time of every Chinese living within its walls. To the energy, vigilance, kindness, firmness and tact of these two men much of the results achieved is to be attributed. The labour of the Roman Catholics living outside the British Legation, it should be remarked, after an unsatisfactory experiment on the part of the committee, was directed by their priests, and by the French, Japanese and others for whom work was done. The registration put into effect in the Fu was modelled after that which had been found to work successfully in the British Legation.

The demand for labour was clamorous and universal. Many of the Legation servants had fled some time before, and others had to be found for their places. All the numerous housekeepers must have a detail of cooks, table boys and coolies; the hospital required a staff always at the command of the surgeons; there were many horses to be fed and watered; the scavenger and other sanitary work was imperative and, like the bakery and laundry, did not admit of irregular depletion of employees. Some educated native Christians, like the scholar class of Chinese, were unused to manual labour and unfitted for it; but every grade and variety of talent was eventually utilized, especially those able to speak English, who could serve as messengers, interpreters, or overseers. A small percentage of men manifested a rooted and chronic disinclination to active effort, but ere long these idiosyncrasies were dealt with on their real merits.

When the incessant calls for labour had first to be met, much confusion reigned for many days. Let an actual case stand as a sample:

At nine o'clock one evening an order came from Col. Shiba, commanding the Japanese in the Su Wang Fu, for ten men and fifty sand bags for immediate use. The superintendent secured the bags, but could find only four available men. He then waked up another gentleman who, being appointed on a wholly different committee had nothing to do with the present exigency, but assisted on general principles. On arriving at the Fu this gentleman learned that Col. Shiba had already got the men needed from the Roman Catholics near at hand.

Meantime a note had come to the British Legation from the American Captain on the wall, requiring twenty men to raise higher the western wall of the eastern barricade, as the Chinese west barricade was firing into it.

The superintendent excused a lad too small to handle the huge bricks on the wall, and sent the same obliging substitute with the three men on hand to aid the band that were kept permanently in the American Legation for emergencies, but happened on this occasion already to have been working all day. When he arrived there the Captain who gave the order had been relieved, and his successor in charge knew nothing about any call for men, but informed the conductor of the workmen that it had been decided to postpone the work until daylight, when it would be done better. The ad interim assistant, the superintendent and the Chinese were then enabled to retire for what remained of the night.

Perhaps a summons arrived from the French to construct an important barricade. No men could be found, for it was late at night, when the labour market, especially the free labour market, is generally closed. A visit to the Fu disclosed numbers of Chinese lying about, but each one proved to have some cherished and dangerous malady. One is the victim of a persistent diarrhœa, another shows by a limp that his lower leg is broken in two places, the crepitation of the bones being, as he alleges, distinctly audible; not, however, to the trained ear of the foreign examiner, who soon ascertains that the man is after all able to walk. Some deserve to be excused, but by degrees, between boys and men, the order is filled and they are sent to work.

The superintendent is no more than back at the Legation, ready for bed after an exhausting day's work in reducing order from chaos, when a request comes for ten men immediately to work all night on a new and important barricade in the Hanlin Yuan. No one but the superintendent can find the men, and to the summons of no one else will they respond. Once more the Fu must be visited and every sleeping room entered with a lantern. In the darkness dusky forms are dimly seen prone upon the k'angs. Here the drafting process is repeated, until at length the required number is obtained, but in transit through so many courtyards and in crossing the canal in the darkness it turns out that three out of the ten have escaped, and being unknown they cannot be identified. At a later period every man had his number not only entered on the register but sewed upon his clothing, so that evasion of duty like this became impossible.

About midnight one hears a great disturbance and angry remonstrances. The weary registrar is roused from his slumbers by an urgent demand for seventeen of the short shovels used by marines, wanted at once by somebody in another Legation. After an hour's hard work and a visit to every place where digging is known to have been prosecuted the day before, some of them are found, but upon being brought in as a part of what is wanted are refused, for they have not the serrated edges of the Austrian shovels. In the renewed search every doubtful spot is approached with a lantern.

"Put out that light," cries a sentry, with the addition of emphatic language. He is informed that the search is being conducted under official orders and will be continued until the required articles are found.

At a later stage, the duty of a ship's yeoman is added to that of the registrar, and the tools, as far as possible, had to be called in at night and kept in a box near the bell tower. Under careless Chinese use, spades, shovels, and picks, of which the supply was originally lamentably small and for which the demand was general and insistent, have their handles broken off and are rendered useless. The assistant registrar afterward added to his many other functions that of general repairer, and as far as possible counteracted the ravages of the wasteful coolie. The Chinese carpenters were kept busy making handles, as also the blacksmiths in their efforts to point iron rods so as to serve as picks or crowbars.

As the result of an orderly evolution of registry every Chinese on the premises came to be known not only by name but by his reputation; the better and more thorough workmen requiring little or no supervision, the lazy and inefficient ones needing constant stimulus. Each man was provided with a ticket good for that day only, entitling him to one meal or to two, according to the amount of work done. When he had finished his work and eaten his meal he returned to his family in the Fu. After the Fu was mostly lost, and it became necessary to remove the Protestants to the vacant houses between the canal and the American Legation, the task of getting labour was much expedited. Those liable to night work were then kept on the premises where they were needed, and where they could not escape. If a man living in the Fu were derelict in his work at the Legation his pass was taken away and he could not get out to return to his family, a punishment generally quite sufficient, as their food depended upon him.

Some Chinese were fortunate or provident enough to have food supplies of their own, which rendered them in a measure independent. In a solitary instance a man of some education after persistently refusing to work, and repeated warnings, was at last tied to a post with his hands behind him, there to remain until his views upon the relation of military law to muscular activity and to rations became materially modified, which happened within a few hours.

The carelessness of the Chinese in everywhere knocking out the burning ashes of their pipes, made it necessary to forbid smoking in buildings. Those guilty of violating this rule were put on duty for four-and-twenty hours continuously. In an especially aggravated case the cook of one of the Legations was discovered to have built a fire of a dangerous and unlawful kind late at night, to see how to take care of his child. At whatever inconvenience to individuals the authority of the committee, found by experience to be just and wholesome, was sustained against all appeals, of which, however, there were but few. Those liable to punishment were sent to whatever work was most urgent; if it chanced that for the time there was none such, they might temporarily escape.

But however perfect the system of registration and labour supply, the simultaneous demand for details of men who were not available necessarily made many hitches in the progress of military work. Thus six men were detailed for labour on fortifications in the Hanlin, but at that juncture a pile of sand bags had fallen in a heavy shower from a hospital window into a gutter, stopping the drainage. The six men were deflected from the less to the more pressing task, but while on the way one of them was called off to carry to the Chinese hospital a woman who in a time of special danger had been shot in crossing the canal from the Fu.

The need of labour made it necessary to require from every able-bodied Chinese two hours' work each day for the public, which often proved irksome alike to servants, mistress and superintendents.

Against this requisition, which was later supplemented by another for the whole time of one or more of the large staff of servants, some employers were disposed to remonstrate vigorously. One gentleman who had at first been very energetic in his coöperation, at a later period asked a detail of men for the purpose of getting his private dwelling ready for a rain, and still later for two labourers to clear up the grounds of the Russian Legation. The unforgetting Registrar recollecting that two of this gentleman's servants had for some time evaded duty, went to his kitchen and called them out. They objected that they were not liable, as they did not live in the British but in the Russian Legation.

"Exactly," was the reply, "there is where you are to work," and the amazed and abused master was then presented with two of his own servants to do his own work in his own Legation!

The work done by the besieged Christians, often hard and exhausting, in no case rewarded with anything more than a bare subsistence, was in general performed with characteristic Chinese patience and perseverance, many of them, under the tireless supervision of foreigners, throwing into it much energy, and in some cases considerable skill.

Indeed their behaviour was almost uniformly admirable. Instead of being a dead-weight to be carried by foreigners as many of these besieged feared they would be, they were soon found to be an indispensable means to the salvation of the rest, and except they had abode in the ship none would have been saved. As in all large bodies collected at random, there were some black sheep, and many speckled ones, but as a rule the patient, uncomplaining fidelity of the Christians in toilsome tasks under dangerous conditions was beyond praise. The steadiness under constant attacks, and in the midst of repeated removals from one unsafe place to another, manifested by the Chinese women, and especially by the 120 and more school girls, were also noteworthy. Many Chinese were furnished with rifles, and fought at the loop-holes side by side with the plucky and soldierly Japanese, winning even their cordial commendation. A good number were killed in posts of danger, many others were struck by the innumerable flying bullets, two of the best helpers of the Methodists—one of them an ordained pastor—falling at the same time.

Many others fell victims to disease, and probably a score or two of poor Chinese children died from disease aggravated by mal-nutrition, but the mothers bore their deep grief with Christian fortitude, and uttered no word of reproach to the Fate in which all non-Christian Chinese have a firm faith, but rather thanked the Heavenly Father for such mercies as they still enjoyed.

Each day there was a gathering both of Chinese and foreigners upon the lawn, to examine the growing pile of clothing and other stuff brought into the Legation. This may be a fitting opportunity to explain in detail the method of dealing with confiscated goods. The area enclosed by the numerous Legations being extensive, it was inevitable that many Chinese families who had no connection either with foreigners or with the Boxers should find themselves gradually encircled with troops, making entrance and exit increasingly difficult, and a prosecution of their ordinary business impossible.

As time went on most of these families became alarmed at the outlook and fled while it was not yet too late, some of them, however, leaving behind trustworthy servants to look after their premises. But numberless dwelling houses and many shops were absolutely deserted, some of the latter being well stocked with goods of many sorts, and many of the former being well furnished. In the confusion of the time it was inevitable that many shops and houses should be exposed to raids from neighbours who remained, as well as from needy Christians, many of

THE "INTERNATIONAL" GUN "OUR BETSEY"

whom had fled for their lives with only the clothing which they wore.

Soon after the general gathering into the British Legation, when it became necessary to check promiscuous pillage and to secure a wise use of the miscellaneous articles thus placed within reach, Dr. Ament was appointed a committee with plenary powers. An impromptu depository of second-hand clothing was established on the tennis court lawn, resembling the storeroom of a Chinese pawnshop. For many days it supplied hundreds of Chinese with clothing and bedding for themselves and their families, until the demand appeared to be fairly met. But many Chinese were unable while at work to guard their possessions, and others ruined their clothes in the heavy rains, or while labouring in the damp trenches or on the wall; these had to be resupplied, yet still the inflow kept on. Foreigners, too, drew liberally from the same source, until the superintendence of the business became a heavy load of responsibility and care.

When there was a scarcity of material for sand bags the Chinese women cut apart many wadded garments, whose legs and arms, filled with earth, were used to add to the prophylactic embankments on the walls and housetops. In quest of bag material, scores (perhaps hundreds) of Chinese houses were entered, but nothing was anywhere taken by force. Some of these dwellings had already been visited and largely despoiled, but others were fresh fields and pastures new. A great variety of articles which at first appeared to have no relation to the wants of a beleaguered garrison, ultimately proved to be most useful, especially tools from a blacksmith's shop and an old Chinese cannon nicknamed " Betsy," or " The International." Some of the abandoned dwellings had been forsaken in hot haste, and contained elegant garments, pieces of silk, furs, valuable chinaware, clocks and curios. A large quantity of such articles was found in the Su Wang Fu. One of the Japanese barricades was largely composed of trunks full of priceless raiment, seized as the most available material; all of this was ruined by contact with earth, or by rains, or was destroyed in the fires.

The Christians lodged in the Su Wang Fu gave early information of the probable concealment of a considerable quantity of sycee silver, which was brought away and stored in the strong room of the British Legation until the close of the siege. Small guns were also found in some of the shops, and also many irredeemable bank bills. On one occasion about seventy taels was discovered in a coal pile, and other amounts were doubtless confiscated by the Chinese on their own account.

The owners of two foreign stores on Legation Street decided to abandon them, bringing into the Legation whatever could be saved. As the siege became closer and the risk in visiting the stores became evident by the whistling of bullets and the killing of one of the workmen, the owner of the larger one gave notice that whoever wished to take any of the remaining articles was welcome to do so. It was an unfortunate and ill-judged step, which for a few days made looting legal, and so facilitated the universal diffusion of intoxicating liquors that an order was soon issued forbidding any one whatever to visit the place without the express permission of the General Committee. Thereafter, the articles rescued were put into the hands of a commissariat and issued only upon due requisition, a course which should have been adopted from the first.

During the brief reign of unchecked lawlessness the general demoralization was very great. Many messes of poor Chinese ate their rice out of broken crockery, but with the addition perhaps of a plate-glass mirror set in a plush frame, or a cut-glass syrup pitcher flanked by a marble clock. The commissariat issued not only stores and utensils but everything which came to hand. All the memoranda of the progress of the siege were entered in note books, with pencil or pen and ink, all of which had been secured by application to the obliging supply committee. One had but to make his necessities sufficiently known to insure such a supply for them as the case admitted, for the besieged in a most literal sense had all things common.

The bulletin boards, where were posted the translations of the "Peking Gazettes" obtained during the armistice, were surrounded for days with a crowd that exhibited the keenest interest in the utterances of that unique publication. Many of these were printed many weeks before, but some of them were highly important, and most of them quite new.

The most important utterance among them was a decree issued the day after the murder of the German Minister, but significantly making no reference whatever to that occurrence. It is a window through which the Chinese side of the international question may be seen. It ran as follows:

"Ever since the foundation of the dynasty, foreigners coming to China have been kindly treated. In the reign of Tao Kuang and Hsian Fêng they were allowed to trade; they also asked leave to propagate their religion, a request which the Throne reluctantly granted. At first they were amenable to Chinese control, but for the past thirty years they have taken advantage of China's forbearance to encroach on China's territory and trample on the Chinese people and to demand China's wealth. Every concession made by China increased their reliance on violence. They oppressed peaceful citizens and insulted the gods and holy men, exciting the most burning indignation among the people. Hence the destruction of the chapels and the slaughter of converts by the patriotic braves. The Throne was anxious to avoid war and issued edicts enjoining the protection of the Legations and pity to the converts. The decrees declaring Boxers and converts to be equally the children of the State were issued with the hope of removing the old feud between people and converts and extreme kindness was shown to the strangers from afar.

"But these people knew no gratitude and increased their pressure. A despatch was yesterday sent by Du Chaylard, Doyen of the Consular body at Tientsin, calling on us to deliver up the Taku forts into their keeping, otherwise they would be taken by force. These threats show their aggressions. In all matters relating to international intercourse we have never been wanting in courtesies to them; but they, while styling themselves civilized States, have acted without regard for right, relying solely on their military force.

"We have now reigned nearly thirty years and have treated the people as our children, the people honouring us as their deity; and in the midst of our reign we have been the recipients of the gracious favour of the Empress Dowager. Furthermore our ancestors have come to our aid and the gods have answered to our call, and never has there been so universal a manifestation of loyalty and patriotism. With tears have we announced the war in the ancestral shrines. Better to do our utmost and enter on the struggle than seek some means of self preservation involving eternal disgrace. All our officials, high and low, are of one mind, and there have assembled without official summons several hundred thousand patriotic soldiers [Boxers], even children carrying spears in the service of their country. Those others rely on crafty schemes; our trust is in heaven's justice. They depend on violence, we on humanity. Not to speak of the righteousness of our cause, our provinces number more than twenty, our people over four hundred millions, and it will not be difficult to vindicate the dignity of our country."

Another Decree, in the "Gazette" of June 21st, expresses the satisfaction with which the Throne has received the report of the Governor General of Chihli, Yü Lu, of the successful engagements at Tientsin on the 17th-19th of that month, and gives much praise to the Boxers who have done great services without any assistance either of men or money from the State. Great favour will be shown them later on, and they must continue to show their devotion. The phraseology of the Decrees already cited serve as an excellent specimen of the Janus-faced utterances of the Empress Dowager in regard to the Boxers. They are violators of treaties, have been often rebuked and must now positively disperse, yet a few days later they are loyal and patriotic, and deserve well of their Empress, who will reward them.

On the 24th of June the Board of Revenue is ordered to give Kang I two hundred bags of rice for distribution as provisions among the Boxers. Still another Decree of the same date mentions, as previously quoted, that since the Boxers—now styled " Boxer Militia "—are scattered all around Peking and Tientsin, it is necessary and proper that they should have Superintendents placed over them (in other words be definitely and fully accepted as in the employ of the Chinese Government). Accordingly Prince Chuang, and the Assistant Grand Secretary Kang I were appointed to the general command, Ying Nien to act as brigadier general of the left wing, and Tsai Lan of the right. All the members of the I Ho T'uan (it is remarked) are exerting their utmost energies, and the Imperial Family must not fall behind in harbouring revenge against our enemies. It is Our confident hope that the desires of each and all be successfully consummated, and it is of the utmost importance that no lack of energy be shown.

On the 27th, Edicts commanded Yü Lu to retake the Taku Forts, and to prevent the foreign troops from creeping northward; and ordered the distribution of one hundred thousand taels of silver to the divisions of troops in the Metropolitan districts, and a like sum to the Boxers assisting them.

During these weeks there are frequent references in memorials and in Imperial Decrees to the general lawlessness which had resulted from the encouragement to irresponsible private individuals, as well as to soldiers, to take vengeance. Were there no other proof, these documents alone would show that the Capital and its environs were under a reign of terror, against which there are numerous protests both from Censors and from the Empress herself.

But the mischief is always laid to those who pretended to belong to the Boxer Militia in order to plunder and kill, and it is these (and not the Boxers as a class) who are ordered to be rigorously dealt with. On the 2nd of July another important Edict appeared, under the ægis of which the slaughter of all foreigners, missionaries not more than others, and the extermination of all native Christians who would not recant, became a duty.

"Ever since Foreign Nations began the propagation of their religion there have been instances throughout the country of ill-feeling between the people and the converts. All this is due to faulty administration on the part of local authorities, giving rise to feuds. The truth is that the converts also are children of the State, and among them are not wanting good and worthy people; but they have been led away by false doctrines, and have relied on the missionary for support, with the result that they have committed many misdeeds. They hold to their errors and will not turn from them, and irreconcilable enmity has thus grown up between the converts and the people.

"The Throne is now exhorting every member of the Boxer Militia to render loyal and patriotic service, and to take his part against the enemies of his country, so that the whole population may be of one mind. Knowing that the converts are also subjects owing fealty to the Throne, we also know that they can bring themselves to form a class apart and invite their own destruction. If they can change their hearts there is no reason why they should not be allowed to escape from the net. The Viceroys and Governors of the Provinces are all therefore to give orders to all local officials to issue the following notification: All those among the converts who repent of their former errors and give themselves up to the authorities, shall be allowed to reform, and their past shall be ignored. The public shall also be notified that in all places where converts reside, they shall be allowed to report to the local authorities, and each case will be settled according to general regulations which will be drawn up later.

"As hostilities have now broken out between China and Foreign Nations, the missionaries of every country must be driven away at once to their own countries, so that they may not linger here and make trouble. But it is important that measures be taken to secure their protection on their journey. The high provincial authorities shall make close investigation into the circumstances of all places within their jurisdiction, and speedily take the necessary steps. Let there be no carelessness. (The above Decree is to be circulated for general information.) "

The putting forth of this Edict was doubtless regarded by its authors as the happy issue of a long and doubtful contest, in which China by a few sweeps of a camel's-hair pencil had now obliterated forty years of the Past, and entered upon a new era!

On the 9th of July Li Hung Chang was appointed Viceroy of Chihli, and Superintendent of the Trade which the rulers of China had by this time extinguished in that part of the Empire. Pending Li's arrival, the former Governor General, Yü Lu, was to consult with Prince Ch'ing as to the best measures to be taken, and the latter are warned against a slackening of responsibility.

On the 12th of July Gen. Nieh, who fought near Tientsin, is severely rated for his failures and blunders and deprived of his rank although retained in command (a favourite Chinese punishment), and in the same sentence his death at the head of his troops is mentioned without comment.

On July 15th the Acting Governor of Shansi quotes a Decree which had been issued on the 20th of June to the several Governors General, and Governors, in which the following significant sentence occurs: " They must suggest plans for safe-guarding the boundaries of the Empire against the aggressive designs of the foreigner, and see that reënforcements be sent to the assistance of the Capital, in order that no disaster befall the Dynasty."

Three days later appeared a Decree which sets forth

another aspect of the international troubles, again refers to the murder of the Japanese Chancellor, and for the first time mentions that of the German Minister, nearly a month previous, carefully avoiding the least information as to the circumstances.

By this time the pressure of events succeeding the capture of Tientsin began to be severely felt in Peking, and the dissensions among the followers of the Empress were at their maximum.

"The reason for the fighting between the Chinese and the foreigners sprung from a disagreement between the people and the Christian converts. We could but enter upon war when the forts at Taku were taken. Nevertheless the Government is not willing lightly to break off the friendly relations which have existed. We have repeatedly issued Edicts to protect the Ministers of the different countries. We have also ordered the missionaries in the various provinces to be protected. The fighting has not yet become extensive. There are many merchants of the various countries within our dominions. All alike should be protected. It is ordered that the Generals and Governors examine carefully where there are merchants or missionaries, and still, according to the provisions of the treaties, protect them without the least carelessness. Last month the Chancellor of the Japanese Legation was killed. This was indeed most unexpected. Before this matter had been settled, the German Minister was killed. Suddenly meeting this affair caused us deep grief. We ought vigorously to seek the murderer and punish him.

"Aside from the fighting at Tientsin, the Metropolitan Department (Shun Tien Fu) and the Governor General of this province should command officers under them to examine what foreigners have been causelessly killed, and what property destroyed, and report the same, that all may be settled together. The vagabonds who have been burning houses, robbing and killing the people these many days have produced a state of chaos. It is ordered that the Governors General, Governors, and high military officials clearly ascertain the circumstances, and unite in reducing the confusion to order and quiet, and root out the cause of the disturbance."

FORTIFIED BRIDGE ACROSS THE MOAT NEAR LEGATION STREET

XXI

DAYS OF WAITING

SUNDAY, July 22.—Early this morning some of the Chinese went out through the water-gate into the southern city to buy fruit, but when others tried it a little later they were fired upon, so that the market is spoiled. Labour on the barricades was suspended at 11 A. M., the first time this has been practicable, as on most of the previous Sundays work has been more urgent than on other days.

The courier to Tientsin with messages got off about noon, and the package was so large that he asked to have its size reduced a little for better concealment. (To many friends of the besieged the word brought by this courier was the first gleam of hope after almost utter despair.) The baby of Dr. and Mrs. John Inglis died during the day, and was buried at nightfall,—one of the six infants who succumbed during the siege.

It is rumoured that the Japanese, always the most enterprising collectors of outside reports, have heard that our troops have already got half way to Peking travelling along the bank of the river. Tung Fu Hsiang is said to have lost his influence, and his men are scattering from him, but according to others he has gone out to oppose our troops. The Chinese have put up a new barricade in the Hanlin. A Chinese soldier has informed some one that we are now surrounded by only about 900 men.

Monday, July 23.—A heavy rain came on in the evening yesterday and kept up all night. There were many collapses of barricades, and in the Hanlin a part of a house-wall suddenly fell, covering the mattresses upon which the volunteers had just been lying. The buildings in Peking are as insubstantial as any others in China, often being composed of small pieces of bricks not larger than one's fist, bound loosely together with mud and a mere suggestion of lime. The result is that whenever a heavy and continuous rain-fall occurs, the walls may be heard falling in all directions—often to the danger of those living within the flimsy structures. The rain is very destructive to the sand bags, especially to the more expensive ones, which are not meant for such a strain as this. Many of them collapse into mere heaps of slush.

Early this morning the Norwegian whose mind had become unbalanced took advantage of the rain, the darkness, and the slumbering guards, British and Chinese, to make his escape over the wall, desirous of speedily falling into the hands of the Chinese, where it is feared he will not fare so well as he expects. It is said that despite the apparent diminution in the number of Chinese troops, they are building new barricades. Yesterday a dog was sent from one of their fortifications to one of ours, with a letter in his mouth—all that is left in Peking of the Imperial Postal Service!

Tuesday, July 24.—It was very hot in the night, so that many could not sleep. The Japanese Secretary of Legation, Mr. Harahara, died of tetanus, greatly regretted both by foreigners and Japanese. He had the reputation of a great knowledge of China, and was universally liked. There appeared to be a severe attack upon the Pei Tang last night, judging by the constant sounds of firing there. On the wall the coolies worked at the barricade till after nine o'clock, when the Chinese began firing on them, and the work stopped.

Notwithstanding the "truce" firing goes on, and four Chinese have been wounded in the Fu to-day, as well as one Italian. A mat-shed has been erected over the defences at the front gate of the British Legation, to prevent it from being ruined by the heavy rain, and only one shot was fired by the Chinese.

After dark a notice was posted that Col. Shiba had seen a Chinese who told him that foreign troops occupied Yang Ts'un on the 17th, and fought a battle on the 19th. One hundred and fifty wounded Chinese of Tung Fu Hsiang's army are said to have been brought to Peking, and foreign troops were forty *li* this side of Yang Ts'un. This news is discredited by Mr. Conger and many others, as being too fast an advance for the time during which troops must have been on the way.

Wednesday, July 25.—About 1 A. M., we were startled by hearing a great many rifle-shots in succession, mainly from the direction of the Mongol market, indicating that a renewed attack was beginning, but it was all over in less than five minutes. It is reported that yesterday a Japanese shot a Chinese who was getting over his barricade, a Chinese in retaliation shot a Chinese Christian, when the Japanese returned the fire; the Chinese then wounded an Italian, on which a British marine killed the man who shot *him!*

Two days ago there were rumours of a large Chinese force from Pao Ting Fu, which would soon attack the Legations. Now it is said that troops are coming in from the Western Park, to be separated into two divisions at two of the Peking gates. There is a rumour that there was an attempt to blow up the Pei T'ang recently, but that it did not succeed, or that at least the Cathedral was not injured. The Chinese soldier who has been giving information to the Japanese, now informs them that a battle was fought on the 24th, between Ts'ai Ts'un and Ho Hsi Wu, lasting from noon till midnight, after which the Chinese retired on Ho Hsi Wu.

A flag of truce was sent during the day to the German Legation with several letters. One of these is to Sir Claude from " Prince Ch'ing and Others " saying that a great many inquiries are being made of the Chinese Government as to the safety of the Ministers. The Chinese Government is willing to send replies from the Ministers to these inquiries, but they must have nothing in them of a military nature, and must be in plain writing, not in cipher. Another document raises once more the proposal of removing the Legations to Tientsin, pointing out that the number of rebellious people daily increases, and that something unforeseen is liable to happen. (It has already happened, however). Travel is temporary, residence is permanent, and an escort could be provided which would make the journey perfectly safe. China does not want war. What means are proposed to stop it? It would be better to settle matters at Tientsin, therefore the Ministers are asked to pack up, and name a fixed day in order that provision may be made for their travel.

A messenger disguised as a fortune-teller was sent out with a repetition of the last batch of messages. The man that was sent to procure a number of " Peking Gazettes " has returned, having experienced some trouble and danger, for which he was rewarded with fifty taels.

Thursday, July 26.—Only a few stray shots in the night, which was very hot and was followed by a day of the same sort. The fortune-telling messenger did not get away after all, being dissatisfied with some detail of his costume. At first his despatches were rolled up in the handle of an old umbrella, but this was criticized as too obvious, and he is now ruminating on a variation of dress for another attempt later.

The Japanese Soldier-Information-Bureau (now ripened into "one of Tung Fu Hsiang's body-guard") to-day offers the very latest. There was another fight at Ho Hsi Wu yesterday, lasting till 3 P. M., twelve hundred Chinese being killed and wounded. The Chinese force included 5,000 soldiers and 3,000 Boxers. Li Ping Hêng is said to have reached Peking, and the plan to deport the Ministers is thought to be his. In the afternoon the Ho Hsi Wu battle was revised so as to have begun at six o'clock, the Chinese being driven back ten *li*. By the same opportunity we learned that 4,800 troops had come in from the west, but they had left to join the Chinese army, with nine guns.

Mr. Conger puts absolutely no faith in any of these reports, but many others give them a qualified credence, "so as to hit it if it were a deer, and miss it if it were a calf."

During the night there were continual isolated rifle-shots to show that we are watched, but no replies came from us.

Friday, July 27.—Much cooler last night. After breakfast there were rumours that a man had arrived from T'ung Chou, with the same man who has come so often before, bringing a report that the Chinese intend to make their last stand at T'ung Chou, and that if they should be defeated there, the Court would retire to Hsi An Fu, the distant capital of the province of Shensi, for which journey carts are said to have been already impressed.

The messenger who was to go out as a fortune-teller has made his second effort to get away and failed. The first time he was let down over the wall, met Chinese soldiers and pretended that he was sent to inspect their camp, but they told him that he could not get there without a pass. Then he pulled the rope, and was hauled up again upon the wall. The next time was at the east gate of the Fu, where he found himself surrounded by barricades and became frightened.

To-day at noon he tried the third time. He had procured a Boxer uniform, but he could not make any use of it. Two soldiers were willing to help him out, one to be the security for the other. The latter remained within our surveillance, while the other took the messenger to a distance of several *li*. When he left the messenger, the latter handed him a small piece of a foreign lady's hair-pin as a pledge, a token unknown to the security who had remained. Upon presenting this hairpin certificate that the safe-conduct had been honourably executed, the two men were paid ten taels. The messenger was to have two hundred taels on his arrival at Tientsin, with his thirteen letters. (It is remarkable that all this elaborate preparation was worse than wasted. There was some little doubt about the trustworthiness of the man, but he was not seriously suspected. When he had got beyond the city he was advised by his brother either to kill himself outright, or go to the headquarters of Prince Chuang, and make a full confession, thus ensuring his own escape from punishment. This he did, and all the thirteen letters were sent out to the translators of the Tsung Li Yamen, who soon put them into circulation in the Imperial Court, where those of them that were not in cipher were doubtless much enjoyed—as so many of their predecessors had already been).

The Ministers yesterday had another meeting to consider what form of sound words to employ in replying to Prince Ch'ing and his "Others," so as to keep the matter in suspense as long as possible, with a minimum of definiteness—an aim for which diplomatic training is supposed to fit everyone perfectly. With regard to the matter of plain telegraphing, it was to-day replied that no Government would accept such telegrams, and no Ministers could send them, for they would not be according to usage, and would therefore defeat the very end proposed, which was to impart information as to the condition of the Ministers. Furthermore, it was impossible to affirm that the families of the Ministers are well, as they have suffered from the five weeks siege, and the lack of accustomed food. As for the omission of military information, this was easy to arrange, as the Ministers had no information in regard to the military situation, and therefore would be under no risk of sending that kind of intelligence.

The Japanese soldier-spy has told them that Jung Lu has five regiments (liang-tzu) at the Pei T'ang, two at the Hou Mên, or North gate of the Imperial city, three surrounding the Legations, while three more have gone to meet the foreign troops. Two hundred carts have been summoned to the Palace for the removal of the Court, and seventy more for Gen. Tung Fu Hsiang.

A Chinese who had beaten his wife was to-day put into a small light cangue, or frame-work about his neck, near the bell-tower, the cangue bearing an inscription: "THIS MAN BEAT HIS WIFE AND IS NOW PUNISHED FOR IT." He is surrounded much of the time by a curious crowd, both of foreigners and Chinese, who regard it as a novelty; indeed, there is reason for supposing that it is the first case in the history of the Chinese Empire—though this is undoubtedly a rash statement to make about anything.

There was a sensation during the afternoon on the arrival of red cards and a quantity of fruit, etc., for the Ministers, and a separate lot for Sir Robert Hart. The approximate census of the provision consignment is as follows: Melons, 150; cucumbers, 100; squashes, 100; flour, 1,000 catties; eggs, 500; ice, 24 blocks. In regard to the acceptance of these Imperial gifts there was, at this as at other times, wide divergence of opinion. Some refused to partake of them in any way, and wished them returned or declined. The controversy was sharply argued on both sides, one of the Ministers being even memorialized by a deputation of ladies against the acceptance of such treacherous bounty.

There was, however, no difference of opinion about the imprudence of using any of the flour, at least until it had first been tried upon a dog,—a suggestion presented by deputations of native Christains, which commended itself to all. It was put aside till urgently required, and had not been touched when the Relief Force arrived, but it was subsequently used with no apparent ill effects. These gifts were as before merely acknowledged by a receipt.

A letter to the Ministers through Sir Claude from the Prince Ch'ing combination suggests that the number of converts in the Legation premises is reported to be large, and the space small. The feeling is now quiet abroad, and the converts may very well be sent out, and directed to pursue their avocations. There need be no doubt and fear. It is requested that the number of them be estimated, and a day fixed for sending them out.

Sir Claude did not consider it worth his while to consult the Christians as to whether they wished to facilitate their own massacre by leaving their only place of refuge, and no reply to this artless communication was returned. In the evenings there are frequent gatherings around the bell-tower for singing.

Several songs have been composed bearing upon the siege, which have become very popular. The Russians sing their fine national air, the Germans "Die Wacht am Rhein," the British "God Save the Queen," and the Americans the "Star Spangled Banner," with great good fellowship.

The messenger reports that a foreigner has been captured by the Chinese, in a very forlorn and unkempt condition. We recognized him as an escaped Norwegian about whom we wrote on the 25th a note of inquiry. He is reported to have been taken to the headquarters of Jung Lu, who examined him and then sent him to the yamen of the prefect of Peking where he now is.

Saturday, July 29th.—The two ponies killed this morning were found to have been preëmpted by a parasite (filaria) in the flesh, making them unwholesome and dangerous. As the Chinese are never deterred by any trifles of this nature, the meat was accordingly sent over to the Fu, and another pony substituted for the foreigners.

A sensation was caused by the arrival of the boy who was sent out on the night of July 4th, disguised as a beggar. He brings a letter to Sir Claude replying to his of the 4th which gave the details of the siege up to that time, and the number of killed and wounded, and which stated that Chinese troops had fired into the Legation quarter continuously since June 20th, and that the Legations were hard pressed.

Notice of the contents of the letter from Tientsin, which is written by the British Consul, is posted on the bulletin board as follows: "Tientsin, July 22nd. Your letter

July 4th. There are now 24,000 troops landed, and 19,000 here. Brig. Gen. Gaselee expected Taku to-morrow. Russian troops are at Pei Ts'ang. Tientsin city is under foreign government, and Boxer power here is exploded. There are plenty of troops on the way if you can keep yourself in food. Almost all the ladies have left Tientsin. D. R. Carles."

The more this strange communication was contemplated, the more extraordinary it appeared. The one vital question to persons in a state of continuous siege is as to when relief may be expected, and on this point the letter not only gave no information whatever, but its phraseology was so ambiguous as to be unintelligible. Even the number of available troops was left a matter of debate, the whole culminating in the singular intelligence that "there are plenty of troops on the way if you can keep yourself in food." This led to the very natural inquiry, what would become of the troops if Sir Claude found that he could not keep himself in food?

It was not until long afterward that it became dimly known that the benevolent purpose of the writer of the letter was to disguise the fact—which it was thought might be fatally depressing to the besieged—that at present there was nothing whatever in immediate prospect for their relief, and that they might as well adjust themselves to these conditions.

The messenger lad reported that he left the Red Bridge above Tientsin July 23rd, and slept at Yang Ts'un in a locomotive boiler. The railway bridge there was not destroyed. That day he saw only Chinese infantry—the main body being at Pei Ts'ang 8 miles west of Tientsin.

He saw no Boxers there. The night of the 24th he spent near Ho Hsi Wu. That day he saw parties of Boxers in the villages, but none on the road. At Ma

DAYS OF WAITING

T'ou the river was in flood, many boats moored, but few in motion. On the 27th he reached the Sha Kuo gate of Peking. The telegraph poles and wire along the river were all gone, the railway was everywhere torn up, and the rails either buried or used for making Boxer swords. The highway to Tientsin was in good condition. The crops everywhere looked well, and the villagers were attending to their farm work. There was a Boxer organization in every village.

When the messenger left Tientsin the foreign troops had not advanced beyond the defence wall. All the yamens in Tientsin were occupied by foreign troops—chiefly Japanese. All Boxers had left the front at Tientsin, because they were so badly punished in battle. The Chinese soldiers despised them because of the contrast between their previous extravagant pretensions to invulnerability and their present flight.

The Japanese subsidized body-guard soldier of Tung Fu Hsiang informs them that there has been "a battle" at An P'ing on the 26th, when there were seven hundred Chinese killed, their army retreating on Ma T'ou. A miltary Harmony has now been constructed with a view to reconciling the dates given by the body-guard expert, with the evidently authentic information of the messenger lad, as follows:

Summary of Battles under the patronage of the soldier of Gen. Tung Fu Hsiang: Ts'ai Ts'un battle, July 24th; Ho Hsi Wu battle, July 25th; An P'ing battle, July 26th; Chinese army at Ma T'ou, July 27th. The messenger boy reports that he slept at Yang Ts'un on the 23rd, Ho Hsi Wu, 24th, Ma T'ou, 25th, Yü Chia Wei, 26th, Peking, 27th. There is thus no material contradiction between these reports.

The word of the intended escape of the Empress Dowager is confirmed by four others, as well as the soldier-spy. Yesterday an experiment was made in getting rude cobbling done by one of the Christians, and watch-repairing by a Roman Catholic refugee.

Sunday, July 29th.—Last night there seemed to be heavy firing about the Pei T'ang, or Northern Cathedral. Early in the morning the intellectually aberrant Norwegian was brought to our lines by a Chinese guard, looking much like a wreck. He had been manacled, and remarked that all the gold in the world would not induce him to repeat the experience. It gradually leaked out that he was asked a great number of leading questions by Jung Lu, and others, showing that they have a very correct knowledge of what is going on inside the Legation premises. One inquiry was about the pits which were being dug, probably the bomb-proofs, and another as to the amount of damage done by the Chinese firing. The Norwegian gave the whole thing away by frankly stating that the Chinese fired too high, and as there was soon after a marked depression of the muzzles of their rifles (and of the spirits of the besieged to match) it was proposed to shoot the man as a deserter and a spy. More temperate counsels prevailed, however, and he was thenceforth kept in a state of surveillance until the siege terminated.

An Austrian marine, who was acting as a cook in his Legation at the time it was abandoned, says that when the order was given to retreat, he was at work in the cookhouse and knew nothing of it, supposing that the firing was due to the Boxers, and was unimportant. Hearing the bullets whizzing he went out to see, and was immediately struck with the total absence of any Austrians at the barricade; he was himself soon hit by a bullet that made a flesh-wound in both legs. Crawling back to the guard-room he wrote his name in his own blood on the wall, explaining that circumstance, lest he should die unknown to the rest. Finding that the Chinese did not enter, he tore up his clothing, made rough bandages ,and crawled to the barricade at the Customs, pursued by bullets. It is now generally recognized by impartial observers that the abandonment of the Austrian Legation at the time was utterly inexcusable.

Mr. Sugi the dispenser of Japanese-Chinese intelligence has taken a small house just outside the Japanese lines, opening on the Customs lane, where he receives messages and whence he dispatches couriers. His body-guard soldier to-day informs him that there are 25,000 Chinese troops at Ma T'ou awaiting the foreign army, which is 30,000 strong and retired yesterday on An P'ing.

A messenger sent out to Ch'ang P'ing Chou, northwest of Peking, met refugees from Tu Shih K'ou. There are said to be Russian troops coming hither by way of Kalgan, but whence is a dense mystery known only to the immortal gods. It is now affirmed that all but two of the gates of Peking are stopped with sand bags.

During the afternoon the Chinese began to build a new barricade along the south side of the bridge which crosses the canal under the walls of the Imperial city. This was at once observed from the north stables, and reported. The Italian gun was sent up there to attack the workmen, and fired several shots, until the gunner (Italian) got a bullet through his hand.

The method of the Chinese was very business-like and effective. There was no one in sight, but now and again a brick or two came around the corner, and then others were thrown on it, until the wall began to show up. Sometimes a box full of earth or bricks was suddenly pushed around adding to the fast growing barricade, but still no one in sight. The shots fired at them did the Chinese no harm, and did not in the least impede their work. Before dark the new wall stretched along the whole bridge front, and during the night it was completed, very high and strong. Much of their work elsewhere was done like this, and having practically unlimited materials and labour, they were able to execute a great deal in a short time. Everyone sympathized with the Russian gentleman who remarked the next morning: "That new barricade makes me very uneasy."

Another and rival messenger just in from Somewhere, tells us that Yang Ts'un was completely destroyed by foreign troops "two or three days ago," they being in steady advance. This makes necessary a revised Harmony of the Peking Anabasis, involving great intellectual labour and highly uncertain results.

A few "Peking Gazettes" have been secured, but there is nothing of commanding interest. The issue of July 23rd contains a long joint memorial from Yü Lu, the Governor General of Chihli, and Gen. Sung Ch'ing, giving confused details of the attacks upon the Foreign Settlement from the 8th to the 11th of July. The "Gazette" of July 11th also had a long memorial of the same description from the Governor General. The Chinese losses are admitted to have been severe, but then those of the enemy were "not small." The Empress Dowager is comforted by information that the Arsenal at the Treaty Temple is not so injured that it can not be repaired. The tone of the later memorial, which was sent two days before the last and successful foreign attack, is much less hopeful, giving details of the numerous foreign forces present and prospective, and each of them makes it plain that "large reënforcements" will be needed.

A paragraph from the former memorial is interesting

DAYS OF WAITING 397

as illustrating Chinese strategy under depressing conditions: "I have consulted," Yü Lu says, "with Gen. Ma Yü K'un, about the mode of continuing the warfare, and we have come to the conclusion that in the first place it is necessary to force the foreign troops to retire from the foreign settlement of Tientsin, and then to attack them at Taku. I have consulted on this subject several times with Generals Ma, Nieh, and Lo, and we hope to be able to take the Taku Forts." A Rescript approves this mode of action (as well it might, considering that it is the Report of a Committee of Civil and Military Rats as to the best Method of Putting a Large Bell on several Foreign Cats now in possession of Our Attic).

In a memorandum by the same Governor published at the same time, he informs the Throne that " Boxers of different places in my province have at different times arrived at Tientsin, and taken part in the battles. At present there is a Boxer-chief of the district of Ching Hai who has come with 5,000 Boxers, and presented himself to me. Seeing that he is a man physically strong and mentally capable, I have ordered him to choose a residence and await instructions. I have also directed that fire-arms and provisions should be distributed to his followers. In case of any merit on his part in future, a special report will be made by me on the subject." A Decree announces that as a reward for the numerous virtues of Jung Lu, he is to be allowed to ride with two bearers through the Forbidden City (a privilege which he was unable to retain for any length of time.)

Monday, July 30th.—The new barricade at the head of the canal commands the whole roadway on each side down to the city wall, and although passage is forbidden, there are many shots fired at the pertinacious Chinese who will take the more dangerous route, instead of the perfectly safe one through the tunnel. A Roman Catholic was killed this morning outside one of the houses near the Fu, along the canal road. A Cossack who was suffering from malaria took this morning a twelfth of a grain of strychnine by mistake for quinia, but he was saved from the toxic effects with some difficulty.

It is a great strain on the human understanding to digest, and especially to coördinate the incessant contradictory reports which come from every quarter. Here is to-day's budget: Col. Shiba's messenger says that he left Chang Chia Wan (three miles from T'ung Chou) at eight o'clock on the evening of the 29th. There had been desultory fighting there from 3 to 8 P. M., and many Chinese were killed. The foreign troops had advanced on Ma T'ou on the morning of the 29th, the Chinese falling back upon Chang Chia Wan, with about 10,000 men. In the afternoon a candy-seller from T'ung Chou, who had been sent out as a spy, returns with the story that there are foreign troops at Yang Ts'un but none this side. As this is not the news we wish, the man is tied up, until he can revise it! He also informs us that Li Hung Chang is here, and has been given three days to make peace. A courier was sent off early this morning with eleven letters, and during the day it was reported that two who had been dispatched yesterday by Mr. Sugi had returned. One of them has brought word of a battle just south of Ma T'ou, on the 29th (or 28th.) These men say that they saw a man who had been in the Roman Catholic village of Chia Chia T'uan, eight miles from T'ung Chou, who reports that foreign troops have come there to relieve the Catholics, who have been standing a little siege of their own.

There are wild and contradictory accounts of what is seen from the American position on the wall, looking down into the southern city, singular movements of carts, horses, coolies, etc., in great confusion. It is said that Sir Robert has received a cipher telegram of nearly an hundred words for which he has no cipher key—so that it is unintelligible.

A reply was sent to-day to the letter suggesting that the Chinese Christians might return to their "avocations," now that the country is quiet. The Ministers mention that in view of this statement they were surprised at the sound of heavy firing at the Pei T'ang, which was evidently being attacked. The barricade at the north canal bridge is referred to, and the fact that a continuous fire is kept up from there, and also against the French and the Russian Legations. There is a strange contradiction between the above professions and the actions described. There are European officers and soldiers at the Pei T'ang. If such attacks as these can not be prevented, it is difficult to see how similar assaults could be prevented on a journey to Tientsin. Explanations are wanted in regard to this matter, before discussing the question of transport.

Prince Ch'ing and his " Others " in reply informed the Ministers that, in the preparation for the journey to Tientsin, the Chinese Government would of course provide carts and chairs for going to T'ung Chou. Brig. Gen. Sun Han Lien with a picked force, and also some of Gen. Sung Ming's troops would be the escort; notice a few days in advance is requested. In reply to the letter just quoted it is explained that the attack on the Pei T'ang was due to the converts going out in all directions to plunder for food. The people joined the crowd of Boxers, and made continuous attacks. A Decree has now been issued that if the converts do not come out to plunder they are to be protected and not attacked. The troops of Gen. Tung were building a road across the canal, and the Legation mistook it for a barricade, which was a misunderstanding on both sides. With regard to the proposed departure, it is not an easy matter to adjust. It was only after much arrangement that it was possible to give guarantees against mischance. The matter is one of the greatest importance, and we could not purposely deceive. We ask you not to be over anxious, but to come to a decision.

Tuesday, July 31.—During the night, there was what one of the British marines called "a tidy bit of firing" down the canal. The Chinese complain that we fired first on them as they were working on their "road" (barricade), which is true. Despite their promise of cessation of hostilities, the Chinese do not suspend their firing anywhere. The supply of eggs has never been large, and now that the Chinese have beheaded a man who was bringing supplies for sale, and the French guards have shot an egg-seller, there are not likely to be any more.

The Chinese soldier-spy brings to the Japanese his usual tale of military news. The foreign army advanced from Ma T'ou fighting, arriving at Chang Chia Wan late on the afternoon of the 30th. The Chinese army is eight miles south of T'ung Chou. The "Ch'ang An Victorious Army" of fifteen regiments, which left Hsian Fu June 27th, is expected at the Southern Hunting Park to-day, and is to make a forced march to T'ung Chou. It is thought that there may be 4,000 or 5,000 of them, and as they are not foreign drilled they will add but little to the Chinese strength in a military way.

The five great armies hitherto controlled by Jung Lu are said to have been turned over to Li Ping Hêng, who had arrived from the south a few days before in obedience to a special summons, and whose influence was at once thrown into the scale in favour of further hostilities, so that they began to be more pronounced in every direction. Tung Fu Hsiang has leave of absence for ten days. Li Hung Chang (who is already in Peking) will arrive at Tientsin in two days. A dispatch from Chi Nan Fu reports that Yuan Shih K'ai, the Governor of Shantung has "revolted and joined the Germans!"

A party of Mr. Gamewell's men who were at work on the fortifications, were to-day called off to make a "brick-proof" for the north-west corner of the Hanlin, where bricks and bottles are coming over almost every minute, and "make the men nervous." The Hague Peace Conference should have included these weapons in its condemnation, along with the "dum-dum bullet." A barricade has been built in the night across the north side of the bridge at the Legation Street. At present the bridge is very unsafe, owing to the perpetual sniping from the Chinese barricade at the upper bridge.

XXII

THE RENEWAL OF THE ATTACK

WEDNESDAY, August 1.—During the night the mentally unbalanced Norwegian broke away from the Japanese Legation where he was under restraint, and went to the Hotel de Pékin. The proprietor brought him to the British Legation at 2 A. M., whence he was sent back to be put under watch again. The barricade at the south gate of this Legation, to protect the crossing of the canal, was finished last night, and we can now breathe a little more freely, but still there is a certain (or rather a very uncertain) amount of danger in going to Legation Street by this route.

The Committee on Food Supply have been very active in getting together everything which could be used, and especially in the steady and most important work of getting the grinding done properly and in season. Upon this the continued existence of all the besieged depends. As the duration of the siege is so uncertain and the matter is one of vital importance, careful stock-taking has been had as to the visible food supply. There seem to be about 600 pounds only of white rice, 11,500 of the "yellow," or old rice, and 34,000 pounds of wheat. If all other supplies were unavailable, it is estimated that the public stores could furnish one thousand persons each a pound of wheat and one third of a pound of rice each day, for five weeks. There are about thirty available ponies re-

BRITISH LEGATION GATE, FUEL SUPPLY COMMITTEE

maining, which at the rate of three every two days would last twenty days.

A visit to the wall shows a vast improvement in the defences there as compared with the period when the first effort was made to build a worm fence of bricks to the top of the ramp. Now this has been completed, and is perfectly safe from shots in any direction. Each of the barricades on the wall is built up very high and strong, and could not be rushed by the Chinese even if they had the disposition, which since the night of July 3rd they have never exhibited. Between the two terminal barricades there is a long path on the wall, protected all the way so as to be entirely safe for passage. The western barricade is held conjointly by Americans and Russians.

Another letter from " Prince Ch'ing and Others " has been received, continuing the subject of the previous correspondence. It says that last night some converts again fired on the posts of the Government troops, wounding two of them. If the converts are not amenable to control, it is to be feared that they will produce a great disaster, and ruin the whole situation. The strictest restraint is requested so as to avoid further hostilities. We hear that the converts have collected in great numbers, and that they do not wish the Envoys to leave Peking, their hope being that they will thus have a perpetual support. The Foreign Ministers ought not to fall into this trap. A reply is requested within two or three days, as to the date of the Minister's departure.

It seemed best to the Ministers to respond as if they were arguing with rational beings, as there was no certainty into whose hands the correspondence might fall. Accordingly a reply was sent to this nonsense the following day. The Legation is defended, not by "converts," but by guards. All day and all night there had been shooting from the new barricade on the north bridge, and not a shot was fired in reply. It is difficult to see why this is kept up. The Foreign Envoys are in great difficulty about the plan to go to Tientsin on a certain day. What security could the Legations have that the firing would not begin *en route?*

It is learned from the telegrams received through the Tsung Li Yamen to-day, that Mr. Conger's telegram of July 17th saying that the Legations had been bombarded by shot and shell for a month, had made a great sensation, and that relief would be sent. It is singular that both the tidings of our distress and the intelligence of the effect produced by the announcement of it, should each have been transmitted through the Tsung Li Yamen. A Shantung Christian named Chang, who was dispatched to Tientsin on the 18th of July, returned to-day with a reply to the Japanese Baron Nishi from Gen. Fukushima, saying that there had been unexpected difficulties in the landing of the 5th Japanese Division, but that most of the troops had already reached Tientsin and the remainder were constantly arriving. The messages sent out from Peking had made the situation there universally known, and many councils had been held as to dispatch of a relief expedition. It was expected that within two or three days from the date of writing, which was July 26th, an expedition would start.

Other letters brought the same or similar intelligence, which makes it clear that the reports which have been coming in so frequently and so regularly from the heavily subsidized body-guard soldier-spy of Gen. Tung Fu Hsiang's are deficient in the element of coördination with other facts of contemporaneous history—in other words they are pure fabrications, which have served their one purpose of holding the attention of the besieged, and

THE RENEWAL OF THE ATTACK

which have kept them studying the map and making estimates of the probable present situation of " our troops." Those who had all along discredited the military narratives, were enabled to say with much and iterative emphasis: " I told you so."

This last messenger, although he had been promised a large reward for executing the commission which he had so well fulfilled, said that he did not care for money, would not accept it, and only insisted that he should be furnished with a return packet of letters as soon as possible. He explained that he was risking his life for the general good, and not for private gain. To the Japanese, as well as to some others, he appeared to be a very eccentric individual. Within two hours he was sent off again on the coveted errand.

A telegram to Sir Robert Hart mentions the results of the fighting at Tientsin July 15th, and states that subsequent to it arrangements for the relief were being hastened, and inquiries whether the Chinese Government is protecting us and supplying us with provisions, etc.

This last sentence exposes the " true inwardness " of the water-melons, egg-plants, and cucumbers, all of which had been sent in not for the purpose of serving as food, but as padding for the dispatches of the Chinese Ministers to various Western Powers, all of whom were now assured that the Government was doing its utmost to make the besieged experience ideal happiness, so that their lot was upon the whole an enviable one.

It is reported from Japanese sources that their losses in killed have been ten, (including the Chancellor of the Legation) of whom five are soldiers, three Legation officials, one an officer, and one a civilian. There have been seven badly wounded, and thirty slightly so. The dead are buried in a special spot in the grounds of the Su Wang

Fu, and when the siege is over the bodies are to be taken up, cremated, and the ashes transferred to Japan.

During the siege a litter of kittens has made its appearance, two of which have been adopted by the marines in the main gate, have had coloured ribbons put on their necks, and sleep serenely in the loop-holes!

Thursday, August 2.—One of the Continental Ministers who was for a long time very timid and pessimistic, remarked in our gate-house this morning: "Well, we are going to get out of this." He seems to think the thermometer is rising.

The two soldier-spies returned to-day, and one gave an account of the retreats of their phantom foreign armies as far as Yang Ts'un! He was somewhat alarmed at finding his fictions rated at their true value. Instead of falling into a passion, as the unskilful Occidental would have been likely to do, his shrewd Japanese employer smiled upon him, and remarked that he was aware all along that the tales were a tissue of fabrications, insomuch that he had never even mentioned them to Col. Shiba at all! Considering that each day a careful abstract of the reports had been drawn up, illustrated with maps, and the whole at once posted on the bulletin board, this was almost as robust a falsehood as the marching and retreats of the imaginary forces from Tientsin. Instead of being dismissed, the soldier was told that he would still be paid, if he would hereafter bring in reports which were somewhat more veracious than any of those which had preceded, but from this date he ceased to be quoted by any one as a military authority.

A man who was sent out for the purpose, returned to-day with a fresh lot of "Peking Gazettes," which contain some crumbs of news.

On the 28th of July a memorial appears from Yü Hsien,

THE RENEWAL OF THE ATTACK 407

the Governor of Shansi, who reports that the district magistrate of the capital of his province, T'ai Yuan Fu, had sent word of a Boxer gathering which invaded his yamen and had asked for troops. Upon investigation the Governor learned that the crowd was a small one, and that only one man had come to the yamen demanding food, and he was not a Boxer. He recommends the dismissal of the magistrate. (There is probably much more in this little incident than appears upon the surface, and it not improbably signifies that Yü Hsien was engaged in inculcating the teaching among his subordinates that Boxers were not to be interfered with, and that any official guilty of obstructing them would be promptly cashiered.)

The same Governor mentions that he was about dispatching four " camps " of infantry and two hundred cavalry to Peking, in obedience to a Decree, but that in accordance with a later Decree their destination was changed to Kalgan. He also reports that he is about to raise fresh regiments. (It was learned later that he marched at the head of his troops for the relief of Peking as far as Huai Lu Hsien, at the entrance to the Ku Kuan pass leading from Chihli to Shansi. Learning that Peking had already been taken, he returned to his own capital, where he later welcomed the Empress Dowager on her flight to the remote west.)

A Decree of which the date is uncertain, but apparently of July 28th, states that Hsü Ching Ch'êng and Yuan Ch'ang, two of the Ministers of the Tsung Li Yamen, had been denounced as of bad reputation, and as given to serving their private ends in dealing with foreign affairs. At an Imperial audience they have made wild proposals, and used the most improper language. Their suggestions have tended to introduce divisions (i. e. between the Empress Dowager and the Emperor) and have been extremely wanting in respect. In order to inspire awe in the minds of other officers they are both condemned to immediate execution. (The above two officials were sacrificed to the fury of the Empress, apparently at the instigation of Li Ping Hêng immediately upon his arrival at Peking. Hsü Ching Ch'eng was the Chinese President of the new Imperial University, had been Chinese Minister to Russia, and was an enlightened and liberal man. At an Imperial audience of unusual importance the Emperor reached over the dais upon which he was seated, grasped the sleeve of Hsü, and exclaimed, " If China is to fight the World, will it not put an end to China?" At this the numerous Manchu nobles present manifested great indignation, and someone cried out that Hsü had laid hands upon His Majesty, and began to revile him openly. He retired as soon as he was able, very much frightened. The same day Li Ping Hêng is reported to have reached the Capital, and the following day both Hsü and Yuan were executed. Their real crime was in daring to advise against the insane course of the Empress Dowager, as urged by Prince Tuan and the rest, in endeavouring to find some way of adjusting the growing difficulties, in alleged truckling to foreigners by visiting the Legations secretly, and in taking up the body of the German Minister when it lay exposed in the street, and encoffining it.) It was at once perceived that this was a most ominous proceeding, displaying the temper of the actual rulers of China as nothing had yet done.

Yesterday preparations were made for extending our line to the southwest of the British Legation, by taking in the ruins of burned buildings near the Mongol Market, and making barricades of them with a view to keeping the Chinese at a greater distance. This was done to-

THE RENEWAL OF THE ATTACK 409

day by Mr. Gamewell and his men, under Lieutenant von Strauch of the Customs (formerly of the German Army), a brave and skillful officer, who threw himself into the new movement with the greatest zeal. The work was designedly begun at a time when the Chinese soldiers are usually torpid (taking their opium and resting after the fatigues of their early rising), and the work was for a long time not even discovered. It has enlarged the area under our control by a space perhaps fifty yards wide to the west, and stretching the entire distance from the Carriage Park on the north to the Russian Legation on the south. Many court-yards were crossed, many houses perforated, and a final barricade made of flagstones in the one furthest west. When at last the Chinese found out what was going on, they made a particularly spiteful attack, piercing a wooden door, and wounding a Chinese, but notwithstanding their utmost efforts they were never able to recover any part of this tract and hold it against the defence.

Toward evening another courier arrived,—the one who took the messages July 23rd, conveying information of the safety of the Legation and the besieged up to that time. The greatest excitement prevailed, both before the posting of the news (which happened almost immediately, as the letters were mostly for the American Minister) and afterwards. The cipher dispatches and letters gave the dates of the military movements for the relief of Tientsin, and information as to the probable order of advance by columns of the relieving force, which did not, however, correspond to the actual movements later on. One of the letters contained the judicious advice to "Hold on by all means," and another said: "Keep heart, aid coming early. Troops pouring in."

The letter of Consul Ragsdale to Mr. Conger, although

very brief, was of special interest to Americans for the welcome glimpse into the doings and feelings of their distant countrymen: "July 28th. Had lost all hope of seeing you again. Prospect now brighter. We had thirty days' shelling here, nine days siege, thought that bad enough. Scarcely a house escaped damage. Excitement at home intense, of course. Our prayers and hope are for your safety and speedy rescue. Advance of troops to-morrow probable. McKinley and Roosevelt nominated. Also Bryan—Vice-President unknown."

A letter from Lieut. Col. Mallory, 41st U. S. Infantry, said: "A relief column of 10,000 is on the point of starting for Peking. More to follow. God grant they may be in time." Under date of August 30th, Maj. Gen. Chaffee announced that he had just arrived at Tientsin.

Some of the other letters mentioned that attacks had been made by Boxers upon Chinese Christians in the districts of Tsun Hua Chou, Shan Hai Kuan, and many other places. That the Russians had been fighting near Chin Chou in Manchuria, and that Newchwang was much disturbed, as all Manchuria seemed to be rising against foreigners, and the hands of the Russians were likely to be full there. The Yangtze valley was said to be also very unquiet, although the two Governors General, Liu K'un Yi, at Nanking, and Chang Chih Tung, at Wu Ch'ang, were doing their best to keep order. Li Hung Chang was still at Shanghai, and his coming north to Tientsin considered doubtful. Tientsin was governed by a joint foreign Commission. Germany and the United States were each to send 15,000 men, and Italy 5,000. Tientsin was full of soldiers, with more constantly arriving. The railway was running between Tientsin and Tongku. Many ladies and children had been sent to the

United States on the transport "Logan." All property at the sea-side resort at Pei Tai Ho was destroyed.

For some time it has been known that there was a stock of Chinese samshu, or strong wine somewhere, but recently it was traced to a shop in Legation Street, where they deal in condiments, sauce, etc. Mr. Tewksbury went there with some men on behalf of the General Committee, and found a sick man asleep above a large wine-jar. He was forced to remove, and the fluid was all poured into the street, which was highly perfumed, to the value of many taels. The jar had been sealed up once before, but the thirsty marines had broken through the seal.

The messenger who brought the welcome news of prospective relief says that, when he reached T'ung Chou, instead of taking the usual route he went east, spending one night on the way with Chinese soldiers. On his return he had his letters sewed into his hat. He left Tientsin by the west gate, making a wide detour so as not to excite suspicion, yet got through in very good time.

Friday, August 3.—The Committee on Confiscated Goods is busy this morning going through the houses which are within the territory captured yesterday, and a great deal of stuff was found which will be of service. There is a fire in the Imperial City, but it is impossible to determine where it is. The following has just been posted:

Census of the British Legation, August 1st.
Soldiers, British and others.................... 73
General Hospital, wounded.................... 40

Legation residents:
- Foreign men 191
- Foreign women 147
- Foreign children 76

  414

Legation residents:
- Chinese men 180
- Chinese women 107
- Chinese children 69

  356

Total 883

This afternoon the Yamen sent to Sir Claude, an undated cipher telegram from Lord Salisbury, in which he complains of having heard nothing since July 4th. The Ministers are trying the experiment of sending cipher telegrams through the Yamen. The latter send notice of the appointment of Jung Lu to escort the Ministers to Tientsin, a piece of impudence which even for the Chinese Government is nothing less than colossal, considering that he has spent the whole summer in trying to kill everyone in the Legations.

In reply to Sir Claude's remonstrances about the incessant firing upon us, the Yamen blandly remarks that it was the result of a misunderstanding, and that it is more or less on the same footing as the morning and evening bells of the temple priests. "It is really hardly worth a smile." In confirmation of the morning-and-evening-bell theory, it is mentioned that the wife of one of the Ministers has been heard to say that, now there is so little firing of rifles and no shelling, she cannot sleep!

Over at the Fu some Chinese coolies have brought

THE RENEWAL OF THE ATTACK 413

rifles and ammunition for sale at one of the out-posts. (This circumstance probably gave rise to the widely circulated story that during the siege a part of the ammunition was bought from the attacking Chinese troops. It was, however, stated as a fact that a Japanese paid one of the Chinese Imperial Guard two dollars for 140 rounds of ammunition, and that within a quarter of an hour the two men were diligently attacking each other!)

Saturday, Aug. 4.—There was much less firing last night than before. The Nordenfelt gun was put up on a high platform at the angle of the newly annexed territory behind the house of the Chinese Secretary, and has a very dissuasive appearance. " Oh, he's little, but he's wise. He's a terror for his size."

The Ministers had a meeting and agreed to ask the Yamen to send mutton and other supplies for the ladies and the sick, but the action was not unanimous, and some of the besieged protest against it vigourously, as a display of uncalled for weakness. A letter was received from the Yamen, informing the Ministers that the various Foreign Offices of the different Nations concerned wish the Foreign Ministers escorted out of Peking, and desiring a speedy reply. Two Russians who were at work in the Russo-Chinese Bank incautiously exposed themselves too much, and were wounded this afternoon, apparently by the same bullet. One of them died during the night.

At an adjourned meeting of the Ministers during the afternoon, the draft of a letter in reply to the Yamen was agreed upon, to be sent to-morrow. The general purport is that the Ministers must be allowed to communicate with their Governments direct, and that they can not receive instructions through the medium of the Tsüng Li

Yamen. Foreign Ministers in China must have the same rights that Chinese Ministers at foreign courts at present enjoy.

With this letter were sent cipher telegrams to the various governments from the Ministers, asking for instructions as to leaving, in compliance with the Yamen's demand. The object of this is to gain time, as the replies at quickest can not be received in less than ten days or two weeks, since the telegrams have to be sent, according to the Yamen's letter of to-day, by courier to Chi Nan Fu, the capital of Shantung. It is understood that at least one of the Ministers incorporated in his dispatch a hint of the object of raising the inquiry at all, with the suggestion that there need be no haste as to a reply. In the interim the Yamen was told that, when these replies are to hand, the Ministers will be in a position to arrange the matter of leaving or remaining—(a prediction and promise which was more than fulfilled.)

Yesterday the Ministers had for the first time tried the experiment of all sending cipher dispatches to their respective governments, to be forwarded by the Yamen, and it is understood that as they have not been returned they have been forwarded.

There is a species of censorship established over outgoing telegrams, to the deep indignation of some of the correspondents who do not wish their opinions revised by a committee.

At the Su Wang Fu soldiers without arms crowd around our sentries in a very friendly way, as the Imperial Edict arranging for the departure of the Ministers is well known and we are supposed to be soon leaving. A soldier who has been useful in getting copies of the "Peking Gazettes" for us, took occasion to observe: "You are

THE RENEWAL OF THE ATTACK 415

alive; we are dead. The foreign army is on the way, and has driven back Gen. Sung Ch'ing, 140 li from here." Rumours among the Chinese say that among the foreign troops there are many "blacks," who are supposed to be from India.

Sunday, August 5.—A report has got around that the Chinese are intending, if the Foreign Ministers do not accede to the proposition to go at once to Tientsin, to attack the Legations in earnest. After nearly three weeks of comparative quiet, with steady preparation under the invariable persistence of Mr. Gamewell, there are many who are quite of the mind of the German soldier who exclaimed on hearing the rumour: "Let them come on!" (Lässen sie kommen.)

There was a hard rain last night for two hours or more, and everything is fresh to-day. No walls have fallen in the Mongol Market addition to our territory, as was feared. This is the first Sunday when no work has been done at all. Several Chinese children died yesterday and to-day. The Roman Catholics are very short of food, —for what reason is not quite clear, as the total stock appears to be good. In the afternoon there were letters from the Yamen again, one of which conveyed expressions of sympathy to the Italian Legation on the death of King Humbert (of which they had not previously heard.) The news was communicated by Lo Fêng Lo, who is accredited both to Great Britain and to Italy. Other letters to other Ministers communicated inquiries as to health, etc.

The following letter was sent out to-night to the Allied forces, and it was through the use of this information that the British and American troops entered Peking so early.

COPY OF MESSAGE SENT TO COMMANDER ALLIED FORCES:

August 5, 1900.

" I enclose map showing Manchu City south wall, with lines in rear, including Legations now occupied by us. Our position on wall is strongly held, is about 300 yards long, and equally distant from the two city gates, and is indicated by flags, Russian and American at each end. The left of the position (American) covers the water gate, an opening under the wall, about forty feet wide and twenty feet high, and through which any number of men could pass without difficulty; arriving within our lines, could take one or both the gates by assault, following down the wall and in the rear from the street. 500 men for each gate would be a sufficient force, especially if assisted by artillery fire from outside. The wall of the Chinese City near the south gate is in bad condition, and far easier to take than any part of the Manchu city wall, which is thicker and higher. The ground from Chinese City south gate up to houses in that city is open. After shelling, an advance up the main street towards the middle gate, then turning to the right in the direction of the water gate, ought to be made without any very great difficulty. I deem this the safest and most feasible entrance into Peking. See Slater's Code, using Ragsdale's code number."

(Signed)　　　　　　　　　　Claude MacDonald.

Monday, August 6.—Between two and three o'clock this morning there was a furious rifle attack, such as we have not had for a long time, beginning with the Mongol Market region and apparently going all around. It continued for perhaps half an hour. It may have been stirred up by the steady work on the barricades in the new terri-

BUDDHIST TEMPLE AND MODERN TRAM CAR

WATER GATE, PEKING, THROUGH WHICH ALLIES ENTERED

THE RENEWAL OF THE ATTACK 417

tory, which are being strengthened all the time. A Chinese barricade fell down at the French Legation, and the Chinese had the presence of mind to set up a great yelling, beating of drums, etc., to distract attention. There was much alarm at some of the houses in the British Legation, and in one of them the second story was abandoned for the night as unsafe.

The alley through which the egg-sellers and the purveyors of news have made their entrance into the Japanese lines, has been walled up, so that we are again isolated from the world, except for the driblets of news—largely of an obituary nature—filtering through the Tsung Li Yamen. During the afternoon another communication arrived from that august body, in reply to those sent yesterday referring to the various home Governments the question of return to Tientsin. The Yamen has forwarded the dispatches, thus recognizing the right of the Ministers to ask for instructions. They also explain the attack of last night by saying that some foreigner made a great noise, so that the Chinese soldiers thought they were being attacked, and replied in kind!

Tuesday, August 7.—The night was much more quiet than the previous one, though there were some shots. To-day is the " Japanese Decoration Day " (the thirteenth day of the Chinese seventh moon), the equivalent of our " All Souls " festival, and they have put flowers upon the eight graves of their dead,—the touch of nature which makes the whole world kin.

The sand bags in the windows of the hospital are all giving way, and are to be taken down and used to fill up the unsightly holes in the tennis-court where earth has been removed. Despite the general quiet there is firing near the Mongol Market, and a Japanese was brought in from the Fu wounded in the leg. A telegram was received to-day from the Yamen with condolence for the death of the Duke of Edinburgh, of which there was no previous information.

To-day after elaborate preparation and many emendations, the Register of the Siege in Peking is published, and put upon the bulletin board. It was originally headed " Commander in Chief, Sir Claude MacDonald," which is understood to have been in accordance with a vote of the Ministers, asking the British Minister, in view of his twenty-four years of service in the British Army, to take the command, which no one else was willing to do. This was the more appropriate, as it was agreed that in the last extremity the British Legation was to be the place for a final stand. Now that the siege seemed nearly over and the unremitting exertions of Sir Claude for the general welfare were about to end, it appeared somewhat ungracious to assert, as some of the Continentals seemed disposed to do, that he was not their " Commander in Chief." Some final appeal in a military way there must of necessity be, and aside from the previous agreement of the Ministers made in the presence of a deadly peril, no more competent or more suitable candidate than Sir Claude was either available or requisite.

In the evening Mr. Squiers prepared a long message to be sent out to the troops, recommending the Southern City as the best point of attack, as being less defended, more easily entered, affording a shorter distance, largely through open spaces where there can be no loop-holing buildings, and having the water-gate accessible. Other letters of this kind have been sent also to the British detachment.

XXIII

THE RELIEF

WEDNESDAY, August 8.—During the night there was considerable firing in the region of the Mongol Market, a few Chinese creeping through the ruins and throwing bricks at the guard on the high platform where the Nordenfelt gun is placed. It was this that gave rise to the story that this post was "attacked." It is impossible for all to look at the matter in the same light, and there are some who are fully persuaded that this addition to our territory, instead of being (as it really is) a source of additional security, is rather the reverse.

There was an auction yesterday of much confiscated property, clothing, furniture, etc., bringing several hundred dollars to a relief fund for the Christians. A French marine accidentally shot another this morning through the lungs, the man dying not long after. Nothing but the grossest and most inexcusable carelessness could have occasioned such a calamity. Work was begun outside the main gate of the British Legation on a trench leading to the canal, where a platform is to be put up for the Austrian gun to command the bed of the canal, down which it would at any time have been possible for a bold and determined enemy to have made an effective rush in the night. On the west side of the Hanlin compound a countermine is being made for the Chinese mine, which has not, however, been discovered.

A meeting of the Ministers was held to-day, and strict economy was enjoined in the use of food. It was agreed to say to the Yamen that in view of the kindly feeling manifested by them in the communication of tidings of the death of kings and princes, it would be greatly appreciated if like kindness should be shown to the women and children here, in arranging for the furnishing of eggs and vegetables. They were also to be asked to take over more than an hundred neutrals who are still within our lines.

In the afternoon a circular dispatch came from the Yamen to announce that yesterday Li Hung Chang had been appointed a High Commissioner to arrange terms of peace between China and the Powers, with the Governments of which he is to correspond telegraphically.

One of Col. Shiba's informants says that there are at present only about 2,500 Chinese troops in Peking—the rest having gone to confront the foreign army. He also reports that another body of 50,000 foreign soldiers has been landed at Taku. It is thought that the appointment of Li as Peace Commissioner may mean that there has been a decisive victory at Yang Ts'un, but one of the Ministers would not be surprised if the expedition had not yet started, owing to difficulties of transportation, etc.

Sir Claude replied to the letter conveying sympathy for the death of the Duke of Edinburgh, remarking that notwithstanding these agreeable amenities it still remained true that he could not put his head out of his own Legation without the danger of being shot! This is the fiftieth day of the siege.

Thursday, August 9.—During the night there was a great deal of firing from the north bridge, not only down the canal but on the British Legation. It is rumoured that there has been a general change of the Chinese soldiers attacking us, the Manchus taking the place of the Chinese, who have been sent out to meet the troops of the enemy. Bullets rattled through the Legation grounds, and during the night a groan was heard, but no out-cry. In the morning it was found that a Chinese Roman Catholic "Brother," whose head was turned to the north and who was asleep on the outer pavilion, had been wounded in the chest by a glancing bullet which perforated his clothing and made a flesh wound near the ensiform cartilage. The man was perhaps stunned, for he did not even wake up, and when he did it was to find himself bloody.

Specimens of the "food" eaten in the Fu have been brought over on a tray, consisting of a mixture of chaff, sorghum seeds, wheat, and the leaves of plants and trees, made into flat cakes. A request has been sent that those who can do so will go out and shoot dogs and cats for the Chinese, to serve as food. There has been a recount of the Catholics in the Fu. The census is 755 women and 546 children, a total of 1,301. The men, who were absent, number 412, making a grand total of 1,713.

Friday, August 10.—About three o'clock this morning there was a sudden and very violent attack begun in the Mongol Market, running all around the circle. It lasted only about fifteen minutes, but during that time it was as vicious as anything we have had. At the signal of a rocket the firing suddenly ceased. Before it began, there had been a Boxer killed and another wounded west of the Market. There was also much shooting down the canal.

In the morning an aged Catholic priest slowly walked the entire distance from the Legation Street bridge to the entrance of the Fu, against many remonstrances, attracting at once the fire from the north bridge. There were twenty-six shots directed at him, but not one struck him. Yesterday some one counted thirty shots fired at a little girl, and an old woman gathering greens became a speedy target. Some Chinese do not seem in the least concerned when fired at, while others are terribly alarmed. One of the Chinese was cautioned not to go into danger, but would not heed, when a bullet pierced his clothing over the abdomen. From that time he became more prudent, but his caution assumed the form of a thick wad of cloth over the place where he had been hit, assuming that the next bullet would strike in precisely the same spot!

One of the diplomatic military authorities says that there were shots enough fired into the British Legation last night to have killed, if properly directed, every person in it. The intention certainly was not lacking, but the execution was imperfect. The trouble began in a corner of the Mongol Market where a bag of powder was found yesterday.

Designs are invited for a Siege medal to be struck in commemoration of the experience. One of the mottoes suggested has been the words "Mene, mene, tekel, upharsin," but one of the besieged was heard to object to this on the plausible ground that "not everybody knows Latin." The total of several auction sales thus far comes to $681.

About three in the afternoon there were rumours of the arrival of a messenger from the troops *en route* to Peking. There was a letter from the Japanese Lieut. General Fukushima, dated near Ts'ai Ts'un on the 8th. The Japanese and the American troops had defeated the enemy near Pei Ts'ang on the 5th, and occupied Yang Ts'un on the 6th. " The Allied forces, consisting of Americans,

British, and Russians, left Yang Ts'un this morning, and while marching north the General received the letter of Col. Shiba. It is very gratifying to learn from your letter that the foreign community are holding on, and it is the earnest wish and unanimous desire of the Lieut. General and all of us to arrive in Peking as soon as possible, and deliver you from your perilous position. Unless some unforeseen event takes place, the Allied forces will be at Ho Hsi Wu on the 9th, at Ma T'ou on the 10th, Chang Chia Wan on the 11th, T'ung Chou on the 12th, and probably arrive at Peking on the 13th or 14th." A letter of a similar tenor was also received from Gen. Gaselee.

The messenger got among Chinese soldiers, who detained but did not search him, and coming back he was forced to help track a boat. Still he made a relatively quick trip, leaving Tientsin Sunday night, reaching the foreign troops Wednesday morning, and arriving at Peking Friday afternoon. He came in through two half-manned barricades disguised as a coolie searching among the ruins of buildings.

Many telegrams were received making inquiries, and others with news. Mr. Conger received one from Washington asking information about his telegram of July 18th, and giving him a name to insert in his reply to establish authenticity. This seems to be an indication that the Yamen is suspected of having sent bogus messages.

There is still no answer from the Yamen in regard to food, except a strange verbal message purporting to come from Jung Lu to the Chairman of the General Committee asking him to make out a list of what he wanted, which Jung Lu would furnish, and for which Mr. Tewksbury could pay him later! The messenger brings a rumour that Li Ping Hêng was wounded in the shoulder at Yang

Ts'un. One of the Ministers thinks it a pity that it had not been a little lower (but the wound eventually proved fatal.)

There was an attack on the German Legation last night, as well as on the British, and this morning a message came from the Yamen apologizing for it, and saying that they had beheaded the man who made it!

A cow was killed the other day, to the great joy of everyone who could get some of it. One of the legation ladies sent for the cow's liver, only to find that it had been calmly appropriated by the marines. An attaché of the British Legation sent up for a part of the cow's kidney as a great luxury, but it had been already distributed. The sympathetic superintendent of the meat apportionment, however, not wishing to disappoint him, sent the man the kidney of a horse, "without note or comment;" afterwards meeting him, he inquired how he liked it. He had enjoyed it greatly, and remarked that while eating it he had forgotten that he was in China!

In the afternoon Lt. von Strauss made a sortie on a Chinese barricade in the Mongol Market addition, which provoked a great deal of retaliatory firing. Showers of bricks came over; one of the British marines had his head cut open, and two Chinese were badly stunned. The bricks are much more dangerous than the bullets. Fortunately the worst brick attack came while the Chinese workmen were at their afternoon meal, so that the most of them could stand quietly under shelter and watch the bricks curve through the air to their harmless destination.

In the evening a hard rain came on, and with it an attack, the firing being especially furious at each loud clap of thunder. It really appears as if it were considered as a signal from the gods for the encouragement of the Chinese.

THE RELIEF 425

Saturday, August 11.—Two ponies were condemned this morning on the ground that they were affected by phthisis, but they were absorbed by the less fastidious Chinese, and another horse and a mule were substituted. Dogs, cats, magpies, crows, and sparrows have all been shot for the Catholics, who got the condemned animals. It is proposed to give the grain directly to each family, instead of having it cooked in a common kettle and divided.

There is some indication of special activity on the wall of the city, where the Chinese flags have been removed, but the number of soldiers seems increased. They have begun firing on the American Legation again, and a ball went through the door of Mr. Squier's office and penetrated the outer door of the (so-called) iron "safe!" Bullets struck some of the other buildings, and one came into the Minister's bed-room. After several weeks of comparative immunity from this kind of attack by day, its sudden resumption by the enemy is peculiarly exasperating.

Sunday, August 12.—There was intermittent heavy firing during the night at no very long intervals, making it difficult to sleep. There were rumours of sharp attacks in various directions. An Austrian and a German were wounded, and a Frenchman killed. A Russian on duty on the wall was slightly wounded. Another Russian died in the hospital yesterday, and also a French marine. Over at the Fu there was a great deal of yelling during the night. Col. Shiba had kerosene tins beaten, and the Italian soldiers shouted, whistled, and cried "Bravo" to one another, to give the Chinese the impression of unlimited numbers.

It was understood yesterday that a deputy official was to come to-day to open a market, but no one appeared.

A man who sells eggs to the French Legation soldiers has told them that there was a battle at Chang Chia Wan yesterday, and 3,000 Chinese were killed. There are some appearances of a panic in the city. Jung Lu is said to have taken poison. It was very hot all day, and it was often remarked how trying this must be for the marching troops.

In the afternoon there was a sudden and savage attack on the Mongol Market defences, to which the Nordenfelt gun replied. The bullets fell thick, and very low. There was a melancholy funeral of two Frenchmen to-day, just on the eve of what we hope is to be the raising of the siege.

The ladies of the United States Legation were busy to-day making sand bags for the German Legation defences. The Austrian gun was taken to the stable-yard. A letter was received from the Yamen saying that the Princes and Ministers would come to the British Legation to-morrow to confer with regard to the cessation of hostilities. The French Captain La Bruce was killed early in the evening in his own Legation, while walking to a barricade. It might have been well to have replied that this Legation is at present a very unsafe place for "Princes and Ministers." Sir Claude planned to receive them in his own house. The Spanish Legation would have seemed a far more suitable place, but at last a mat-shed was put up outside the front gate. The Chinese do not believe in receiving them at all.

It is reported that a Chinese gun at the Ha Ta gate has been firing blank cartridges, so that the Germans did not think it worth while to reply with rifles. At a loop-hole in the Mongol Market region, two nights ago, a bullet cut clean through the small board over the opening, so that the bricks dropped down without having been

THE RELIEF

hit. It is becoming a favourite plan with the Chinese now to keep on firing away at a loophole and its neighbourhood, until the wall gives way. Sometimes they get the range, strap the gun tight, and keep blazing away at one spot. Our Nordenfelt yesterday knocked down a section of the Chinese barricade in this manner, but the hole was promptly filled up with sand bags.

Monday, August 13.—The attack which was expected came off, and was practically continuous all night, and very violent. The Chinese soldiers and their rifles seem to be different from those before used, and the bullets (Männlicher) have much more penetrating power. Many barricades were much weakened and must be repaired. It is marvellous that no one in the British Legation was hit during the night. The firing was more consecutive than at any time since the siege began, and strangely incongruous with proposals for peace,—another of the many glaring absurdities of our situation. The impression given by these repeated and furious onsets is that, the time being short, they must annihilate us immediately. The shooting was much lower than hitherto.

There was a meeting of the Ministers in the forenoon to consider the place of receiving the Yamen Ministers. It is difficult for the Ministers to refuse an interview with the Yamen, because it was on the ground of being useful in helping on such negotiations that they declined to go to Tientsin.

At half past ten o'clock, however, came a letter from the Yamen to say that the Ministers have reopened hostilities (!), by killing an officer and 26 men in the region of the Board of Works (just west of the British Legation), and as "the Yamen Ministers are busy," they can not come as agreed! There was no reply as to the purchase of food, and not an atom of news from outside.

Both the German and the American Legations were attacked last night, the former at very short range. Notice is posted that arrangements have been made to take photographs of the siege positions, etc., with a camera which belongs to a Japanese, and there are fortunately enough photographic chemicals available for the purpose.

Some Chinese cavalry leaving the city yesterday by the Ch'ien Mên were fired at several times from the wall, but this is not the alleged resumption of hostilities, but the fact that men were killed on the west of us. The Chinese officer who was shot is said to be a Captain who had guaranteed to take the Legation within five days, which time was up yesterday. This, however, is not authenticated. The American and Russian flags have been put up on the wall to-day, and a staff prepared for the British flag.

About eight o'clock in the evening there was, as expected, a furious attack in the Mongol Market region, which was kept up for a long time and only died down to be again resumed. An hour or so later there was a second, likewise very furious and vindictive.

Tuesday, August 14.—The distinction between to-day and yesterday was entirely obliterated, as no one could sleep, and very few made any pretence of even going to bed. The battery on the wall of the Imperial City began firing Krupp shells during the night, about ten shots in all. One of these fell in a dressing-room off Sir Claude's bed-room, and made a complete wreck of it. Three others struck in the front gate fort, one of them coming through the gate-way and knocking over by its concussion those who were at hand.

Between eleven and twelve o'clock there was an alarm on the bell of a " general attack," and every one turned out—the first experience of the kind for nearly six weeks.

THE RELIEF

Sir Claude was on hand and, after waiting to see how many appeared, dismissed them after a brief delay as if it were a mere drill.

Three hours later there was a second alarm, which was caused by the fear that the Chinese were about to make a rush into the Mongol Market defences. Volunteers were assigned their positions, and the attack was as savage as those which had preceded, and as unsuccessful. It was alleged by some of the Volunteers that the Chinese officers were heard urging the men to make the long-expected rush, crying "Don't be afraid—we can get through," to which after a short interval there was the response, "It can not be done."

In preparation for this attack all the big guns had been made ready, the American Colt's Automatic in the main gate, as usual, the Nordenfelt on its high platform back of the house of the Chinese Secretary, the Austrian and the "International" in the Mongol Market addition. In firing the latter, owing to its recoil and uncertainty, it was necessary to have a large porthole, and Mitchell, the American gunner, had his arm shattered by a rifle-ball while discharging the piece. When the shell-gun opened fire on us, the Colt's replied, and the gun was eventually silenced, or at least suspended operation.

All through the night at irregular intervals could be heard the deep baying of the Nordenfelt, the irresistible and simultaneous discharges of which must have been very depressing as well as exasperating to those within its range. The attack at the Fu was fierce as elsewhere, but it did not drive the Japanese from their position, for the Chinese did not charge. The same was the case in the Hanlin, and likewise in the French Legation, between 1 and 2 A. M.

A French priest and the Belgian doctor were slightly

wounded during the night, at the British Legation—among the very few casualties to civilians within that area during the whole siege. The Japanese doctor at the Su Wang Fu had a ball through his leg, a British marine was wounded in the shoulder, and a German who had been wounded previously and had recovered, was killed, also a Russian on the wall. It was understood that yesterday the Yamen had notified the Ministers that whatever Chinese officer reopened hostilities should be court-martialed. The proceedings of this fearsome night were a singular commentary upon this imaginary truce.

Between 2 and 3 A. M. there was distinctly heard the sharp rat-tat-tat of a machine gun far to the east, and it was at once concluded that the foreign troops are at hand. The yard, even at that early hour, swarmed with eager groups discussing the probabilities. The question was raised whether the machine-guns which we heard might not be in the hands of the Chinese themselves, and it was remembered that Li Hung Chang had ordered a large number of them many years ago. (It was not then suspected, what was afterwards said to have been a fact, that these particular guns had been captured from the Chinese, and were probably a part of the very equipment referred to.)

Many excellent designs have been sent in for the proposed commemorative medal, and to-day they are represented by drawings placed on the bulletin board, and votes are solicited as to the material, the pattern, the inscription obverse and reverse. A limit of time is also fixed. Unfortunately for the best effect, the all absorbing interest in the impending relief deprives the mere pictorial symbol of much of its interest, so that the voting halted, and was soon altogether abandoned.

In spite of the heavy firing none of our barricades were

overthrown, and the strength of those most threatened in the Mongol Market tract had been almost doubled within twenty-four hours. During the forenoon it was learned that the shell-gun on the Imperial city, which fired so much last night, had been taken away, which indicates activity of some sort. Our Austrian Maxim has been removed to the north stable court to be ready for it, however, should it begin again.

There has been a sound of heavy cannonading to the eastward all the morning. From the wall the Southern City seems to be quiet, but Chinese troops are hurrying in through the Ch'ien Mên, instead of going out, as yesterday. The bulletin-board has a notice that " the sentries in charge of the south gates have received orders not to allow any civilian to leave the Legation without a special permit from the officer in charge of the defences, since in case of a general attack by retreating Chinese the services of every available volunteer will be required."

Another order announces that " women and children and persons not on duty are requested as far as possible to keep within doors to-day, as there will probably be considerable danger from dropping fire."

From the city wall an excellent view is to be had of the bombardment of the Ch'i Hua gate, upon which thus far not much impression seems to have been made. There is also a heavy attack at the Tung Pien Gate, and all the time the deep rumbling of the heavy booming guns of " our troops." " Blessed are the people that hear the joyful sound." The troops on the wall thought those outside would " be lucky if they got in to-morrow night."

Soon after two o'clock, Mr. Moore, who was on the wall, reported to Capt. Hall that he saw foreign troops in the distance; though this was doubted, it soon proved to be the case, and he was sent post-haste to convey the news to Sir Claude MacDonald. It was at first erroneously supposed to be the Germans who had been sighted, but they soon showed up as British.

The excitement was now at its height, and the few who had leave to do so, not being on duty, hastened out through the Russian Legation to the street, only to be told that the troops were already making their way into the Tartar city through the water-gate. There was at the time very little water, but the mud rendered the entrance through the narrow passage somewhat disagreeable, yet it was only for a few rods and unworthy of mention as a difficulty in a march.

The regiment which made the first entry, was the 1st Sikhs and then the 7th Bengal Rajput Infantry, and Gen. Gaselee was one of the first officers to be seen. The banks of the canal were lined by Chinese, and the few Europeans present, among whom was Sir Claude, tried to raise a cheer, but their voices were unequal to the task and it was a feeble failure!

On reaching the British Legation there was such a riot of joy as is seldom seen in Asia, and such as was never seen in the Capital of the Chinese Empire. Everybody swarmed out to see the glorious spectacle. The Rajputs cheered as they marched, till they brought up on the tennis-court, beyond which there seemed to be nowhere to go. The next regiment was the 24th Punjab Infantry (Frontier Force), who went cheering past the hospital filled with brave but disappointed, yet happy, men who had lived through it after all, and now saw the day of rescue.

It was remembered that the 1st Sikhs regiment is descended from the one which helped take Peking forty years ago. The 1st Bengal Lancers came next, having had to

"HERE THEY COME," GENERAL GASELEE ON THE RIGHT

FRATERNIZING ON THE TENNIS COURT

THE RELIEF

wait for the Ch'ien Mên to be forced; then a detachment of the Royal Welsh Fusileers, the 23rd Field Battery, the Hongkong Regiment, and the Royal Marines.

By this time the limited available spaces of the tennis-court and the Legation roads and paths was more than exhausted, and the whole place was one complicated tangle of Sikhs, Rajputs, Lancers and Fusileers, with Chinese and the besieged Occidentals everywhere at once.

In the midst of this wild welter the American 14th Infantry arrived, to add to the joy and the chaos, and everyone is asking to know where some one else is, and what is going on in that segment of creation outside of the Peking Legations.

The troops were no sooner in the courts than Gen. Gaselee relieved the sentinels on duty with his own men. One of them (a Sikh), was assigned to the front gate fort where the Colt's Automatic was pouring out its reckless welcome in a thunder of rat-tats. There he was immediately hit by a bullet through a loophole and went promptly to the hospital. The tumultuous cheering of both the besieged and the relievers roused the Chinese from their afternoon nap, and they began the fusillade with renewed vigour, but apparently without any notion of what the altered conditions denoted. For a time the bullets were falling thickly all over the Legation, and the wife of a Belgian engineer was wounded in the leg,— the only case in which a lady received any injury from shot or shell during the whole siege.

In a very short time a large hole was blown into the Carriage Park through the thick wall to which we had owed so much, and in a brief time that expansive enclosure was filled with the jaded horses of the Lancers. The Chinese shots grew less in vigour, fewer in number, more distant in space, and died away to nothing. The men who had so long manned the barricades facing us "folded their tents like the Arabs, and silently stole away" (except that so far as they had any tents they left them in situ), and were to be seen and heard no more.

XXIV

FROM THE TAKU FORTS TO THE RELIEF OF PEKING

AS the military events connected with the progress of the Allies from the coast to the capital have been detailed at length by more than one competent observer, they will be sketched here only in the briefest manner,—though of the deepest importance and interest.

While the clouds were thickening about the all but doomed city of Peking, a splendid fleet had for weeks been proudly riding at anchor off the mouth of the Peiho. There was good reason for indecision as to their movements.

By the middle of June it was obvious to everyone that the political complications were so grave that no peaceful solution was at all likely. The Mephistophelian cynicism of the Edicts of the Chinese Government, the fact that the regular troops and the Boxers were everywhere fraternizing, and the increasing evidence that the Throne was privy to the councils of extermination, made the situation difficult beyond precedent, surpassing the flight of the wildest imagination previous to this experience. Peking was already cut off from the world. There was an unknown body of Chinese troops between the capital and Tientsin, where the McCalla-Seymour Expedition was soon to be fighting for its life against overwhelming odds. Gen. Nieh was somewhere, and there was a great camp of his troops at Lu T'ai, which could be brought to bear upon the line of communication of the fleet with the Settlement of Tientsin. There were signs that those troops were about to move, that the river itself was being mined with torpedoes, and that the Taku Forts were to be strongly reinforced, so that their capture without enormous loss would be out of the question.

On Saturday, June 16th, the Admirals held a Council and under these exigent circumstances determined to send an ultimatum calling for the disbandment of the troops, and announcing that if it was not complied with before 2 A. M., the United Squadron would destroy the forts. Admiral Kempff, representing the United States, dissented from this step, but that fact did not influence his subsequent actions.

The questions in what is termed "International Law" thus brought to the front, have served for much debate, and many vigorous editorials ever since. But at the time, and under the circumstances, it is difficult to see what else the Admirals could have done with any self-respect, or with any regard to the interests of their respective Powers. It is quite true that it was this ultimatum which directly led to the corresponding order to the Legations to leave Peking within four and twenty hours, and it is likewise a fact that the effect of the attack upon the Taku Forts by the Allied Forces was to fire the Chinese national feeling, as nothing else had ever before done. In some respects it is comparable in its consequences to the effect of the assault upon Fort Sumter upon the people of the North, at the opening of the American Civil War.

Nevertheless, if the Taku Forts had not been taken within a few hours of that time, it is a moral certainty that not only would the Legations in Peking have been even in far greater peril than they were placed by this act, but that it would have been hard to save the lives of a single man, woman, or child of the large numbers who were at Tientsin, and who as it was were rescued from deadly peril only with the greatest difficulty.

The Chinese Commander of the principal Fort acted with more decision and courage than was expected, and an hour before the time limit had expired opened fire upon the fleet, and hostilities had begun. The Forts were for the third time assailed by foreign guns, which in 1858 had taken them within the compass of twenty minutes, while the succeeding year the Forts had been able to beat back a combined squadron of thirteen British and French gunboats. On the present occasion the fight lasted about six hours, when the last gun was silenced and the north Fort was stormed, the British and the Japanese entering simultaneously, and the other contingents a little later, the Chinese soldiers prudently abandoning the position in hot haste.

A shell from the British "Algerine" exploded a magazine in the south Fort, which blew up, with a magnificent column of black smoke, 500 feet in height, the wreckage falling for miles around. By 7:30 all the Forts had been taken, with a loss of 21 killed and 57 wounded on the part of the assailants. But for various errors of judgment on the part of the Chinese, and their lack of resoluteness, the results might have been very different.

The situation at Tientsin was now serious, but no information regarding it had reached Taku, the communication having been completely cut off. It was imperatively necessary to get word to the fleet of the dire distress of the foreign settlement. In this emergency James Watts, a young Englishman of 22 years, volunteered to ride with despatches through forty miles of country swarming with Boxers. He started under cover of darkness on a pony, with three mounted Cossacks, for a journey of twelve hours, knowing only three words of Russian. He had to speed through villages where men were sitting with rifles and fixed bayonets, his flask was shot away, and the lives of all were in momently peril. The horses swam a creek near a hostile village and reached Taku, where the despatches were delivered to the Russian Admiral. This brave act saved the lives of the besieged at Tientsin, and was subsequently rewarded with a decoration.

From Tangku to Tientsin the railway was largely torn up by Boxers, and the last part of the distance was made with extreme difficulty by the relieving forces. They were welcomed by the besieged with great joy, a full week after the Forts had been taken.

In case relief did not come, the military authorities had seriously debated the question of the necessity of abandoning Tientsin altogether, and retreating upon Taku.

The relieving body had no sooner reached Tientsin than a party was sent out to rescue in turn the force of Admiral Seymour which though but a few miles from Tientsin was unable to move on account of the large number of the wounded and the strength of the enemy. To the fortunes and misfortunes of that famous expedition it will be desirable to devote a little attention.

Early in June Admiral Seymour had proposed that the senior naval officers should consult in regard to mutual protection, and the first meeting of this kind was held June 4th, the officers of eight nations being present. Two days later at another consultation it was agreed that if communication with Peking should be cut off, it should be reopened with whatever force was necessary.

On the 9th another conference was held owing to the

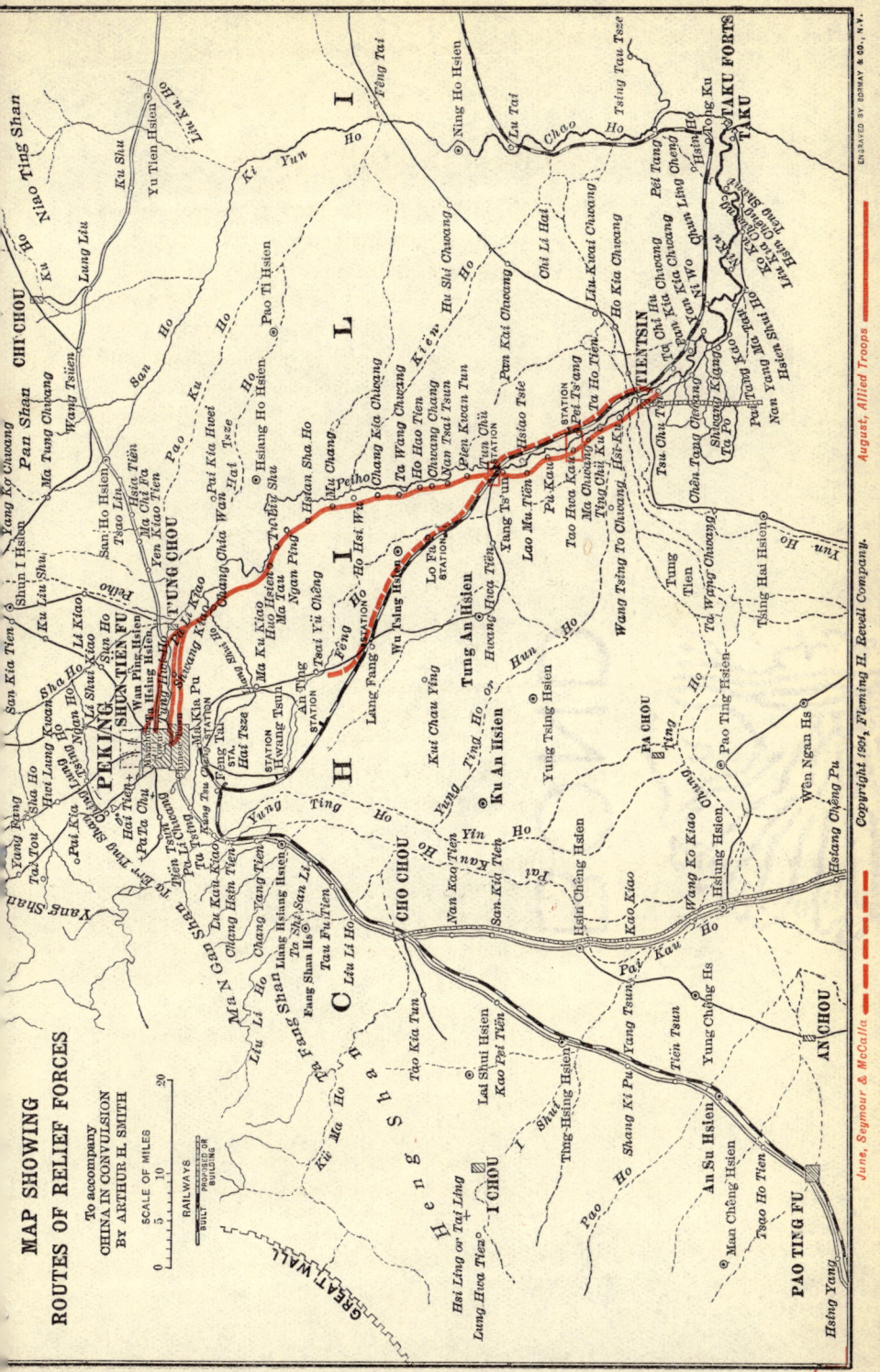

FROM TAKU TO RELIEF OF PEKING 439

receipt of an urgent telegram from Peking, the Ministers saying that unless they were soon relieved it would be too late. Capt. McCalla was resolved to go to the relief of the United States Minister, and Admiral Seymour in like manner declared his intention to start at once, and expressed a hope that the rest would coöperate.

The force which left on the morning of the 10th was composed of 300 British, 112 Americans, 40 Italians, and 25 Austrians. The train proceeded to Yang Ts'un where it had to stop for repairs. There it remained for the night, and there two more trains joined the expedition, making a total number of 112 Americans, 25 Austrians, 915 British, 100 French, 450 Germans, 40 Italians, 54 Japanese, and 112 Russians. This was increased the next day by the addition of 200 Russians and 58 French, to a total of 2,066 men.

On the 12th a guard having been left at Lo Fa, it was found that the line was much cut up in front. A party was sent out to An Ting to prevent more damage and to hold the station there. The party was attacked three times by Boxers, who retreated with the loss of fifteen men.

About the middle of the forenoon there was another onset by 450 Boxers, who advanced with great courage and enthusiasm, but who were repulsed with a total loss of about 150. As the party at An Ting was out of ammunition a retreat was ordered.

On the 13th Maj. Johnstone was sent towards An Ting, but was attacked in a village adjoining the railway. The Boxers lost about 25 men killed, while there were no foreign casualties. The party returned to the main body on the evening of the 14th. On that day there was a fierce and determined assault by Boxers in great numbers on the train at Lang Fang. They advanced in a loose formation, with the utmost courage under a withering fire, and some even reached the train before they were killed. Their loss was about 100. Five Italians who were on an exposed picket in an abandoned village were killed.

At 5:30 P. M. a messenger from Lo Fa in the rear reported that the guard was being attacked by a large body of the enemy. A train was taken down the line to assist them, when it was found that the fight was over, and that the Boxers were retreating having left about 100 killed. Two small cannon had been captured from the Chinese. Two seamen were dangerously wounded, one of whom died later.

On the 15th the line was repaired under a strong guard, but the road below Lo Fa to the rear was reported broken up, and the Boxers were concentrating on Yang Ts'un to cut off the retreat of the expedition.

On the 16th a train endeavoured to get through to Tientsin, starting at 4 A. M., but returned at 3 P. M., because the line was too much damaged. Both provisions and ammunition were now running short; the expedition was entirely cut off from its base and since for three days there had been no intelligence from Tientsin, it was ignorant of what was occurring elsewhere. It was vital that the rear should be protected; but when on the 17th a train reached Yang Ts'un it found the station demolished, communication more than ever cut off, and no supplies obtainable. Messages had been sent back to Tientsin with orders for junks and provisions to be sent to Yang Ts'un, but no couriers had got through, and even if they had done so no boats could have been sent. From the 13th of June to the 26th there was no communication from the Admiral to Tientsin or *vice versa*.

As an advance was now felt to be an impossibility the recall of the trains in the front was determined on.

The following day—June 18th—a new aspect was put on affairs by a strong attack at Lang Fang, not as heretofore by Boxers, but by the regular troops of Tung Fu Hsiang, who had been stationed in the Hunting Park south of Peking, and who now began to "bear a hand" in a decided manner. The force including cavalry was estimated at not less than 5,000 men, armed with the latest magazine rifles. This gave the first definite knowledge that Imperial troops were arrayed against the expedition. They were driven off, but rallied, and when repulsed were supposed to have lost 400 killed. The loss of the Allies was six killed, and 48 wounded.

At a conference the next day (19th) it was decided to abandon the railway trains, and to withdraw to Tientsin, marching by the left bank of the river, conveying the wounded and the necessaries in boats, four of which had been taken by the Germans below Yang Ts'un. A start was made at 3 P. M. A six-pounder gun had to be thrown overboard before one of the junks would float. The men were unskilled in handling the clumsy boats, and no Chinese were to be had. The enemy opened fire, but were driven back. Several villages had to be carried by rifle fire or by bayonet charges, which were invariably successful. A one-pound gun used by the enemy was harassing, but its position could not be located. The distance made this day was eight miles. The Chinese cavalry hovered about all day firing occasionally, the enemy using artillery which was replied to in kind. Several villages had to be taken by fighting, the enemy being strongly posted in Pei Ts'ang. It was decided after a rest to make a night-march.

On the 21st the enemy made an increasingly stubborn resistance, and their gun-power was augmented so that but six miles were made. The lighter containing the guns filled and sank, and had to be abandoned, only the Maxims being saved.

At 4 P. M. the expedition arrived opposite the Imperial Chinese Armory at Hsiku. A party of 100 men under Maj. Johnstone was sent across the river to rush the position, and at the same time a German detachment crossed lower down, capturing several Krupp guns. The two parties soon cleared the Armory, the main body crossing the river and occupying the place, which was commodious and defensible by the numerous captured guns. The provisions remaining were sufficient only for three days at half allowance, but the next day when there was an opportunity to make a search, 15 tons of rice were found. This set at rest all fears of starvation.

Renewed efforts were made to communicate with Tientsin, but in vain. The Chinese made a most determined attempt on the 23rd to retake the Armory, but were wholly unsuccessful. Immense supplies of guns, ammunition, and war material of the latest pattern were found there; thus the great want of food and ammunition being suddenly met it was possible to hold out for several days. The number of wounded was about 230 and on this account it was impossible to force a way to Tientsin, now but a few miles distant. The couriers had all been either killed or stopped. Guns were mounted and a Boxer stronghold down the river was attacked with such good effect that thereafter the enemy was more quiet.

A courier succeeded on the 23rd in getting through to Tientsin. Although captured and tied for a time to a tree, he had destroyed his message and was released.

FROM TAKU TO RELIEF OF PEKING 443

A Chinese soldier taken prisoner the next day said that Gen. Nieh's army was much discouraged at their failure, having attacked with 25 battalions of 300 or 400 men each. On the 25th the relief column under the Russian Col. Shirinsky appeared in sight, to the joy of all. The wounded were transported across the river, and the whole force followed later, bivouacking on the bank for the night. On the 26th, after the return march had commenced, Lt. Lowther-Crofton, and Mr. Davidge, Gunner, remained behind to destroy as far as possible the contents of the Armory, which were of the estimated value of three million pounds sterling. After the work of destruction had been accomplished the officers recrossed the river, mounted ponies which were in waiting, and overtook the main body.

During the whole sixteen days it was difficult to estimate with precision the numbers of the enemy. At first they were simply Boxers armed with spears, but later the Chinese regulars, and perhaps the best fighting men to be found in the Empire, joined them. It was unforeseen that these soldiers would join in the attack, and this alone made the whole enterprise impracticable.

The gallantry and steadiness with which it was conducted by this mixed contingent are worthy of all praise. Admiral Seymour in his official report especially commends the conduct and services of Capt. Von Usedom of the Imperial German Navy, whom he had nominated as his successor in case of accident, and also Capt. McCalla, each of whom were wounded.

The dramatic incidents of this attempted relief expedition attracted universal attention, and whatever else the enterprise may have accomplished it disposed once for all of the favourite proposition so often advanced that it would be possible for a small but well organized and thoroughly equipped foreign force to march through China from end to end without effective opposition.

An important result of this failure to force a way to Peking was the profound conviction on the part of many military authorities that the Capital could not now be reached without an enormous army prepared for all contingencies, and able to hold open communications with their base against any possible force which the Chinese could bring. Extreme confidence in foreign ability to deal with Chinese opposition, thus gave way to a much juster estimate of the difficulties to be faced when the Chinese were thoroughly aroused and poured forth in practically illimitable numbers.

The story of the Siege of Tientsin deserves far more space than can be devoted to it in these pages, for taken altogether it is perhaps not less remarkable than the Siege in Peking.

It should be remembered that the Foreign Settlements, French, British, and German, lie along the Peiho, beginning a mile or so below the native city and extending for another two miles or more, with an average breadth of perhaps half a mile. An earth rampart fully ten miles in length surrounds the settlements, the native city, and the suburbs. The vicinity of the city itself and that of all the settlements, was crowded with Chinese villages, each of which became a natural and a convenient nest for Boxers and for Imperial Soldiers in their attack.

The rampart which, could it have been held, would have made an excellent defence, was partly within and partly without the lines, and the handful of foreign soldiers, aggregating about 2,400 when reënforced by the Volunteers, was totally inadequate to guard so long a line, attacked by perhaps five thousand Chinese troops, with an indefinite number of coöperating Boxers.

FROM TAKU TO RELIEF OF PEKING 445

Instead of making a strenuous attack in two places at once, the Chinese contented themselves with a galling rifle fire from across the river, and indeed from every direction. The bombardment by shells began on Sunday, June 17th—the day of the fighting at the Taku Forts—by a plan evidently preconcerted, and continued with occasional intermittence until the city was captured a month later.

The miscellaneous foreign community retreated to the Municipal Hall, a lofty structure in the Norman style, well adapted to serve both as a fort and a hospital.

The larger part of the non-combatants gathered there under siege conditions, but a considerable number of the missionaries were invited by Mr. Edmund Cousins, the hospitable agent of Jardine, Matheson & Co., to his compound, where also the native Christians to the number of over 500 found accommodation in the expansive godowns. As in Peking, so here at the beginning of the siege, the Christians were regarded as a menace and a nuisance, and as in Peking so in Tientsin, it was not long before it was perceived that without their help the necessary labour simply could not have been performed as practically all other Chinese quit their work and fled.

The whole settlement was barricaded with bales of goods from the godowns, a task which, owing to the long distances and the number of cross-streets, involved a great amount of exhausting labour. The men among the Christians carried water, ammunition, and provisions, and dug the numerous graves, the women did the hospital washing, picked over the camel's-wool for pillows, and performed much other useful service, winning in the end unstinted praise.

The arrival of the relief force at Tientsin did not prove the immediate deliverance of the Foreign Settlements from perpetual attack, as had been expected. The enemy was numerous and gradually became aggressive. After a fierce and bloody contest, the Eastern Arsenal was taken on June 27th, a slightly inaccurate report of which by Yü Lu, the Governor, found its way into the "Peking Gazette," and enlightened the darkness of the besieged in the Legations. The military relations were, it is true, sufficiently harmonious, but that did not lead to the vigorous action which any one or two of the detachments would have been likely to take by themselves.

A Fort situated at the junction of the Peiho and the Grand Canal was the key of the position, for it commanded the native city, the suburbs, the settlements, and the line of advance to Peking by rail or river. The difficulties of the Allies were enormously increased by the inexplicable lack of suitable artillery, theirs being far inferior to that of the Chinese. Many of the Chinese guns were difficult to locate, and practically inaccessible, but their range was excellent, and their attacks most annoying. On a single day six shells were thrown into the Temperance Hall, occupied as the head-quarters of Gen. Dorward and his staff. One shell went through the dinner-table while the officers were at tiffin, followed immediately by another equally well aimed.

It was unsafe to appear anywhere upon the streets on account of random shots, the steady rifle fire, and the constant shooting from loopholes in Chinese houses in the French settlement and elsewhere, at every foreigner who showed himself. The settlements were full of spies, many of them posted in foreign houses deserted by their owners, whence they kept up a perpetual fusillade. Some of them even acted as signalmen for the Chinese gunners at a distance, indicating at what places to direct their fire, and it proved practically impossible to detect and dislodge

BLACK FORT AT TIENTSIN, OUTSIDE VIEW

BLACK FORT AT TIENTSIN, INSIDE VIEW

FROM TAKU TO RELIEF OF PEKING 447

them all, but as many as were caught were immediately executed.

The center of the fighting and the key of the position on the east side of the river was the railway station, the holding of which was recognized both by the Chinese and the Allies as vital. The courage and persistence of the Russians at this point more than once saved the day. They guarded the pontoon bridge, and bore the brunt of the heavy fighting in the exposed positions between the river and the captured Arsenal. On one occasion engines were urgently needed down the line. There were locomotives at the station, but the problem was how to get them out under the heavy shell fire. Russian infantry made a wide feint attack to attract the enemy's attention on the left, while two engines on which steam had been got up, and three trucks were to make a dash over a mile of exposed embankment.

Hardly had the first puff of white smoke appeared from the funnel, when the Chinese saw what was going on and at once turned their guns upon the train. Four shells whizzed over it and then two fell just short; speed was gathered and the gunners did not again get so near, but the gauntlet had to be run for a mile or so, and it was made warm for them all the way. It was a daring deed dashingly done, and the most exciting incident of the day.

On the 5th of July transportation was provided and the ladies and children who were still left in Tientsin were sent to Tangku, on the way to some safer place than a settlement which was daily being shelled. A previous party had escaped just in time to witness the attack on the forts, and to be within range of the fire,—to their imminent peril, from which they all happily escaped.

For a summary of the following events, as for some

which have been previously mentioned, we are indebted to the graphic and trustworthy narrative of the Correspondent of the " London Times," who called attention to the surprising and unique fact that 10,000 European troops were being held in check by about 15,000 Chinese braves, the former paralyzed by the lack of long-range guns; thus repeating the lesson which England had paid so dearly to learn in South Africa—the importance of heavy artillery.

The inactivity of the Allied forces encouraged the Chinese to renewed efforts. Not content with vigorously shelling the settlements, they were busily engaged in pushing out their lines in a south-westerly direction, until eventually their flank rested on the ruined building at the race-course, their left remaining as before on the mud wall where the Lu T'ai canal flows through it. Their lines thus stretched from north-east to south-west over a distance of about six miles, in a rough crescent or semi-circular shape, having the settlements for a centre. A British battery of naval guns on the mud wall at the extreme west of the northern line of defence was in a precarious position, being under a harassing fire from front and rear, besides being enfiladed. The settlements, now become one huge camp, were subjected to a severe cross-fire, in addition to being bombarded from the fort near the city and from the batteries on the north bank of the Lu T'ai canal. The practice made by the Chinese gunners showed signs of considerable improvement, so that an increasing amount of damage was done and the casualties in barracks grew frequent. Inactivity was no longer possible; something had to be done.

The most pressing need was for the clearance of the rear and flank of the battery of British guns on the mud wall, and this was accomplished on the 9th by a combined wide flanking movement to the south-west, working around eventually to the north-east until the West Arsenal was captured and cleared. This was accomplished by the Japanese blue-jackets and the American marines, who entered together, the Japanese flag flying over it soon after. The whole movement was well planned and well executed by the British, Japanese and Americans in combination, the naval battery was relieved in flank and rear, and the settlements were subjected to no further cross shell-fire.

The next day passed quietly, the Chinese even refraining from attacking the outposts at the railway station, which had not before happened since the siege opened. They began again on the 11th, and were only repulsed after three hours' sharp fighting, in which the French and Japanese lost heavily, and the British and Russians slightly. The Boxers had bayonets, and as they got into a string of railway trucks lying outside of the foreign lines, the soldiers had to turn them out at the point of the bayonet. The difficulties in getting the Allied artillery into position were great, owing to the lack of material, tools and machinery. These were at length overcome, and on the 13th it was arranged that a combined movement of the Russians, assisted by the Germans, should be made on the batteries of the Chinese at the Lu T'ai canal, with a force of perhaps 3,500. Another body of about 4,500, consisting of Japanese, British, Americans, French and Austrians, was to advance under cover of the western battery of British naval guns and attempt the capture of the city of Tientsin.

The forces of the Japanese and British, under General Fukushima and General Dorward, started at 3 A. M., making a wide flanking movement similar to the one on the 9th.

At daylight the British batteries attacked the Chinese position. The Allied troops converged on the West Arsenal about a mile from the south gate.

During the morning there was a terrific explosion caused by the blowing up of a vast quantity of brown prismatic powder stored in a magazine connected with the East Arsenal and situated near the Lu T'ai canal. A colossal cloud of smoke stood up white and still against the clear blue sky—a "wonderful and beautiful sight." In the settlements nearly every one got the impression that his house had been struck by a shell, and many, running out to see what damage had been done, found this marvel in the sky.

The plan was to advance against the south gate, which the Japanese were to blow up and so effect an entrance; on their right were the French, and later, through an error, the Americans under Col. Liscum; on the left were the British.

The day was hot, and so was the fire from the British battery as well as from the Chinese guns and the innumerable rifles on the wall. The plain is dotted with tumuli each representing a Chinese grave, but they afforded very little shelter for so many soldiers at so short a distance from the enemy. Col. Liscum fell pierced by a bullet, and the loss of the Americans, as well as of the other detachments, was very great, perhaps amounting to ten per cent. of the forces engaged, and including a great number of officers. If the Chinese infantry and cavalry which during the whole morning had been seen drawn up on the plain to the westward had taken an active part in the operations, matters would have been still more serious. As it was, the failure of ammunition and the difficulty of making effective headway made the situation bad enough.

Hour after hour passed, but the blowing up of the south gate did not take place. At length Gen. Fukishima sent word to Gen. Dorward that he should himself occupy his present position throughout the night, to which Gen. Dorward agreed. Meantime no report had come from the Russians whose operations on the north were a principal part of the work of the day. It later appeared that they had been very successful. After heavy fighting they had captured the batteries on the north bank of the Lu T'ai canal, and pushing on to destroy two Chinese camps, left a force to attack in the dawn, the main body returning to camp with the loss of about 150 men.

At three o'clock on the morning of the 14th, the Japanese crossed the city moat, blew up the entrance to the bastion of the south gate, scaled the walls, and opening the gate itself from the inside, admitted the rest of the force. The Japanese, French, British and Americans poured into the city, the Chinese dispersing like clouds before a strong wind. The Chinese position, had it been properly defended, was one of irresistible strength, but Chinese troops are incapable of resisting a resolute attack of Western or Japanese soldiers and had virtually abandoned their defence before there was any external evidence of that fact.

The city was no sooner captured than a Tientsin Provisional Government was organized by the Military Commanders, and installed in the yamen of the Governor General, who had fled, and who seems to have killed himself and his whole family at Yang Ts'un.

From the occupation of the city onward for a period of nearly three weeks, the whole world, especially the tiny segment of it imprisoned in the Peking Legations, was anxiously waiting to know what was next to be done toward their relief. The correspondence in regard to the matter would fill volumes, and there is more between the lines than in them.

Considering the proximity of Japan and the completeness of her military preparations, it appeared to many that, in the dire emergency, that Power would surely be intrusted with the task of rescuing the besieged of all nations, lest by undue delay they should all be massacred together. Japan was ready to do the work, provided she were asked to do so by all the other Powers. The "other Powers" had their own ideas, some of which were expressed and some of which were repressed. In case Japan were to execute this commission, what was to prevent her from retaining the territory which would be once more hers by right of conquest? Every one had vivid memories of the events following the war between China and Japan, when the latter Empire was defrauded of the fruits of her victory by "diplomacy," in other words by superior force.

The result was what every one, even the besieged themselves, anticipated, and diplomatically next to nothing was done beyond exchanging notes and ascertaining by slow processes of conference, proposition and explanation, iterated and reiterated, what the Powers respectively were *not* prepared to do. Troops meantime were pouring into northern China from the uttermost parts of the earth, with more and ever more to follow.

There was not wanting evidence that delay might be fatal to the success of the relief of the Legations, but the inevitable difficulties attendant upon the movement of large bodies of troops in a foreign land under unpropitious conditions, especially when as now flying several different flags, made it unlikely that anything would be done before September. The effect of the repulse of Admiral Seymour, as already remarked, was to inspire

WALL OF TIENTSIN AFTER BOMBARDMENT

GATE THROUGH WHICH ALLIES ENTERED TIENTSIN

extreme distrust of any but the most thorough preparation, especially as it was thought that the Chinese might be able to mass perhaps fifty thousand troops to oppose the Allied advance. The Americans and the British were alike impatient for a forward movement, but nothing seemed decided upon.

It became known at a later day that the influence of Jung Lu had been exerted in Peking to minimize the unavoidable attacks upon the Legations, and that, while he could not repress he could in some degree neutralize the vicious energy of Tung Fu Hsiang; and in this he was to a considerable degree successful. Jung Lu was in communication with trusted Chinese at Taku and at the Pei T'ang Forts, who perfectly comprehended the situation. It was learned from messengers who left Peking at the time when the capture of Tientsin was first known there, that the party of Prince Tuan and Tung Fu Hsiang was practically irresistible, and that it would not do to wait till September to start the army of relief. This information was communicated to Mr. Detring, one of the commissioners of the Imperial Customs, and by him to the Allied Commanders.

On the 3rd of August a five hours' conference of the Allied Generals was held, at which it was decided to start the next day, despite the fact that it was in the midst of the rainy season when the difficulties of transport are likely to be almost insuperable. As it was they were truly colossal, and were greatly augmented by the heterogeneous nature of the Allied forces, and the endless variety of their equipment. The latter was at all points insufficient, even that of the Japanese, who had to provide for a division instead, as originally planned, for a brigade. The road was blocked with carts of all sizes and kinds, from the light little wagon used by the

Japanese to the heavy army wagons of the Americans, drawn by four enormous mules and capable under any ordinary circumstances of hauling immense loads. The total number of troops was in the vicinity of 20,000, of whom the Japanese had about 10,000, the Russians 4,000, the British 3,000, the Americans 2,000, and the other Powers each but a few hundred. All the larger contingents were provided with artillery, the Japanese alone having perhaps as many guns as all the others combined.

On the afternoon of the 4th the British and American troops moved out toward Hsiku, where Admiral Seymour's expedition had taken the Armory. The route lay through the endless series of villages which line the Peiho on either side. Heavy rain had threatened, and on the way it began to fall, making the roads slippery and furnishing a foretaste of what might be expected if the fall should be heavy and continuous.

Before the village was reached the rain had stopped. Gen. Gaselee took up his headquarters with the British troops to the left of the place, and the Americans to the right. Orders were issued for an early start on the following day, and the force lay down on the wet ground to snatch what sleep they might before the impending fight. The British troops consisted of four companies of the Welsh Fusiliers; the 1st Bengal Lancers; the 12th Field Battery and the Hongkong Artillery, with two naval 12-pounders and four Maxims; the 1st Sikhs, 250 of the 24th Punjab Infantry, and 400 of the Rajputs. The Naval Brigade was to coöperate with the Russians and French, preparing the way for an attack on the enemy's left.

The American force under Gen. Chaffee consisted of 450 marines, the 14th Regiment, 1,000 strong; the 9th Infantry, 800 strong; two Hotchkiss guns, and the Fifth

FROM TAKU TO RELIEF OF PEKING 455

Field Battery under Capt. Reilly. The Japanese division was under Gen. Yamaguchi, Gen. Fukushima being Chief of Staff, with three field batteries, and six mountain batteries. The Russians had two infantry regiments with a nominal strength of 2,000, two field batteries (eight guns each) and some squadrons of Cossacks. The French, only a few hundred in number, were infantry from Tongking, with two mountain batteries firing melinite.

The enemy were intrenched in a position running roughly north-east and south-west across the river and the railway, their right resting on an embankment, their left five miles away on the other side of the river, near the fifth railway bridge, beyond which the country was inundated. The main strength of their position was in the centre where it crossed the river. Here was a skilfully concealed series of rifle pits and trenches from which it would have been exceedingly difficult to dislodge a courageous enemy. On the left bank of the river their position was protected along its whole length by a canal.

The combined forces of the Japanese, British, and Americans were to operate against the enemy's position on the right bank of the river, the Japanese leading the attack, the British supporting, and the Americans in reserve, while the Russians and French, assisted by the guns of the Naval Brigade, were to operate on the left bank.

About 3 A. M., the Japanese moved forward and captured a battery which would have enfiladed a front attack on the enemy's centre. There was an artillery duel for a time, when the Japanese under a galling fire made a charge for which the Chinese did not wait, although they inflicted severe losses on the Japanese before taking flight. The whole army advanced, the Americans on the left, the British in the center, and the Japanese on the right. Here and there the Chinese made some slight resistance at long range, and it was expected that they would make a stand near Pei Ts'ang where they were supposed to hold strong positions, but while they had the positions they had not the disposition to stick to them. The fight was practically over when the first trenches were rushed. Before 9 A. M., the Japanese occupied Nan Ts'ang, after which all firing ceased.

The Japanese had borne the brunt of the fight, and their losses were all out of proportion to those of the other forces engaged, being estimated at about 60 killed and 240 wounded. The British lost four killed and 21 wounded, while the Americans lost none. The Russians on the left bank had six wounded. The Chinese loss in men was not large, owing to their being protected by a mud wall, but they lost " face " and lost heart, a far more important matter than the actual number killed.

The whole army spent the night at Pei Ts'ang. On the morning of the 6th there was another encounter with the enemy at the ruins of the railway station of Yang Ts'un which lasted for about four hours, the Chinese being driven back on the town of Yang Ts'un, the Russians shelling them, and the Bengal Lancers clearing them out of the villages. The effect of the previous day's action was throughout apparent, the enemy fighting in a very half-hearted manner. The heaviest losses were sustained by the Americans, 65 killed and wounded in the 14th Regiment, and nine in the 9th. The British losses were under 50, the Russians had seven killed and 20 wounded.

The troops were exhausted after their two days of marching and fighting in excessive heat, and it was decided to remain at Yang Ts'un during the whole of the following day, to rest the force and to wait for supplies.

The advance was resumed on the 8th, the whole force to march thereafter on the right bank; the Japanese in front, the Russians next, the Americans following, the British bringing up the rear, while the French were to remain at Yang Ts'un. The Japanese were quick marchers and the Russians slow, slouching along with frequent halts at a pace hardly exceeding a mile an hour, which greatly embarrassed the Americans in their rear, who were often compelled to halt on the sandy plains in the hot sun, while the Russians were resting in the umbrageous villages in front. This fact was of importance as accounting for the large number of casualties which they suffered from the heat, the Americans and the British being obliged to do the heaviest marching in the hottest hours of the day.

The superior organization and equipment of the Japanese were everywhere conspicuous, and their position in the front of the column gave the enemy no time to rally, so that their retreat was in reality a long and rapid flight before the agile men from the Land of the Rising Sun, who gave them no respite and no pause. Gen. Fukushima, the moving spirit of the pursuit, was asked if his troops were not very tired, and replied: "Yes, but so are the enemy."

His plan was to keep them on the run at all costs, and it was carried through perfectly and with great success. His cavalry and mounted infantry were usually pushed ahead about three miles in advance of the main body of infantry. Whenever they got into touch with the enemy they dropped back upon the infantry, which was then extended and sent forward to go thoroughly through all the villages to the right and left of the line of march. While the infantry rested after this, the cavalry pushed on again, and the process, to the consternation of the pursued, was repeated.

On the morning of the 9th the Japanese shelled the Chinese out of Ho Hsi Wu, who after some skirmishing fled, leaving the place to the Japanese. The same day the Bengal Lancers and the Japanese Mounted Infantry came on a body of 200 Chinese cavalry, scattering them, killing about fifty, and capturing four banners of Gen. Sung and Gen. Ma.

On the 10th the main body was at Ma T'ou, and though the march was not a long one the road was lined with stragglers. The place where the Chinese had breakfasted in the morning was strewed with melon rinds. They had no commissariat and lived on what they could pick up, such as melons and Indian corn.

The next day the weather was a little cooler, and to the great relief of the troops, rain fell. The army brought up at Chang Chia Wan, and the Japanese shelled the enemy out of a position south of T'ung Chou, from which they retired into that city.

Early on the morning of the 12th (Sunday) the Japanese advanced to assault the east south gate, and found the city evacuated by the Chinese troops and no resistance offered to an entrance, though the city wall is strong and high and could easily have been defended. By way of saluting their own general the Japanese blew in the outer gate of the enceinte, and the city was quietly occupied. Gen. Yamaguchi issued a proclamation assuring safety and protection to non-combatants, and promising to respect the rights of the people in their homes. The Japanese took the southern half of the city, and the French, who had now reappeared, the northern part.

The Allies spent the night of the 12th at T'ung Chou, and on the next day began the last march to Peking, now only twelve miles distant. The Japanese advanced along the stone road leading to the Ch'i Hua gate, the Russians south of them, but to the north of the canal, on the road to the Tung Pien gate of the southern city. South of the canal, on the road to the same gate, marched the Americans, and still farther south, the British.

It had been arranged that at a distance of three miles from Peking, the four columns were to halt, and that another conference should be held to decide on a plan of attack. But the Russians, instead of halting, marched close up to the city walls, and meeting no opposition thought it possible to effect an entrance. But they had not reached the gate before a hot rifle fire from the corner of the northern city wall met them, and their loss was heavy, including the Chief of Staff, Gen. Vasilewski. They became tangled up inside the Tung Pien gate, which had been forced open, and for many hours made no progress.

The Japanese advanced to the vicinity of Ch'i Hua gate early on the morning of the 14th, working under cover of houses toward the vicinity of the gate, which they hoped to blow up. But the rifle fire from the wall was so sharp that the Japanese suffered severely, and it was decided to bombard the wall. The bombardment began about 10 A. M., and continued for some hours without much visible impression being made. Only the heaviest artillery would have breached the wall of the gate, and the number of sharp-shooters made impracticable any approach to blow it up. More than a thousand shells were wasted, as well as the whole day, and nothing had been gained. It was decided to wait until night to blow up the gate. It was then successfully accomplished, the lofty tower being set on fire, and the Chinese troops driven from the wall with great slaughter. All honour to the brave troops of every nation, and most of all to the sturdy Japanese!

The American troops had come early in the forenoon to the corner of the southern city wall, near the Tung Pien gate, where some of the men scaled the wall. The main body came in at the Tung Pien gate, as the Russians had done before them, and found themselves within the southern city exposed to a heavy fire from its northern wall. Their detachment entered the southern city at about the same time as the British, but they missed their way, and it was many hours before they reached the water-gate, entering the British Legation some time after the British, a part of each of these forces forcing open the Ch'ien Mên, or main gate of the wall between the cities.

The British were fortunate in finding the Sha Kuo gate, on the east face of the southern city, almost entirely undefended, though a party of Chinese cavalry had first to be shelled out of a village in front of it. A small guard was left to hold the gate, the 24th Punjab Infantry was sent to occupy the Temple of Heaven, and the remainder of the force advanced along the main east and west street of the city, more than half the way to its centre, when they turned north in the direction of the water-gate, in accordance with the advice previously quoted in a letter from Sir Claude MacDonald to the Commander of the Allied Forces. When the British advance emerged from the houses to the south of the canal, at some distance from the water-gate, there were still Chinese riflemen posted at the Ha Ta gate to the east, who opened an ill-directed and ineffectual fire. The

COURT, TEMPLE OF HEAVEN,
BRITISH HEADQUARTERS

TEMPLE OF HEAVEN,
BRITISH HEADQUARTERS

first officer to enter through the gate was Major Scott, of the 1st Sikhs, accompanied by four of his men, with Capt. Pell, and Lieut. Keyes, Aides to Gen. Gaselee, who with his staff was close behind.

From the water-gate by way of the Russian Legation (the only safe route) to the British Legation, was but a few minutes' walk, where the deliverers were welcomed with an outburst of joy, which to those who experienced it can never be other than a vivid recollection while life itself lasts.

The Siege in Peking was raised! Once more the Occidental had met the Oriental in a face to face death struggle, and by means of intrepid resourcefulness, indomitable perseverance in the face of obstacles, supreme courage confronting deadly dangers, and the Superintending Providence of God, had been victorious. It was the dawning Twentieth Century victorious against the Middle Ages, a potentially glorious Future vanquishing an inert and lifeless Past. In it was the seed of a New China, and Hope for the Far East.

XXV

THE FORTIFICATIONS

TECHNICALLY speaking, the Siege in Peking was over, although much still remained to be done to render the relief effective. Before adding anything on that head it may be well at this point to mention in somewhat fuller detail, a topic to which no justice has yet been done, but which can not be omitted altogether—siege house-keeping.

Under the abnormal conditions of the siege, the exigencies of domestic life (if such a thing could be said to exist) deserve to be depicted by a woman's pen. Every building on the grounds was crowded, sometimes almost to the point of suffocation. The mess of Lady MacDonald was generally about thirty-five in number, and the whole establishment was literally turned inside out for the benefit of the besieged; Sir Claude's office and library became a hospital, the smoking-room was occupied by gentlemen by night, and the ball-room by ladies, while for weary officers there was, during the day, an overflow into the sleeping apartments of the ladies of the house. It would have been difficult to suggest anything for the comfort of the sick, or for the welfare of the besieged, which was not promoted by the administrators of this hospitable establishment.

The quarters of the legation doctor, ordinarily occupied in the summer by one European, or at most two, suddenly became the abode of eight and twenty men,

THE FORTIFICATIONS 463

women and children, distributed into four different messes. Their servants' quarters absolutely swarmed with Chinese, and the minute back yard was always overflowing with eager candidates for participation in the next kettle of rice, always just about ready for distribution.

The Customs mess (in the Escort quarters) was of variable size, the number ranging between thirty and forty, and as the dining-room was small it was necessary to serve the meals to five different detachments, when all were on hand. But a large part—perhaps one-half—were members of the Customs volunteers, assigned to duty in various parts of the defences, oftenest in the Su Wang Fu, for a period of twenty-four hours at a time. Food had then to be sent over to them three times a day. This greatly augmented the care of so large a family, yet two capable English ladies ably and successfully managed it all.

The number of American missionaries who came in from the Methodist compound was about seventy. They were assigned to the occupancy of the church, a rectangular structure situated near the median line of the compound, measuring forty-three feet in length by twenty-five in width. On each side of the entry was a small closet, and one of these was provided with a winding staircase to the loft. The rear of the audience room was occupied by a platform, surrounded by an altar-rail and furnished with a lectern. Passages on each side led to the small robing-room in the rear. Most of the available space in the main room was absorbed by more than a dozen large wooden seats, each with a book support in front.

Trunks of all sizes were piled at the entrance, and outside under the projecting eaves. The mattresses were spread for the night wherever there was room, the disposition for sleeping much resembling the ground plan of a box of sardines. Some of the gentlemen found temporary and precarious lodgment on the edges of one of the pavilions, and later, as already mentioned, in the smoking-room of the Minister's house. The two closets on each side of the entrance were soon cleared out and turned into wash-rooms, every superfluous article being relegated to the loft.

At a later stage this attic was itself transformed from a lumber room into a dormitory. A high platform in the middle (representing the arch in the ceiling of the church) and the surrounding spaces in front, in the rear, and on either side, were found choked with the accumulation of the entire Legation for decades. Among the mass may be mentioned the balls and pins of the bowling-alley, huge packing-cases, iron bed-steads without their ropes, scores of windows used for winter fittings to the dwelling-houses, punkah fans, shelves, trunks, boxes, relics of the Queen's Jubilee in the shape of transparencies, lanterns by the hundred, theatre scenery, rush-mats, reed-screens, cubic yards of copies of the somewhat useless treaty between Great Britain and China, and piles of legation archives and accounts, running back to the ancient days of the East India Company,—all profusely decorated with hoary cob-webs accumulated under successive ministries.

Under the energetic superintendence of a few gentlemen and ladies, much of this material was removed elsewhere, leaving space for narrow bed-rooms in which nearly twenty persons found much better accommodation than had been before available. The loft was built to conform to the general Chinese architecture of the Legation, having windows upon the east side only, making a

THE FORTIFICATIONS

circulation of air an impossibility—a circumstance little adapted to promote comfort in the heats of July. Yet despite a due allowance of sand-flies, fleas, and mosquitoes, it was discovered that the inconveniences almost amounted to luxuries, and by mutual exchange of quarters the sick and the weary could always find some haven of comparative rest and quiet.

The small room in the rear of the church, already mentioned, was made to do duty as the only store-room for such provisions as had been gathered, or at any later period turned up. At first even a part of this was used as a ladies' bath-room, which was replaced later by the little lamp-room at the front entrance. Sergeant Herring obligingly gave the mess his own kitchen—a tiny one at the back of his quarters, with a small Chinese range—and had his own meals prepared on a Chinese stove on the door-step, or wherever he might be.

In the effort to get all the needed articles cooked at once on this minute range, the cooks were forced to exert themselves to the utmost, every hour of the day. A small kerosene stove and a little spirit lamp were in constant use as accessories, but as there was no oven it was only possible to bake biscuit in a kerosene tin. To get quantities of food cooked at one time under such conditions, without perpetually having some of it scorched, would appear out of the question—yet it was accomplished.

One of the greatest and most serious perplexities, sufficient to drive an Occidental cook to complete distraction, was the incessant demand upon the kitchen for hot water. It was wanted for cooking the regular meals, it was called for by the occupants of the house to which the kitchen belonged, by the marines, by the mothers of sick babies, and by the Chinese *ad libitum*. Fortunately two large braziers were brought, which materially relieved the pressure on the kitchen, so that tea, coffee, and a certain amount of hot water could be provided near to the church—the kitchen being distant from it half the width of the Legation compound. It is to be borne in mind that while many were able to drink the water from the principal wells without even filtering, perhaps half of the company were less fortunate, and had to be supplied with that which had been thoroughly boiled.

The indispensable utensils for cooking on a large scale were happily provided from the stock distributed by the owners of the foreign stores. Yet the provision was far from complete. There was a great lack of large dishes, and it was sometimes necessary to soak beans, or to make biscuit, in a wash-bowl. The dishes must often be washed in cold water, when there was no other. For it must be remembered that the first contingent of about thirty-two persons were summoned to breakfast at 6.30, and must finish their meal and make way for the second section, who at no long interval gave way to the third. (Later the three divisions were condensed into two.)

Sideboards for this large company there were none, except the altar, and all the surfaces—seats, book-rests, window-sills—were uniformly aslant, affording no support for crockery, which had to be continually passed out through the window to be rewashed, a task of some difficulty during the frequent heavy rains. A similar embarrassment was felt on rainy days, in drying the dish-cloths, the supply of which never seemed to run short, being mysteriously recruited from odds and ends which turned up (table-cloths and napkins being practically and happily unknown).

All this unceasing round of work was carried on by three different sets of cooks and servants, each of which

THE FORTIFICATIONS 467

had always to hasten its work so as to be out of the way of the next relay; yet there was never a quarrel, and no friction worthy of the name.

During the height of the rainy season, the only place in which to put away food was a small wire-screen safe, about a foot and a half square—there was no ice-box and no ice. A few rods distant was the slaughter place for ponies, haunted by millions of flies, and the only way to keep meat from their attack was to have it always covered with a cloth—a very temporary device in the hot damp days of July.

There was a standing committee of three ladies who planned the menu for the three daily meals, and two others—changed each day—attended to setting the tables and saw that each meal was ready on time. The ingenuity of this committee in so planning an extremely limited diet as to make the most of it, was positively marvellous,—a housewifery that frequently served up the flesh of tough mules so that no one would have suspected its origin, and that made tasty puddings without milk, butter, or eggs.

The lady in charge of the hospital kitchen also showed great skill in making palatable dishes for the wounded, and if at any time there happened to be a little left which would have spoiled before the next morning, she was invariably able to make such arrangements as to forefend that catastrophe. Little committees of the foreign Christian Endeavor children busied themselves in carrying around whatever might be left on hand, distributing to those in need, and to the sick Chinese, who were always so hungry after their perpetual diet of porridge that all scraps from a foreign table were welcomed with joy.

Much of the time there were sick ones among the mess who could not eat the coarse brown bread and the old yellow rice, and for such, whatever the stress of other work, appetizing dishes were always ready. There were also wan little babies, for whom their mothers had to cook in a passage-way so narrow that if one stooped down no one else could pass, and for many, many nights these tired mothers were kept awake by the moaning of their own infants, or perhaps by the cries of some of the others, for whom no other place was open and for whose ills there was no respite and no help. In the recapitulation, all these disadvantages and inconveniences appear most formidable, but at the time they were submitted to with a patience and a courage which never once failed, and which was not a little promoted by a daily half-hour service of prayer and praise in which many passages from the Psalms, the prophecies, and the epistles, were made to become luminous with a new light, glowing like a diamond in the dark.

Although this is in no sense a military history of the Siege in Peking, yet a few words in regard to the fortifications of the British Legation must not be omitted. These it may be remembered were early in the siege put in charge of the Rev. F. D. Gamewell, whose education as an engineer proved a unique qualification for a unique work. At the request of Sir Claude MacDonald he also undertook in a few instances work outside of the area of the Legation and its precincts; but this was exceptional.

The barricade on the west side of the Legation Street bridge was made eight feet thick, with five feet of earth intended to stop cannon balls, for which it is probable it would have sufficed. One of the military engineers considered that such an elaborate defence, each of the double walls being of the thickness named, was quite unnecessary, but after the German losses had become very heavy

GATEWAY TO BRITISH LEGATION, MOAT AND BARRICADE

THE FORTIFICATIONS 469

he wished it continued. There was a similar experience of change in military opinion as to the value of thorough-going fortifications, in the Mongol Market, where the bullets penetrated fifteen and eighteen inches of rubble—or common Chinese wall.

The Russian Legation was practically not fortified at all, for what reason it is difficult to comprehend, although there were barricades in some parts of the premises.

At the south end of the Mongol Market lane, the barricade built was five feet thick, and solid. The north and south walls were reënforced so as to be always eighteen inches thick, and in no case was dependence placed on a single line of bricks, where there are sure to be many cracks, and where there is always a chance of penetration by a stray bullet. This reënforcement continued up to a point opposite the house of the First Secretary. Beyond that the outer line began with a thickness of two feet. The importance of this was illustrated by the fact that on the very day on which Mongol Market defences were finished at 11 A. M., by 4 P. M. the Chinese had every house opposite loopholed, and twelve loopholes in a single building.

The ordinary penetrating effect of the Mauser bullets on Chinese bricks was from one-half to three-quarters of an inch; but in the case of the Männlichers used during the closing days of the siege, the damage was much greater,—the bullets leaving deep pits, and rapidly cutting away any wall. On the last Monday morning of the siege Mr. Gamewell was called up to build extra walls to check this destructive and corrosive fire.

The courts next beyond the one last mentioned were protected in the same way, under constant attack. During all the building of fortifications, at which probably an average of fifty men were employed every day except

Sunday, only one man was killed, and that was due to his total disregard of repeated cautions not to expose himself unnecessarily. The barricade immediately to the west of the south stable-court was four feet in thickness, aside from the outer yard wall, and was one of the strongest in the whole line, as it was one of the most exposed to attack. It was a marvel that the two-storied house in the stable-court did not fall. Behind the stable-yard gate was a barricade three feet thick slanting to the north-west, and next beyond that was a platform built for the Italian gun, the wall being very solid, and eight feet thick. The next wall was twenty inches thick, independent of the original outer wall, and very strongly built. Beyond this was a sort of fort, with five loopholes, very securely put up, and after that a rubble wall four feet in thickness, reënforced by still another substantial wall.

Further to the north stood " Fort von Strauch," which was the situation of the " International " gun at the close of the siege. The gunner, Mitchell, stood behind it when he was wounded, and not to one side. Directly to the west of this, and not more than fifty feet distant, was the Chinese barricade. Still further beyond is a court which is directly under the wall of the Carriage Park.

The death of the marine who was killed at the stable-court early in the siege first called the attention of the military men to the need of sand bags. Before that time they said they had enough, but it was discovered later that the director of the work of fortification was right in his consistent declaration that there would never be enough of them until the relief column reached the Legation. After a time every officer was converted to the value of sand bags, and made frequent and liberal calls for them.

Behind the Students' Library a deep trench was dug as

THE FORTIFICATIONS 471

a countermine, between ten and twelve feet deep, and only ten inches from the wall of a two-storied building whose foundations were only three or four feet below the ground. Digging this trench was at great risk of undermining the building, but the risk of being blown up was also a serious one, and it was risk against risk. The trench was not absolutely continuous, but the main sections were connected by cavities which went from one to the other, or as nearly so as the roots of a large tree would allow. It was almost certain that this digging would have detected any Chinese mine, as it was 12 feet deep, and at that time of year the water line was thought to be about 13 feet. In the first court of the Hanlin a countermine was begun which extended some distance into the Carriage Park, but it was discontinued as superfluous, and was a standing jest for a long time.

In the Hanlin grounds the line of defence was at first weak. The second line, however, had a two foot brick wall very strongly propped, and reënforced to stand artillery fire. Being short of bricks, the workmen used a great number of the wooden plates of books, mostly poetical works in the Hanlin Library. From this point eastward to the north stable-court the whole line of wall was likewise reënforced for withstanding artillery, and there was a trench 12 feet deep just behind the defence for the whole length.

In case this should have been rushed by the Chinese, the pavilion immediately to the rear had a loophole three and a half feet in thickness to enfilade the enemy. This pavilion, itself, by the way, was perforated with solid shot from the batteries on the Imperial City wall, seven shots striking within the space of ten feet. One of them went through a heavy post, 16 inches in diameter, and shattered one of the marble tablets let into the wall. The book-cases of the Hanlin had been set up in the yard, and covered with tar-paper simply as covering-screens, so that the Chinese should not be able to detect the movements of the defence. A smaller pavilion in front was loopholed to prevent the approach of the enemy unseen, and there was a second strong line of defence behind. The larger of the two pavilions (called the Ching I T'ing) was named "Fort Strouts." Another smaller one to the north was loopholed in the same manner.

At the east end of the Hanlin the artillery defences were carried up two-thirds of the way to the top, but were never wholly completed. The most eastern of the fortified positions was styled "Fort Oliphant." Immediately in front of this the defences were very strong, consisting of an enormously thick wall, eight feet through at the base, and a trench 13 feet in depth. The steps up to the elevated sentry-posts were made of the wooden cases which when found contained the great Ming Dynasty Encyclopædia, "Yung Lê Ta Tien", but were now packed solidly with earth. The strength of the Hanlin position as finally fortified was great, and if the Chinese had been able to screw up their courage to the point of a desperate charge, the positions could have been captured only with the greatest difficulty, and with the sacrifice of a great number of lives, for which happily they were at no time quite prepared.

The defences of the eastern side of the Legation (the Hanlin being on the north) received perhaps more laborious consideration than those of any other quarter. On the 29th of June—only nine days after the siege began—Col. Shiba informed Sir Claude that at the outside he should not be able to hold the Su Wang Fu more than two or three days longer. Sir Claude communicated to Mr. Gamewell the information, with the comment, "You should know this." The result was a most elaborate plan of defence which was a surprise alike to Chinese and to foreigners, who were perpetually asking "What is the use of all this work?" The use was to guard the British Legation at its weakest point, in case the Su Wang Fu should be abandoned, and the Chinese should plant artillery on the high mounds of the Flower Garden belonging to the Fu, which was separated from the Legation only by the width of the canal road. The Chinese would have been able to mount guns within fifty yards (or less) of the residence of the British Minister, and it was difficult to see how any part of the Legation grounds could have then been held for an hour.

The fortifications by way of defence against this danger began at the end of the north stable-court, and extended in an unbroken line to the Escort Quarters, a little north of the main gate of the Legation. The post on the roof of the cow-house at the north end was a very strong position, and a very exposed one, being much nearer to the batteries on the wall of the Imperial City than any other, as well as close to the enemy's positions which attacked the northern end of the Fu. The wall of the stables themselves on the canal front was about fifteen inches thick, and with great labour this was reënforced by a wall five feet thick, strongly braced both at top and bottom throughout its whole length. At the upper end of the stable-court there were countermines, lest the Chinese should attempt to blow up the post. The tunnel was run to the west about five feet, thence north twenty-five feet, and then east the same distance, but no sign or sound of Chinese mines was found, and the very existence of the countermines was not generally known. From the stables to the Escort quarters the same plan of defence against possible cannonading was pursued throughout,—thick and high walls made of earth well rammed down, and stoutly braced by the heaviest available timbers against the buildings opposite at every point.

The cannon balls and shells of the enemy received on this side did much damage. One of the three brick columns in the second story veranda of the Minister's house was knocked down into the yard below, but extra posts were put in under the supports of the roof, so that it did not give way. On the last night of the siege one of the smaller roofs of a room adjacent to a bed-room in the Minister's house was crushed in by a shell, as already mentioned, but the injury throughout the siege from this source was surprisingly small.

The discerning reader will perceive that, amid so many military men at a time of such peculiar strain, the task of a civilian charged with one of the most important duties of the defence, was one of peculiar difficulty and delicacy. The sense of responsibility was at times almost overwhelming, and, aside from sometimes working twenty hours a day, the necessity of having the most discouraging military secrets confidentially imparted was enough to wear out the constitution of one in the most robust health.

Perhaps in no other order throughout the entire siege did Sir Claude MacDonald exhibit to better advantage sterling good sense, than in placing Mr. Gamewell in a position absolutely free from military interference of any kind, with responsibility to the Commander in Chief only. When this fact was thoroughly established, all occasion for friction disappeared, and the civil and the military defence dove-tailed into one another in an admirable and most effective way. At the close of the siege Mr. Gamewell received a cordial letter from Sir Claude acknowledging the common obligations to him

THE SIX "FIGHTING PARSONS" AND
SERGEANT MURPHY AT FORT COCKBURN

for his services, and Mr. Conger in a similar note justly added that "to you more than to any other man we owe, under God, our preservation." A few days after the relief forces arrived, one of the British subjects who had been through the siege took occasion to ask Gen. Gaselee what he thought of "our infant fortifications?" Gen. Gaselee replied that he was greatly surprised at the extent and the effectiveness of the defence conducted, and especially with the amount of work done in the time at the disposal of the besieged; and that the fortifications and everything connected with the defence were "beyond all praise."

In the official report of the events connected with the siege of the Legations, Sir Claude MacDonald states that an important effort to betray the Legations was only discovered after they had been relieved. "Among some documents seized by the German troops was found a letter addressed to the General commanding at the Ha Ta gate on the subject of mines. The writer had been a teacher at the British Legation in the employ of Her Majesty's Government for four years, and was well known to the student interpreters; together with all other teachers he disappeared about the middle of June. The letter was dated the beginning of July, and pointed out that the General's methods of attacking the Legation were faulty, and were bound to lead to considerable loss in the future as they had done in the past. The proper method of attack, the writer said, was by mining; to assist the General in his attack he enclosed a correct plan of the British Legation, with which he was well acquainted, and marked on the plan the most suitable place for the mine to be driven. Eager inquiries have been made, since the siege was raised, for the writer of the letter, but as yet he has not been found." The fact that with such detailed treachery as this freely offered to the Chinese, they failed to drive a single mine under any part of the long front of the British Legation, adds one more to the already long list of surprises connected with the defence.

In view of the supreme importance of the subject it may be worth while to devote a little space to a brief summary of some of the foregoing aspects of the defence of the Legations, by a competent military authority, Lieut. Col. Scott-Moncrieff, of the Royal Engineers, who contributed an article on the subject to the " Royal Engineers Journal " (April, 1901.) Only a few points can be selected. The reader is indebted to him for the excellent map of the defences which accompanies this volume.

" The first thing which strikes one on looking at the plan of the whole defensive position is the enormous number of buildings crowded together on the ground. Even in this respect the plan comes short of the truth, for if the houses had all been actually drawn it would have added to the confused mass of buildings shown, in such a way as to obscure essential points.

" Some of the Legation compounds and yards have many trees standing in them. The trees were both a help and a hindrance to the besieged. They obscured the look-out, tended to spread conflagration when a fire broke out, and falling branches were often a source of danger; but they afforded some protection, and prevented the enemy from seeing in. The massive and heavy roofs of the Chinese buildings though giving considerable command were not much taken advantage of by the assailants. The two-storied houses in the Legation, though heavily bombarded, acted most efficiently as traverses, so that it was quite possible to move about freely inside the defended area. This was very much noticed by the relieving force when they entered. The noise of the musketry and machine guns was incessant, projectiles of all sorts were whistling overhead, yet on the lawn-tennis court of the British Legation ladies were moving about so freely that it was like a garden-party. The defences of the British Legation were, by all consent, the strongest and best of any of the works in any part of the position. The engineer who devised and superintended them was an American missionary, the Rev. F. D. Gamewell. He was one of a considerable number of American missionaries who were sheltered during the siege in the Chapel of the British Legation, and whose skill in organization and cheerful energy contributed largely to the comfort and well-being of the garrison.

"There were no engineers, military or civil, among the garrison of the British Legation. Mr. Gamewell made it his business to be always working at and improving the defences. Walls liable to artillery fire were strengthened and strutted. Walls supporting roofs, or in any way doubtful, were propped and buttressed, traverses were made in every possible passage, openings and communications were made freely throughout the defensive line, barricades and flanking caponiers were made in every place where it was possible they might be needed, deep trenches were sunk across every part where the enemy might be expected to mine, the upper stories of houses were barricaded, loopholed and strengthened, and above all in every place ample head cover was given to the firing line, so that only as much of the man as came opposite the loophole was exposed.

"On the west of the British Legation in one of the large sheds of the Imperial Carriage Park, the enemy began a mine, the failure of which is very instructive. They started in the direction of a strong barricade and breastwork inside of our works in the Hanlin. They were heard at work, and a countermine was started, which however, did not go far. The enemy apparently heard the countermine, and changed direction to their right, heading for the Students' Quarters, a double-storied building close to the boundary wall. They seem to have lost their bearings, and kept edging off to the right, so that they worked round in an almost complete semi-circle, and ultimately were heading away from their objective. This was afterward discovered, when, after the relief was accomplished the mine was opened. It was found that the atmosphere in the mine was so foul that it was impossible to keep a light burning, and as the Chinese were probably working in the dark, it is little wonder that they missed their way. The difficulty of keeping the true direction of a small mine gallery, even when one has the aid of lantern and compass, is well known, and in this case the enemy were probably unable to use any such assistance. Some empty powder-boxes and powder-hose were found in the mine, but no charge.

"The last and most furious assault on the Legations was delivered on the 13th and 14th of August, when the enemy knew it was their last chance. But the defences were sound and the hearts of the defenders good, for relief at last was near. The closeness of the attack may be gauged by the fact that when Major Scott and his Sikhs, who were the first to enter the Legation, relieved the Marines of the Legation Guard at the Mongol Market barricades, and were greeted with cheers, they at once received a volley of brickbats from the enemy a few yards off!"

It was gratifying intelligence to all who were interested in the work of the siege and its results, to know that so many who took an active part in it were promptly rewarded by a due recognition of their services.

THE FORTIFICATIONS

The last six pages of the British White Book, (China N. 4, 1900) are exclusively occupied with dispatches from Sir Claude MacDonald to the Marquis of Salisbury, calling attention to the singular services of a great number of individuals, both military and civil, including almost every nationality. Among those selected for honourable mention were Capt. Halliday, already mentioned, who fought with conspicuous courage at close quarters; Capt. Poole, who was not absent from duty for a single day or night during the whole 55 days; and Capt. Strouts, who was killed. The British Volunteers, among whose number David Oliphant and Henry Warren were killed, are highly commended.

Mr. Dering, Second Secretary of the British Legation was in charge of important defences. He was always alert, and had also the difficult task of deciding what ponies or mules should be killed for food, each of the owners naturally being desirous of reserving his own as long as possible. Mr. Cockburn, Chinese Secretary, was both a Volunteer, and in charge of the very important correspondence between the British Minister and the enemy. His house was an especial target of shells and rifle bullets. He was ably seconded by Mr. Ker the Second Chinese Secretary. Capt. Percy Smith, a retired officer, was especially useful on the city wall in difficult and dangerous circumstances. Mr. Clarke-Thornhill, formerly of the Diplomatic Service, was an active and willing Volunteer.

The Rev. Frank Norris, Chaplain of the Legation, rendered invaluable services outside of his especial duties, in work with pick and shovel in the trenches and on the barricades; and also in taking charge of and encouraging the Chinese converts in their work on the defences. He was always ready, willing, and cheerful; though severely wounded by the explosion of a shell in the Su Wang Fu, he stuck to his work, and was at all times a splendid example to those about him.

Mr. Tours of the Consular Staff, and Mr. Tweed of the Hongkong and Shanghai Bank, were indefatigable as captains of the Fire Brigade, which several times saved the Legation. The former had such arduous duties that at the close of the siege his health gave way completely, and for a long time he hovered between life and death.

Dr. Morrison, Correspondent of "The Times", acted as Lieutenant to Capt. Strouts, and rendered most valuable services. Active, energetic, and cool, he volunteered for every service of danger, and was a pillar of strength when matters were going badly. By his severe wound on the 16th of July his valuable services were lost to the defence for the rest of the siege.

All the Student Interpreters are warmly praised. They behaved with pluck and dash, yet a steadiness under fire worthy of veteran troops. The Volunteers belonging to the Imperial Maritime Customs likewise distinguished themselves, and soon after the siege received the promotion which they had so well earned.

Mr. Nigel Oliphant took an important part on several occasions until he was seriously wounded, on the 18th of July.

In another supplementary dispatch Sir Claude asks that the thanks of the British Government be conveyed to Lieut. Baron von Rahden, of the Imperial Russian Navy; Capt. Myers, U. S. Marines (wounded); Lieut. Darcy, French Navy (wounded); Lieut. Baron von Soden, Imperial German Marines; Lieut. Paolini, Italian Navy (wounded); and Lieut. Hara, Japanese Navy. In addition to these, the skill, tenacity, and courage of Lieut. Col. Shiba, of the Japanese contingent, are mentioned as worthy of all

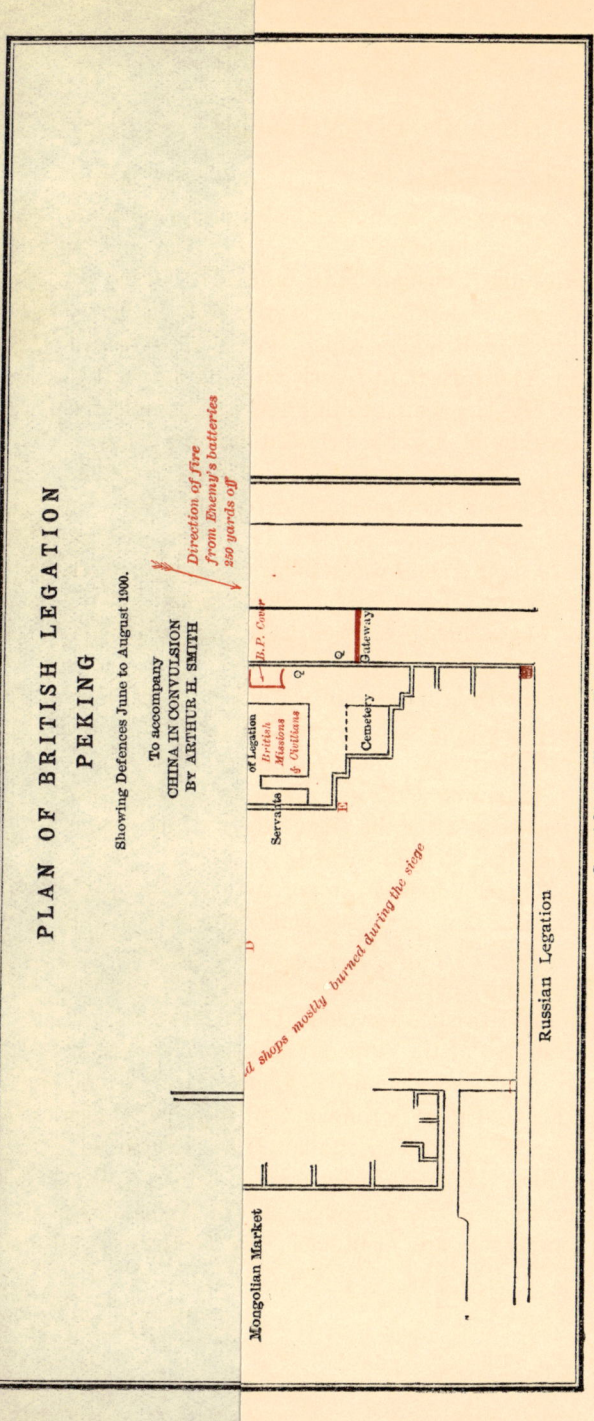

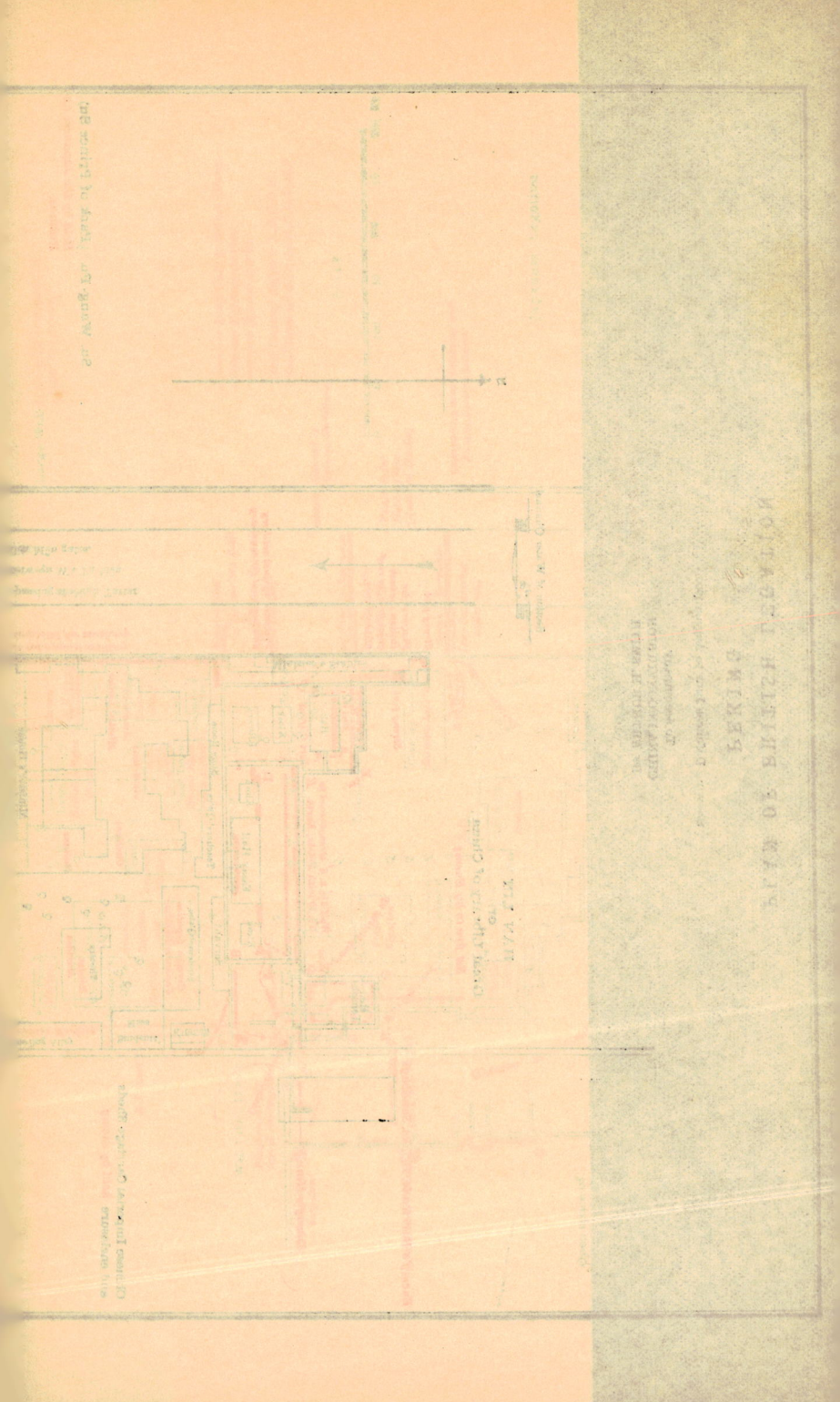

THE FORTIFICATIONS 481

praise. His dispositions were taken with the greatest skill, and he contested every inch of ground, thereby giving time for the defences of the British Legation to be put in order; and as a direct effect of this the lives of very many of the garrison were saved.

Don Livio Caetini, Second Secretary of the Italian Legation, is commended to his Government for his devotion and ability, having never once quitted his post, which was a barricade exposed to a very severe shell and rifle fire. M. von Strauch, a member of the Imperial Maritime Customs, formerly an officer of the Prussian army, was in command of the Customs Volunteers, and was of the greatest assistance to Sir Claude, who was much struck by his zeal and intrepidity. He and Dr. Velde of the Hospital are especially commended to the German Government. M. Fliche, an ex-officer of the French Cavalry, was an orderly constantly under fire, and for his gallantry was recommended to the notice of the French Government.

The United States has few methods, aside from the vote of special thanks by Congress, of accomplishing the highly desirable objects aimed at in the decorations and honours thus worthily bestowed. It was therefore the greater gratification to the besieged and their friends to find in Washington telegrams of Jan. 4th, 1901, the following: "The British Ambassador has communicated to the Secretary of State a dispatch recently received by him from the Marquis of Lansdowne, commending the gallant conduct of certain Americans who distinguished themselves last summer during the attacks on the Legation quarter in Peking. The text of the dispatch is as follows:

"My Lord: With reference to my preceding dispatch of this day's date, I have to inform you that Sir C. Mac-

Donald has brought to my notice the conduct of certain gentlemen who particularly distinguished themselves during the attacks on the Legation quarter, and who gave invaluable assistance both to him personally and to the defence in general.

"Sir Claude mentions the names of the Rev. F. D. Gamewell of the American Methodist Mission, and Herbert G. Squiers, Secretary of the U. S. Legation. He states that the Rev. F. D. Gamewell carried out the entire defences of the British Legation, and that these defences have excited the admiration of the officers of the various nationalities who have since inspected them. As a tribute to their excellence he mentions that notwithstanding a constant rain of rifle-fire during the five weeks of the siege, not a single woman or child in the Legation suffered. He adds that a deep debt of gratitude is owed to him by all the besieged.

"Herbert Squiers acted in the capacity of Sir Claude's Chief-of-Staff after the death of Captain Strouts of the Royal Marines. Sir Claude says that his earlier services in the United States army were of great use in the defence, and that he can not speak too highly of his zeal and ability. The barricades on the Tartar wall were designed and carried out by him, and under Sir Claude's orders he drew the plan for the entry of the troops which was conveyed to Gen. Gaselee by a messenger let down from the wall.

"I request that you will bring the names of these two gentlemen to the favourable notice of the United States Government, and express the appreciation felt by Her Majesty's Government of their eminent services.

(Signed) LANSDOWNE."

This series of graceful recognitions of merit is fitly

THE FORTIFICATIONS 483

concluded by the following dispatch to Sir Claude Mac-
Donald, published in the White Book relating to the
siege in Peking.

FOREIGN OFFICE, *Feb.* 10th, 1901.

"As the present report completes your account of the
siege and relief of the Legations, I desire to take this
opportunity of stating how highly His Majesty's Government value these admirable and exhaustive records of an
episode of the deepest historical interest. The gallantry
with which the siege was maintained by all the foreign
forces engaged, more especially after the failure of the
first relief expedition, and the consequent disappointment
of the besieged, coupled with the energy and courage with
which the efforts of the regular forces were seconded by
the Legation Staffs and other civilians, has commanded
the admiration of the whole civilized world.

"His Majesty's Government desire also to place on
record their appreciation of the important part borne by
yourself throughout this crisis. On the 22nd of June at
the request of your colleagues you took charge of the
defence, a position for which from your military training you possessed exceptional qualifications; and from
that day you continued to direct the operations of the
garrison until the relief took place on the 14th of August.

"Information has reached His Majesty's Government
from various sources that the success of the defence was
largely due to your personal efforts, and more particularly
to the unity and cohesion which you found means of estab-
lishing and maintaining among the forces of so many
different nationalities operating over an extended area.
Competent eye-witnesses have expressed the opinion that
if it can be said that the European community owe their
lives to any one man more than another, where so many

distinguished themselves, it is to you that they are indebted for their safety.

"I can not conclude this dispatch without asking you to convey to Lady MacDonald the thanks of His Majesty's Government for her unceasing and devoted attention to the welfare of the sick and wounded. Her work and that of the ladies who assisted her have earned the lasting gratitude not only of those who were benefited by her ministrations, but also of their relatives in Europe who were kept for so many weeks in a condition of most painful anxiety and suspense.

LANSDOWNE."

XXVI

AFTER THE SIEGE

WHEN the relieving columns marched into the Peking Legations they received a glad welcome from all the besieged, who had been looking for their coming with such mingled fears and hopes. But it was soon evident from the bearing of the rescuers, as well as from their remarks, that they were considerably disappointed in us. They found a large number of gentlemen and ladies going about as they would have done under ordinary circumstances, except that many of them were on sentry duty. The specific occasion of the disappointment felt and expressed seemed to be that the besieged did not look sufficiently pinched with hunger, and that some of them—especially the ladies—were far too well dressed, and met the relieving army with glad smiles and cheers, instead of bursting into hysterical sobs. As one of the bright young women phrased it, "they seem to have expected to find us lying gasping on the ground."

Several of the besieged were only visitors in Peking who had been caught in the effort to leave on the very day when trains finally ceased to run, and these ladies, at least, had lost none of their belongings. All the rest, however, displayed the singular feminine talent for making a little go a great way in dress, as they had done in food, and even under the most depressing circumstances of lack of changes of raiment, of persistently rainy weather and absence of all ordinary facilities for washing clothes, not to say for starching and ironing, often blossomed out in attire which showed no signs of hard usage or of age.

All the ladies alike appeared to rise to the occasion in a way to make one proud of the civilization of the West, which has found so large a place for the energy and the diversified talent of the fair sex. The wives of the American and the Russian Ministers were especially assiduous in working for the comfort of those who were wounded and in the hospital, giving up anything and everything for their comfort. When the detail for cleaning the hospital failed to appear, Madame de Giers one day seized the mop herself and more than made good his place.

Many of the women, through the entire siege, were quite as cool and as courageously hopeful as the men. During the severest attacks they sat diligently working on the sand bags without pause, nor was there ever anything in the smallest degree approximating a panic. Nothing at the time (nor in subsequent calm review) appeared more surprising than the cool way in which everything about the siege was taken as a matter of course, and the facility with which the necessary adjustments were swiftly and tactfully made by all the women alike, and pre-eminently by those who chanced to have any especial responsibility placed upon them.

During the whole of the siege the numerous children played about the grounds, and seldom with any restraint upon their movements. They paraded as " Boxers," and as companies of soldiers sent to arrest Boxers. The smallest mites had their little flags and cartridge-belts, and joined in the incessant sport. They made deep holes in inconvenient situations, but as these were said to be for " bomb-proofs " they could not be disturbed. They tugged at heavy bricks and timbers which were placed in preposterous positions to be regarded as defences. They filled tiny sacks, made for their especial use, with earth, and heaped them up *passim,* to guard the works which they had constructed.

On one occasion a redoubt of this sort built by infants of the "Number four" size, was totally demolished by some of those of the "Number ten" variety, to the indignation of the justice loving mammas, who remonstrated with the big boys for their harsh treatment of the little ones. But the leader of the attacking party drew himself up proudly and replied: "In time of war they ought to have put a guard over their works, or else they might expect to have them captured!" As there seemed to be some reason in this military view of the case, the matter was dropped. On another occasion some children of missionaries were seen throwing stones at another company of lads, who were returning the compliment; but upon inquiry each side hastened to explain that "They were trying to break down our barricades, and we wouldn't let them."

It has been already mentioned that there was a foreign child born during the progress of the siege, a circumstance which was commemorated in the name bestowed upon him—"Siege Moore." There were probably several Chinese babies introduced into the world at the same inauspicious epoch, but of these there is no record. More than one of the Chinese schoolgirls was married during the early days of the imprisonment, as their parents could not take care of them, and they could not otherwise go to their prospective homes.

Of the number of Chinese who died of wounds, or of illness, it is impossible to speak with any accuracy, as it was impracticable to collect satisfactory information. It has been already mentioned that the mortality among Chinese children was very heavy. Six foreign infants succumbed to the hardships of the time. The following semi-official table of casualties among the defenders of the Legations is of great interest, but it ought to be understood that it does not represent the final account, which is perhaps not to be had in a completely accurate shape. When the marines left Peking, a few too weak to be removed remained in the hospital. The very first British marine to be wounded (Sawyer) was the last one to die, long after his comrades had gone back to their ship. Something similar may have been true of some of the wounded in other detachments. As soon as the terrible strain of the siege was over, most of those who were able to do so left Peking, and many of them left China. Among them were several who seemed to be in perfect health, only " a bit tired."

CASUALTIES AMONG VOLUNTEERS DURING SIEGE IN PEKING.

LEGATIONS.	Killed.	Wounded.	Total Killed.	Total Wounded.
American	....	1	7	11
Austrian	....	....	4	11
British	[4]3	6	6	26
French	2	6	13	42
German	[1]1	[2]1	13	16
Japanese	[3]5	8	10	29
Italian	....	...	7	12
Russian	1	1	7	20
Totals	12	23	67	167

[1] Baron von Ketteler, German Minister.
[2] Mr. von Cordes, Chinese Secretary, German Legation.
[3] Including Surgeon Captain Ando.
[4] Including Mr. Wagner, a Frenchman in the Imperial Maritime Customs.

CASUALTIES DURING THE SIEGE IN PEKING.

LEGATIONS.	Officers.	Men.	KILLED OR DIED OF WOUNDS.		WOUNDED.		PERCENTAGE OF CASUALTIES.			Illness.
			Officers.	Men.	Officers.	Men.	Killed.	Wounded.	Total.	
American	3	53	....	7	2	8	12.5	17.3	30.3	....
Austrian	5	30	1	3	3	8	11.4	31.4	42.8	....
British	3	79	1	2	2	18	3.7	24.4	28.1	....
French	3	45	2	9	....	37	22.9	77.1	100.	....
German	1	50	....	12	....	15	23.5	31.4	54.9	....
Japanese	1	24	....	5	....	21	20.	84.	104.	....
Italian	1	28	....	7	1	11	24.1	41.4	65.5	....
Russian	2	*79	....	4	1	18	4.9	23.9	28.3	2
Totals	19	388	4	49	9	136	....	....	....	2
Average	....	....	....	....	....	....	13.1	35.6	48.7	....

PEI T'ANG.

French	1	30	1	4	....	8	16.1	25.8	41.9	....
Italian	1	11	....	6	1	3	50.	33.3	83.3	....
Totals	2	41	1	10	1	11	....	....	....	....

*Including 7 Cossack Legation Guards.

A fearfully long list of deaths has to be added to these tables, which cannot without danger of serious omissions catalogue those who, in places widely distant from each other, and at intervals of weeks or of months, lost their lives as a direct consequence of the Siege in Peking. The tables will therefore be understood to refer to the time when the siege was raised, and not to the final result.

The incidental references to the International Hospital, which constituted so important a part of our recuperative energies, should be supplemented by a few notes, most of which are culled from an article by a British lady physician well qualified to write on the subject.

The large proportion of the medical faculty represented among the besieged was truly remarkable. Altogether there were, of all nationalities, twenty men and women with medical and surgical degrees, including Dr. Ts'ao, a Chinese physician of the American Methodist Mission, and a retired naval surgeon.

The Hospital was opened on the day after the siege began, Drs. Poole and Velde being the staff. The women doctors were asked to nurse, which they gladly did. There were two trained nurses, and other ladies to help. The physicians who had to leave home at an hour's notice had of course few drugs and dressings. The British Legation was poorly stocked, as Dr. Poole had only just come out. Fortunately Dr. Velde had a large supply, all of the German army type,—iodoform gauze tied up in little packets very much compressed, to be cut into strips, with white muslin gauze squares, about five inches each way, folded and compressed into another very small package. He had also a sterilizer, which later had to be used when muslin curtains took the place of the white gauze, and bags of peat or saw-dust that of wool. Instruments were always sterilized for operation.

To most of the assistants the experience of shot and shell was new. The hospital first occupied two rooms in the Chancery bungalow, but gradually, as the number of the wounded grew, more rooms had to be taken over, until there were an operating-room with two tables; five wards and beds for five patients in the hall; a convalescent ward for officers and civilians in Lady MacDonald's house, and another for marines elsewhere. Three American ladies superintended the kitchen and stores; they were beyond all praise.

The Hospital had of course first claim to commissariat stores, but nowhere else was there such fragrant pony-soup, such really eatable mule stew. Officers and men appeared to think it worth while to be slightly wounded to get a few days' good feeding. Owing to the difficulty of "diverse tongues" the men were "warded" by nationality wherever possible,—at any rate no man was in a room where he could not talk to some one. Italians and French were together, with a French Sister in charge; Russians were in another room, where they were most tenderly cared for by Madame de Giers, herself. The Germans were often put with them and one room was always full of the bright, interesting little Japanese. English and Americans naturally went together. There was one ward for officers and civilian volunteers, and here were nursed British, American, German, French, Italian, Austrian, Dutch, Australian, and Russian.

It was wonderful how the stores and supplies came in —beds and bedding, shirts, and all that was necessary. They represented very much self-denial on the part of some, and exhibited many expedients. The under pillows were made of straw from the packing of wine bottles, eider-down quilts were cut up for soft pillows, a long piece of Chefoo silk found in the Mongol Market made shirts, as did best damask linen and bright yellow cotton. " Imperial " shirts these were called.

There were very few bedsteads; matresses were placed on the floor, but every man did have a mattress from somewhere, as well as sheets and pillows.

The families of some of the Legation people went without mosquito curtains for the whole siege, that the men in the Hospital might be supplied with this luxury—almost, indeed, a necessity. Some of the marines had first-aid dressings in their haversacks, but the civilian volunteers had none, so that their wounds were not cared for until their arrival at the Hospital.

The character of the wounds was not that of open warfare, for the fighting was all behind barricades. Consequently the proportion of head injuries was large. Secondary operations, undertaken on account of symptoms, often disclosed bits of material—shirt or trousers—which had been driven into the wound, or the missing bullet or fragment of shell. The proportion of shell wounds was small, only one, of the face proving fatal. There were three perforating wounds of the larynx. Two cases of compound fracture of tibia developed tetanus, each of which was fatal.

A case of strychnine poison has been already alluded to. Chloroform inhalation, continued for two and a half hours, followed by the stomach pump, brought about recovery, and the second day the man was dressed, returning to duty the day following.

Towards the close of the siege several cases were invalided with diarrhœa and dysentery. Among the Russians there were two deaths from the latter, but they were

AFTER THE SIEGE

known to be exceedingly careless about their drinking water. There were three cases of typhoid, one of which died after removal to Tientsin. With the exception of the two tetanus cases, there was during the siege no death of any one who survived his injury twenty-four hours.

No hospital notes were kept during the siege, which was a cause of regret, but no one had the time. At the Pei T'ang, explosion from mines was the cause of most of the casualties.

In his dispatch to the Marquis of Salisbury regarding the conduct of the defences, Sir Claude MacDonald makes especial reference to the Hospital, and to the two physicians in charge. During the siege 166 cases passed through the Hospital, twenty suffering from illness, the rest surgical cases. Owing to the devotion and skill of the two medical officers, 110 of the wounded were eventually discharged cured. Dr. Poole was indefatigable at his work, always sympathetic and cheerful. The wounded of all nationalities spoke most warmly of his devotion and skill. At the conclusion he was struck down with fever of a very dangerous description, and had to be invalided. The sick-bay steward, Mr. Fuller, is highly commended for his care and gentle treatment of the wounded, and the willing and cheerful manner in which he carried out his duties. Miss Myers and Miss Brazier daily filtered the water for the Hospital (a task by no means easy with a hand-pump filter) and carried it there themselves, often with bullets and shells bursting in the trees overhead. Several of the ladies received, for their tireless labors in nursing the sick, the well merited order of the Red Cross. Miss Jessie Ransome was personally decorated by King Edward, while Miss Lambert of the Anglican Mission, Miss

Abbie Chapin of the American Board, and Miss Dr. Saville of the London Mission, received the decoration in China.

Immediately upon the conclusion of the siege, the Americans met and adopted resolutions recognizing their obligations to the Marines by whom they had been defended for so long a time, to Sir Claude MacDonald, Her Britannic Majesty's Minister, and to Minister Conger. From the latter the following communication was received at about the same time:

" PEKING, *August* 18, 1900.
" The Besieged American Missionaries:

"To one and all of you, so providentially saved from threatened massacre, I beg in this hour of our deliverance to express what I know to be the universal sentiment of the Diplomatic Corps, the sincere appreciation of and profound gratitude for the inestimable help which you and the native Christians under your charge have rendered toward our preservation. Without your intelligent and successful planning, and the uncomplaining execution of the Chinese, I believe our salvation would have been impossible.

"By your courteous consideration of me, and your continued patience under most trying occasions, I have been most deeply touched, and for it all I thank you most heartily. I hope and believe that somehow, in God's unerring plan, your sacrifices and danger will bear rich fruit in the material and spiritual welfare of the people to whom you have so nobly devoted your lives and work.

"Assuring you of my personal respect and gratitude, believe me,   Very sincerely yours,
E. H. CONGER."

INDEX TO GROUP OF AMERICAN MISSIONARIES.

1. Rev. G. W. Verity
2. Miss Amy Brown
3. Mrs. A. H. Smith
4. Rev. W. T. Hobart
5. Rev. John Wherry, D.D.
6. Rev. W. F. Walker, D.D.
7. J. H. Ingram, M.D.
8. Rev. H. E. King
9. Rev. G. R. Davis
10. Rev. A. H. Smith, D.D.
11. Rev. C. A. Killie
12. Rev. W. B. Stelle
13. Rev. Gilbert Reid, D.D.
14. Miss Grace Newton
15. Miss Luella Miner
16. Miss Nellie Russell
17. Miss Maud Mackey, M.D.
18. Miss Elizabeth Martin
19. Mrs. F. D. Gamewell
20. Miss Gertrude Gilman
21. Miss Anna Gloss, M.D.
22. Mrs. C. M. Jewell
23. Miss Gertrude Wyckoff
24. Miss Ada Haven
25. Mrs. Howard Galt
26. Mrs. J. H. Ingram
27. Rev. F. M. Chapin
28. Miss Janet McKillican
29. Mrs. Gilbert Reid and child
30. Miss Eliza Leonard, M.D.
31. Mrs. C. A. Killie
32. Miss Alice Terrell
33. Miss Jane Evans
34. Mrs. C. Goodrich
35. Mrs. W. F. Walker
36. Miss Emma E. Martin, M.D.
37. Mrs. C. E. Ewing and child
38. Mrs. F. M. Chapin
39. Miss Mary Andrews
40. Mrs. J. L. Mateer
41. Rev. C. Goodrich, M.D.
42. Miss D. M. Douw
43. Miss Ruth Ingram and sister
44. Miss Grace Goodrich
45. Miss Esther Walker
46. Miss Marion Ewing
47. Miss Dorothea Goodrich
48. Master Carrington Goodrich
49. Master Ernest Chapin
50. Master Ralph Chapin

The following American Missionaries were not on hand when the picture was taken: Rev. F. D. Gamewell, Dr. G. D. Lowry, Rev. C. E. Ewing, Rev. W. S. Ament, D.D., Rev. and Mrs. C. H. Fenn and family, Rev. J. L. Whiting, Dr. and Mrs. J. Inglis, Rev. Howard Galt, Miss Bessie McCoy, Miss Abbie Chapin, Miss A. H. Gowans, Miss H. E Rutherford and Miss Grace Wyckoff.

GROUP OF AMERICAN MISSIONARIES PRESENT DURING THE SIEGE

AFTER THE SIEGE

Three days previous to this, Sir Claude had written to the Chairman of the General Committee, as follows:

"BRITISH LEGATION, PEKING, *Aug.* 15, 1900.
"Dear Mr. Tewksbury:

"I have been busy these last few days, and feel quite worn out, otherwise this letter would have been written before.

"I want to express to the American members of the Committee of General Comfort my high appreciation of the good work they did during the siege, and of the ready and loyal manner in which they anticipated my every wish.

"With such men to work with, work becomes a pleasure, and is bound to be crowned with success. This remark applies to all the American missionaries who took part with me in the siege. Their work and support were unstinted, intelligent, and most loyal, and I have no hesitation in saying that I consider that their presence in the Legation saved the situation. Yours very truly,
CLAUDE M. MACDONALD."

A few days later, the following telegram from the President of the United States was received by the Minister:

"The whole American people rejoice over your deliverance, over the safety of your companions of our own and other nations, who have shared your trials and privations; the fortitude and courage which you have all maintained, and the heroism of your little band of defenders. We all mourn for those who have fallen, and acknowledge the goodness of God which has preserved you, and guided the brave army that set you free.
WM. MCKINLEY."

Two days later the following communication from the Queen was received by Sir Claude MacDonald.

" Warmest congratulations on your safety, after such a terrible time of anxiety to us all. Trust you, Lady MacDonald, and children are well as well as the others.
V. R. I."

A separate telegram was sent from the same source.

" To the Officer Commanding the British Marine Guard:

I thank God that you and those under your command are rescued from your perilous situation. We, my people and I, have waited with the deepest anxiety for the good news of your safety, and a happy termination to your heroic and prolonged defence. I grieve for the losses and sufferings experienced by the besieged.
V. R. I."

* * * * * * *

The siege in Peking was scarcely raised before many of those whose homes were in the city, hastened to visit the sites of their dwellings, to see in what condition they then were. Most of them were found to resemble the premises of the Methodist Mission, where the Americans had been in a state of semi-siege for twelve days. On these spacious grounds, in three distinct divisions, separated from one another by intervening streets, had been seven dwelling houses, three chapels, two boys' schools, one large girls' school, two training schools, two hospitals, two dispensaries, and eight native houses. The University of Peking was a large two-story building enclosed by a high wall, on extensive grounds.

AFTER THE SIEGE 497

When it became possible to revisit this familiar spot, one could have ridden on horse-back everywhere except where the cellars of the buildings had left dangerous pits. It was difficult to find anywhere a whole brick, and aside from occasional sheets, or parts of sheets, of galvanized-iron roofing, it was difficult to find anything whatever to suggest for what the premises had been used. From all the compounds together not enough splinters of wood could have been gathered to kindle a fire. The outer walls of the premises, as well as those of the buildings, had been excavated down to the bottom of the foundations, to remove every brick, and every tree had been not only cut down, but dug up by the roots, so that the exact situation of each could be determined by the deep and irregular holes. The only exception was a fine old tree standing just within the main gate, upon which the notices and bulletins had been daily posted during the semi-siege. Why this was spared is somewhat of a mystery, unless it may have been supposed to be the abode of a spirit; but it served as a landmark without which it was difficult to determine where anything had once stood.

On the University campus a flock of an hundred sheep, intended for the use of the troops, were quietly grazing. Few Chinese were anywhere to be seen. Many of the neighbouring dwellings were destroyed together with the Mission property, either through accident, from revenge, or in gratification of the wild instinct of promoting universal ruin. Most of the neighbouring court-yards were found full of bricks and other looted material, but only a trifling fraction of that which had been lost could be recovered. The large bell of the church had been buried but was afterwards exhumed, on the locality becoming known. This process of sepulture for compromising articles was one of which the Chinese made great use, especially in the concealment of rails and ties from the railway, but in many cases unfriendly informers made the last state of those who had ventured upon this method far worse than the first.

The condition of the Methodist compounds may serve as a type of all the premises destroyed in Peking. In a few instances walls were left standing as if to mark where the buildings had once been, but this was exceptional. In almost every compound there was the same monotony of absolute and total destruction, unrelieved and hopeless.

The total amount of property destroyed belonging to the various Protestant missions in Peking, has not been exactly ascertained, but approximately it may be said to comprise thirty-four dwelling houses, eighteen chapels, eleven boys' schools and one university, eleven girls' schools, four training schools, eleven dispensaries and eight hospitals, besides more than thirty summer-houses at the western hills, and several others at the sea-side.

Within a few days of the arrival of the troops, the Protestant Cemetery at the southwest corner of Peking was visited, and it was found that the tales which had been told of its condition were only too true. All the enclosing walls had been pulled down, and even the foundations were dug up. The long avenue of trees, nearly forty years old, had been destroyed, monuments had been overthrown and broken into fragments, and thirteen of the graves had been opened and the bodies removed; some of them had evidently been used for a bonfire, only a few fragments of bones and here and there a metal button remaining to tell the tale.

This savagery, so alien to the usual Chinese respect for the dead, differentiates the Boxer rising from any

RUINS OF METHODIST MISSION, PEKING

RUINS OF PRESBYTERIAN MISSION, PEKING

anti-foreign movement which had preceded it, and may serve as a gauge of the violence of the volcanic forces deliberately let loose. The Russian Cemetery received the same treatment, which indicated that despite the apparently exceptional relations existing between Russia and China, at the crucial moment there was no discrimination between one barbarian and another.

On the 19th of August a memorial service was held for Baron von Ketteler in the German Legation, with military honours, the body having been brought back in the Chinese coffin where it had been deposited by the kind intervention of one of the members of the Tsung Li Yamen who was not carried away by the prevailing insanity of the hour. On the 6th of September a still more impressive memorial service was held on the IIa Ta great street, the coffin being deposited at the spot where the German Minister had been basely shot seventy-eight days previous. Some companies of German soldiers were in attendance, with a band, and many members of other Legations. A part of the brief exercises was a stirring address delivered by a Chaplain named Kessler, reviewing the career of the late Minister, and enforcing the obvious lessons to be drawn therefrom.

It was a strange and an impressive spectacle, taking place as it did on one of the great arteries of the ancient Capital of the Empire, which with all its experience had never witnessed conditions like these. The chair of the Baroness, in deep mourning, stood beside the coffin; the streets were lined with interested European spectators, and with impassive Chinese, perhaps dimly wondering what it was all about. What a change of circumstances within that two and a half months, and what a wonder that events shaped by an unseen Hand had brought about such a surprising revolution, for the man who fired the shot was already in the custody of the Germans, admitting the act, but explaining that he was obeying the orders of his immediate superiors.

During the entire siege more than seventy Chinese Peking carts stood in the British Legation, a reminiscence of the expectation that an overland journey to Tientsin would be soon undertaken, and they would all be wanted. As soon as the besieged began once more to go upon the streets, there occurred one of those surprising alterations of conditions to which despite their perpetual recurrence it was difficult to become accustomed. The city was flooded with foreign troops, and such Chinese as had remained soon began to perceive that nothing would be safe in merely Chinese possession. Accordingly many of them who had foreign friends among the besieged, or even mere acquaintances, hastened to confide to them the carts and mules which in the sudden and universal demand for transportation, it was impossible to save from confiscation. Thus was realized the Chinese adage which says: " Nothing to eat in the morning, and at night a horse to ride."

The disagreeable and dangerous pervasiveness of some of the Continental soldiers became so obtrusive and intrusive, that it was necessary to remove the Chinese Christians, especially the school-girls, from their siege quarters to safer and more secluded places. The quest for suitable headquarters occupied some of the guardians of these helpless wards for many weary days. In many cases Chinese who had been in good circumstances were more than willing to put their property at the disposal of any foreigner whom they knew, to prevent it from being despoiled.

In two instances considerable bodies of Chinese Christians were lodged by the consent of the military and legation authorities in the palaces of Manchu Princes, which had been abandoned by their owners in terror. As the extensive complicity of all the Manchus in Peking with the Boxer movement became established as a fact, it seemed increasingly probable that the property in these places would be promptly confiscated. In accordance with the express advice both of the British and the American Ministers, it was decided to sell the property thus abandoned, and to use the abundant proceeds for the support of the destitute Christians, the number of whom continually increased as refugees from distant places began to have courage to come into the city.

This step gave rise to much misapprehension, and when the story was repeated with unconscious exaggeration by those ignorant of the peculiar circumstances, led to the propagation of much absolutely unsupported scandal. It would have been quite possible to have refused to enter these places at all, but having entered them, the only way to preserve the property from miscellaneous looting was to take possession of it under the highest authority then in existence, and to use it in ways which that authority approved.

With the flight of the Empress and the Court, the whole Chinese army disappeared from vision, dispersed in many different directions, harrying the people through the regions where they passed, and anon congregating in Pao Ting Fu and other centers, only again to scatter. The mere occupation of Peking was probably regarded by them simply as an untoward incident, and by itself accomplished little or nothing toward the settlement of the numerous and intricate questions arising upon every hand. The extensive supplies of arms which seem to have been sent to Peking during the siege, were concealed in a great variety of places, many of them coming to light in unexpected localities. Young Fargo Squiers with a companion discovered a great number of cases of Männlicher carbines; two of these they conveyed to the American Legation, but upon returning for the rest, it was found that the French had seized them. Mr. Tewksbury learned through a Buddhist priest that in a temple a short distance outside of the Chang I gate of the southern city there were stored several cases of $3\frac{1}{2}$ inch shells belonging to the captured Krupp guns. On reporting this to the United States officers, a Major and a guard were sent to take possession. Similar finds were made in other quarters.

One of the most interesting discoveries was the mode of construction of the elaborate gun-platforms which the Chinese had put up inside the south-eastern corner of the Imperial City, for attacking the Legations and the Su Wang Fu. These were built of pine poles of large size carefully and strongly lashed together, supporting a platform about twenty-five feet in height, with an area of about twenty-five by forty feet. A long ramp led up to each one, for dragging the guns into position. A careful count showed that not less than seven hundred poles had been required for each platform. They were provided with strongly built roofs of two inch planks and the port holes, which had been dug through the coping of the city wall, were protected from rifle-firing by doors of 3-16 inch iron as bullet shields,—apparently some of the plunder from the electric light works. Either one of these batteries properly worked ought to have made the British Legation and the Fu untenable after two hours firing; yet, except during the final night of the siege, the execution actually done was trifling.

The water-gate directly below these gun-platforms had been most securely barricaded with bricks and stones, as

BRITISH LEGATION WALL

CHINESE GUN PLATFORM FOR FIRING ON THE LEGATION

if to prevent the besieged from making a rush on the Imperial and Forbidden cities, and capturing the Court! At the same time, the corresponding gate in the southern wall of the northern city, through which as already mentioned, the first foreign troops actually entered, was left wholly unguarded, some of the iron bars being altogether lacking, and the remainder easily removed.

By far the most interesting sight in Peking after the relief, was the Pei T'ang, or Northern Cathedral, which had been defended with supreme courage from the 16th of June (four days before the Legation siege began), until the 16th of August (two days after the Legations were delivered), when the first entry, singularly enough, was made by the Japanese troops. The extensive grounds are adjacent to the west wall of the Imperial City, and had been attacked from a gun platform similar to the one just described, situated at the north-west corner of the wall, but on the outside, as well as from rifle-platforms only a short distance off. Just beyond the north wall of the orphanage premises was situated a large magazine stored with sulphur and other materials for the manufacture of powder, of which the Chinese made incessant use.

During the sixty days of uninterrupted attack there occurred four explosions, due to the mining of the Chinese, which was indefatigable and on a large scale. Two of the four were very severe and resulted in great loss of life, especially among the Chinese children. In one of these explosions the roof of a building fell in and buried an Italian officer five feet deep in the debris. It was supposed that he was of course killed, but some hours after, when there was leisure to attend to it, excavations were made, and he was found to be uninjured!

The Cathedral was terribly battered by shells, but most of the bullets were fired far too high to do much execution. During the whole two months of the Cathedral siege, the attacks of the enemy were never intermitted,—as was the case at the Legations—and in all that weary time no messengers were able to get out, and no outside news was received. During the period of semi-truce at the Legations, those besieged in the Cathedral, hearing no more artillery, naturally concluded that the Chinese had been victorious, and that the Legations had succumbed.

The total number of foreigners imprisoned in the premises was about ninety, of whom forty-three were officers and marines. There were several thousand Chinese, and a very inadequate food supply, as Bishop Favier had expected that they would all be rescued within a short time after the siege began. At the close there was absolutely nothing to eat, the besieged having been reduced to two ounces of food a day; and when the relief arrived even this morsel was not available, and the civilians had agreed to go without food that what there was might be given to the fighters. The Mother Superior, a venerable lady of great age, never wavered in her conviction that the Lord would assuredly save His little flock. She lived through the siege to see her prophecy fulfilled, and then quietly passed away in peace.

The accurate foresight of the Bishop in forecasting the coming storm was equalled by the heroism of all those who passed through this frightful ordeal, which on some accounts was much worse than that experienced by those in the Legations, as its duration was longer, the attacks continuous, the resources more meagre, the defenders a mere handful against vast numbers, and the harrowing suspense in regard to what was taking place outside was never once broken. Whatever may be the fate of Christianity in Peking or in China, the Northern Cathedral will always remain as a witness of what Christian men and women, Chinese as well as Europeans, can do and suffer for a faith to which they have given their whole selves, and for which they would gladly have given their lives.

The following additional notes upon the Siege of the North Cathedral are condensed from an account by Rev. Gilbert Reid.

There were congregated there 30 French officers and marines, 10 Italians, 13 French Fathers, 20 Sisters, and 3,200 native converts.

There was food enough for about 500 usually living on the place, but the task of feeding six times that number was a serious one.

At first the Chinese had eight ounces of food each day, but toward the end this was reduced to two ounces. The men worked well as long as their strength remained, but afterwards could not do much more than crawl about and keep up a mere existence. The supply, such as it was, chaff, grass, and leaves of the trees, could only have lasted a few days more, and then famine and pestilence would have occurred. The foreigners fared better as their strength was indispensable for the defence.

The attack, at first by Boxers, began on June 15th, when forty-eight of the enemy were killed. By June 20th, Chinese soldiers appeared, and ever afterward continued to be the chief factor. On that day they also began cannonading, firing with one gun straight into the main entrance of the Cathedral grounds. The marines made a rush upon the enemy and captured the gun, which was the only artillery they had during the whole siege. The cannonading thus began earlier than at the Legations and was more severe. For three days the Cathedral was under fire from at least fourteen guns, while the number was ordinarily not less than four, including one from the Palace grounds, and another from the palace of Prince Li.

There were twenty-eight successive days of shelling,—being four days more than the whole period in which any of the Legations were shelled. During these days as many as 2,400 shells were fired, and on June 24th, 380 shells burst in the grounds.

The only defenders of the Cathedral and its vast crowd of helpless refugees were the forty marines who were sent from the foreign guard, stationed at the six different places where the fortifications were made strongest. The French were supplied with 2,000 rounds of ammunition, but the Italians had less. As soon as one of their number was killed a Chinese would take his place. Night and day this small number had to keep watch, and be ready to resist every device of the enemy.

The shelling left its marks on every other building as well as on the Cathedral itself. But the greatest effect was from the powder explosions. As many as eighty persons were killed in one explosion, and 400 in all, of whom 120 were children. The loss among the natives was mainly from these mines. The Foundling Hospital was a total wreck, a fitting illustration of the designs of the enemy.

At the beginning as many as 600 of the native converts were armed with swords and spears, but when the Chinese soldiers began firing shot and shell, such equipment was useless. Forty rifles and one gun were the defence against perhaps 2,000 rifles and a dozen guns.

However superior the strength and number of the enemy, they made no attempt to assault and enter the place. The shots of the French were too well aimed to encourage such an attempt. A kind Providence rested over the place, and the united prayers of each morning brought their blessing in rich munificence.

The enemy who fought, and the Empress and advisers who schemed, had clearly one intent, and that was the annihilation of the body of Christians who never fired a shot except in self-defence. To the credit of Catholic France and Catholic Italy the calamity was prevented.

The defence was one of sublime heroism. The head of the Mission, Bishop Favier, was the leader of courage. While untrained to martial deeds, he maintained cheerfulness and hope, and by calmness of spirit and trust in God, kept in check any panic among the converts, and all despondency among the marines. Half of the Italian defenders, and both of the French officers, with three marines, were killed, or one-fourth of the total. However desperate the position, the Bishop never lost heart.

The Siege in Peking, from whatever point of view it is regarded, will always remain a memorable experience in human history. It was the culmination of a movement without any parallel in the annals of the past, and which is not likely to be repeated under any future conditions. There is much about it which is obscure, and much which will perhaps remain so. But as an example of the steadfast, patient courage of a handful against a host, of the sagacious use of slender resources, of the bravery of men and the fortitude of women, of unfaltering trust in God, and of a great deliverance wrought by Him against all human probabilities, it is a story, however inadequately told, which the world will not willingly let die.

XXVII

THE HAND OF GOD IN THE SIEGE*

FREDERICK the Great is said to have inquired of his Chaplain what he considered to be the proof of the authenticity of the Bible. The Chaplain replied: "The Jews, Your Majesty." Should any one ask what is the evidence of a Providence which watches over the affairs of men, the compendious answer might well be: "The Siege in Peking." Instead of submitting the case to argument, it is better to confine our attention to a few outline facts.

1. The preservation of the lives of the foreigners in Peking before the Legation guards arrived. There is probable, but not certain, evidence that the Grand Council held a meeting at which the question of exterminating all Occidentals in Peking was discussed, and nothing but the vacillation of Prince Ch'ing seems to have delayed the act.

2. The arrival of the Legation guards by the very last opportunity. Had they been two days later, the utter and irreparable ruin of the railway and the general blaze throughout the country would have prevented them from coming, as it prevented Admiral Seymour a few

---

* The substance of this address was delivered at a Union Thanksgiving Service, held in the British Legation grounds, Peking, Sunday morning Aug. 19th, after the arrival of the relieving army.

COMING OUT OF CHURCH, PEKING

THE HAND OF GOD IN THE SIEGE 509

days after. This would have insured the massacre of every foreigner at once.

3. The immunity from attack while foreigners were unaware of their serious peril. Many were scattered in distant parts of Peking, and some even at the Western Hills, as if nothing were wrong. They were gathered in by the 8th of June. The largest part of all, twenty-four in number, travelled without escort thirteen miles, from T'ung Chou, through a region seething with animosity to foreigners, not only without attack, but with no threatening symptoms of any sort.

4. These Americans just mentioned, with others to the number of seventy, took refuge in the large premises of the Methodist Mission, where for a period of twelve days they were in a state of semi-siege, a time which was a most important rehearsal of the coming period of far greater trial. An elaborate organization was at once effected, committees of many kinds chosen, fortifications and defences begun, sentries mounted, the Chinese Christians drilled and armed, so that when the whole body of foreigners assembled at the British Legation, and the British Minister desired the active coöperation of the Americans, the whole machinery was in order, and it was only necessary to slip the belt on the wheel for it to begin to work.

5. The safety of the native Christians. When the sudden murder of the German Minister led to the order that all foreigners should repair to their Legations, nothing was said in regard to the native Christians. They were regarded as outside the sphere of influence of the Ministers, who took no action in regard to them at all. To many they were an unconsidered and a negligible quantity. Largely through the agency of the lamented Professor James, who was killed at the very time of the

entrance of the Christians to the palace which he had helped to secure for them, they were graciously and marvellously provided for, at a time of dire extremity, in the Su Wang Fu. Little as most of us realized it at the time, this palace and its grounds were absolutely essential to our salvation. Without it the British, Spanish, Japanese, French and German Legations could not have been held, and without the services of the Chinese Christians the work of defence could not have been prosecuted. It might have been said, " except these abide in the ship, ye cannot be saved."

6. In round numbers there were probably three thousand persons to be fed during the siege, exclusive of the many hundred marines. Many foreigners came into the Legation, as did nearly all the Chinese, without any provision whatever. It was inherently improbable that any considerable food-supply could be obtained within our lines, for a siege of unknown duration. Yet in a grain shop on Legation Street was discovered between one hundred and two hundred tons of wheat of this year's crop, recently arrived from Honan. Besides this, there were mountains of rice, white and yellow Indian corn, pulse, and much else. All the shops in Peking dealing in foreign goods were within our lines, and their stores were immediately available, and during the whole siege were absolutely essential.

There was a large supply of ponies for the races, as well as mules, most of which were consumed for food, while nearly all the remainder were needed for hauling, grinding grain, etc. The food for all these animals was supplied as remarkably as that for men and women. Considerable sorghum and beans were discovered, besides a huge pile of millet-straw close to two dwelling-houses which had been burned,—one on either side of the straw,

THE HAND OF GOD IN THE SIEGE 511

which was not disturbed. Many old residents of Peking were surprised to find the water of the eight wells in the British Legation was of great excellence, and it was abundantly proved that it could be safely drunk without being filtered or boiled. While there were heavy drafts on these wells during the great fires, they never once failed us.

The fuel supply was absolutely unlimited, though had it been absent nothing could have taken its place. We were surrounded by hundreds of thousands of pounds of coal, which had only to be brought a short distance. Wrecked buildings afforded all the kindling needed and abundant timbers for fortifications.

7. Miscellaneous supplies were procured from the foreign stores; and clothing for many foreigners, who had not even a change of garments, was found at tailor shops near by. One of the greatest, most imperative, and constant needs, was material for sand bags, of which perhaps 50,000 may have been made. At first, legation curtains, damask tablecloths, and any and every fabric obtainable was used. Later the supply from the foreign stores and Chinese sources seemed literally inexhaustible, and to the end never gave out. From Chinese dwellings within the lines, or without, were procured enormous quantities of clothing most useful for the destitute Chinese Christians, until their wants in all directions were amply supplied, much being sold at auction for their benefit.

Materials for the defence were discovered in many places, notably in a blacksmith's shop, where were obtained an anvil, bellows, smelting-pots, and best of all, an old Chinese cannon which proved invaluable. It was mounted on an Italian carriage, loaded with Russian shell refilled by the British armourer, charged with Chinese powder, and fired by an American gunner—justly termed the "International Gun." In many shops and houses were found britannia-ware to the extent of several cart-loads, much of which was used in making balls for the cannon, and shot for the Italian one-pound gun, besides many bullets. Of all the miscellaneous stuff which came to hand, very little proved amiss in the end.

8. The restraining hand of God upon the Chinese. When foreigners were on their way to the Legations, and everything was in a chaotic state, the Chinese might readily have annihilated the whole body at a blow. While the Chinese held the city wall, they could easily have made every Legation uninhabitable if they had used the right means. Rifle shots alone would have been sufficient.

Then they adopted well-chosen plans to burn the British Legation, by the spread of fires set on the outside. Of these attacks, three were fierce, persistent, and dangerous in the extreme. Yet in the end they not only all failed, but we were left in each case in a stronger position than before. More than once the wind suddenly veered about, saving us from what appeared to be imminent destruction. Buildings being removed which sheltered the enemy and which might spread fires in our Legation limits, we were better protected. The destruction of the Hanlin Yuan was the means of extending our line of defence a considerable distance, the position being later made almost impregnable.

More terrible than all else was the threat of mining. This we knew to have been actually begun in two places, and perhaps elsewhere, one mine in a building in the Carriage Park, and one on the wall near our most advanced post to the west. Why were these mines never finished?

THE HAND OF GOD IN THE SIEGE 513

The Chinese might at many different times have made a sudden and a violent attack at a weak point, from which it would have been difficult to defend ourselves, the lines being very long and the defenders few. Had we been attacked by European or Japanese troops, they would certainly have crept down the edge of the Canal in the dark, where our rifles could not command them, and have rushed the front gate. Only two days before the siege was raised, was a platform completed for the planting of a gun to prevent this, though, owing to the greater peril elsewhere, the gun was never mounted upon it. A few hundred Chinese, willing to throw away their lives to ensure the capture of the Legations, would have taken them at any moment during the first month of the siege. Why was it never done, or even attempted? The Chinese were in some way kept from following up the principal advantages which they gained.

At the very beginning of the siege nearly all the Legations were abandoned in a panic, but the Chinese did not enter, and the positions were reoccupied. At another time the city wall was abandoned, but the Chinese did not find it out until too late, and it was at once retaken. When the new battery had begun to play on the house in the south stable court, a few shots threatened to bring the house tumbling down. Rifles attacked the battery and it was withdrawn, and never replanted there.

At a later date shells were thrown into the house of the Chinese Secretary in a way to threaten the whole Legation, as well as that one dwelling. Again the rifles assailed the gunners, and after five shots the battery was withdrawn permanently. Time after time, when the gunners appeared to have got the exact range, the shelling ceased. The very last night of the siege the shells were most destructive, but only ten shots were fired, and the next day the gun was gone. The most terrible engines of destruction were rendered comparatively harmless.

It has been estimated that between a million and a half and two million bullets must have been discharged at us. In some of the earlier attacks, when we appeared to be surrounded by several thousand foes, there seemed to be 124 shots a minute, or more than two a second. Yet excluding men at the loopholes, only three or four persons are known to have been injured by these bullets in the crowded British Legation, where there were probably never less than 800 persons on an average, and sometimes over 1,000. One marine was killed in this way, and two or three others wounded, and the last day of the siege two civilians were scratched. After the relieving force had entered the Legation, the only injury received by any lady took place. No child was hit, though the yards swarmed with them.

Careful count shows the number of shells and shots fired at all the Legations during the siege to be about 2,900. In the British Legation it is believed that no one not on duty at the loop-holes was ever really injured by any one of these, although a few Chinese were hurt by bricks knocked down by cannon balls. Hundreds of solid shot fell in the Hanlin courts, in the Ministers' houses, and in other crowded places. Why were these innumerable missiles so harmless? For a long time there appeared to be from twelve to fifteen guns playing at once. Thirteen bomb-proofs were laboriously dug, but so far as is known not one of them was ever entered to escape from a shell.

9. The restraining hand of God in warding off disease. The overcrowding was excessive, the conditions most unwholesome. Orientals are impatient of sanitary re-

THE HAND OF GOD IN THE SIEGE 515

straints. Whooping-cough, measles, typhoid and scarlet fevers, as well as small-pox, have all been experienced during the siege, by both foreigners and Chinese, but there was no contagion to speak of, and no epidemic. What an opportunity for the development of Asiatic cholera! Bad and insufficient food had caused considerable mortality among Chinese children, and the aged, but in general the vital statistics have been extraordinary. There was no known case of heat-stroke, and for this latitude the weather throughout was phenomenal.

The physicians available for service were exceedingly numerous and skilful. One of the most intelligent patients declared that in no hospital in the civilized world would better care and more tender nursing be secured. Lady doctors laid aside all professional etiquette, and were content to act simply as nurses. Under the circumstances, the percentage of losses in the hospital cannot be considered large, especially among so many serious cases.

10. The Lord sent a spirit of confusion among our enemies, who feared us far more than we feared them. Their most savage attacks seemed designed to prevent us from making sorties which they exceedingly dreaded and tried in every way to prevent.

On our part there was a spirit of unity rare to see. Greek, Roman Catholic and Protestant Christians fraternized as never before. We represented every country in Europe except Turkey and Greece, besides three in Asia, and the United States. What a Noah's Ark! Yet the thought of Plato and the hint of Cicero, concerning "the common bond" which links the whole human race was seldom more strongly felt, realizing the idea of Paul that we are all members one of another. Amid political and military jealousies this fact will remain a precious memory. The harmony of the defended was well matched by the bravery of their defenders.

In all these things we see the Hand of God in the Siege in Peking. In many of its aspects it is fully and comprehensively anticipated in Psalm CXXIV, especially the seventh verse, which was sent home as a telegram the day after relief came. We honour the living for their heroism in defending us. We cherish the memory of the brave dead. But most of all we thank the Lord who brought us through fire and water into a healthy place.

XXVIII

THE PUNISHMENT OF PEKING

FORTY years have elapsed since the first occupation of the capital of China by European troops, in 1860. At that time, every consideration was shown to the feelings of the Chinese: the city was left uninjured, and within a month of their first entry the troops were withdrawn from within the walls. Great things were hoped from the blow to the national pride involved in this brief occupancy. It was confidently expected that it would prove the death-blow to the old stubborn arrogancy that has so long looked down upon the foreigner as an outcast and a barbarian, and made Peking a closed city to the outside world.

But after more than a generation of intercourse with Europeans, Peking must still be called an anti-foreign city from first to last.

Although the Yamên Ministers have gone to the Legations for occasional banquets, it has always been noticeable that there were no return visits at their own homes, and the effort to introduce such an innovation a few years since was a blank failure. Except in the case of the missionaries, it is still true that the homes of the city are tightly closed to the outsider.

The number of treatments in the various hospitals, especially in the pioneer one of the London Mission, has amounted to hundreds of thousands—perhaps even to a million or more—and many wide and effectual doors have thus been opened to the Chinese heart; but, taking Peking as a whole, it has remained irreconcilable in its contempt and hate.

It has long been known that the native pundits who teach foreigners the language would not recognize their pupils on the street should they meet them, because, whatever their private views might be, to do so would cause the pundit to lose "face," or self-respect. And what was true of scholars was to a considerable degree the case also with the tradesmen, who were willing enough to absorb the foreign dollars, but who despised their owners. The same was also true to a large extent of the working class—even the coolies—who felt themselves immeasurably the superiors of those for whom they toiled —a view not, perhaps, unlike that entertained by the Jews in Babylon toward their conquerors.

The southern city of Peking has always prided itself upon being far more pronouncedly anti-foreign than the Tartar city. It has steadily resisted every effort to buy a foot of its sacred soil for missionary purposes, and if there have been occasional exceptions in the success of such attempts, they have but served to emphasize the general rule.

Such has been the response of the capital to the first foreign occupation, when leniency and magnanimity of treatment were scrupulously observed. The second occupancy has occurred under circumstances widely different from the first, and with consequences never to be forgotten by the Chinese. If the crimes that led to it were of a singular atrocity, their punishment also has been of a singular completeness.

When the Boxers first arrived in practically limitless numbers, they were distributed like soldiers all over the city, and fed, as soldiers often (but not always) are, at

POLICE STATION, PEKING

RAILWAY STATION, PEKING

THE PUNISHMENT OF PEKING 519

the expense of the people. This would have been a heavy tax, but it was followed by much worse. In order "to guard the Legations," the large detachments of the troops of Jung Lu, Commander-in-Chief of the provincial army, and of General Tung were brought in. These soldiers were related to the Boxers much as scorpions to grasshoppers.

Between them the city was reduced to an acute pitch of misery such as it had never known since the arrival of foreigners. Many families were extinguished, and in others only one or two out of eight or ten members remained alive. Hundreds of house doors were walled up entirely, which often meant that there was no one left. The savages from the province of Kansu who followed General Tung speak a strange dialect almost unintelligible to the Pekingese, but they have written their names in blood. They are to the Chinese in Peking what the Chaldeans from afar were to the ancient Jews, "a hasty and a bitter people."

The ruin of all Christian property was but the beginning of destruction. During the week of burning, the relatively few foreign houses by no means sufficed to quench the unquenchable thirst for places to loot and to destroy. On some days one could count six or eight distinct fires in different quarters, the greatest of them all being the destructive conflagration outside the Front Gate, in the southern city, where were situated the richest shops and the most flourishing trade of Peking.

When it was once more possible for foreigners to traverse the streets of the city, the desolation which met the eye was appalling. Dead bodies of soldiers lay singly or in heaps, in some instances covered with a torn old mat, but always a prey to the now well-fed pariah dogs. Indeed, dead dogs and dead horses poisoned the air of every region. The huge pools of stagnant water were reeking with putrid corpses of man and beast; lean cats stared wildly at the passer-by from holes broken in the fronts of shops boasting such signs as " Perpetual Abundance," " Springs of Plenty," " Ten Thousand Prosperities," and the oft-quoted maxim from the Great Learning, " There is a highway to the production of wealth." One might read over the door of a place thrice looted, and lying in utter ruin, the cheerful motto, " Peace and Tranquillity." For miles upon miles of the busiest streets of the northern and southern city not a single shop was open for business, and scarcely a group of persons was anywhere to be seen.

But the capital of the Chinese Empire had no sooner been occupied by the Allies and its territory distributed for purposes of patrol among the several military contingents represented, than the Chinese began to adapt themselves to the new relations with the same ease with which water fits itself to the dish into which it is poured. The Japanese, having the command of the Chinese written language, were the first to enter this new field, and in three days the whole city was inundated with little flags with a red disc in the middle, and thousands of doors began to be ornamented with the legend: " Compliant subjects of the Great Japanese Nation." For some time it was common to meet Chinese with such flags, the upper space blank, and only the words " compliant subjects " inserted, the nation to which they gave their adherence being left to be filled in later—a striking commentary on the " patriotism " of the Chinese. Of ten men on the streets, eight would probably be furnished with flags of different lands (in cheap imitation only, and much the worse for a heavy shower). The advice so often given by Chinese to one another not to " follow

THE PUNISHMENT OF PEKING

foreigners" has, then, brought about this result, probably unique in the history of mankind.

Not only were flags made the symbol of allegiance to other and unknown countries, but the English language was tortured to compel it to announce this allegiance. "Belong Japan" was the notice on an old shed in the great Ha Ta street. "Noble and good Sirs," read another placard, "please do not shoot us. We are good people." Surely never was there stranger and more unanticipated fulfillment of the prophecy that "the sons of them that afflicted thee shall come bending unto thee," than the circumstance that within a few doors of a temple which served as a Boxer headquarters one read the surprising legend, "God Christianity men," while the remainder of the alley was decorated with the reiterated petition, "Pray officer excuse. Here good people."

There was not only no business doing in Peking in the early months of the occupation, but the very sources of commercial prosperity had been cut up by the roots. In the northern city were four allied banks, each with the character "Hêng," denoting Perpetuity, and the syndicate (supposed to be owned by a eunuch of the Palace) was considered as safe as the Bank of England. In the third week in June the Chinese soldiers plundered each of the Perpetuities, which have ceased to exist—as for a time did all other cash-shops and banks. The streets were abundantly supplied with bank-bills, which blew hither and thither with the gusts of wind and the swirls of dust, and were impartially nosed over in the gutters by the few surviving dogs.

It was not many months, however, ere the shrewd Chinese had a system of cash-shops once more in operation, greatly modified by the inrush of foreign dollars which now became the standard currency of the city.

During the extreme political uncertainties of the winter, it sometimes happened that the price of silver in terms of Peking cash suddenly advanced, at one time to the extent of twenty-five per cent within a period of about three weeks. This was supposed to be because silver can be buried with facility, while brass cash is much too bulky, and it was considered only prudent to confide one's bullion to Mother Earth, who, when not tampered with, is practically the only safe banker in the Empire.

That the gates of Peking, so intimately associated in the minds of all Orientals with the safety of the people, suffered severely during and after the siege has been already mentioned. The Boxers were responsible for indirectly igniting the outer tower of the Ch'ien Mên during their costly conflagration of June 13th, and the inner tower was set on fire accidentally through the carelessness of a signal party after the British troops were in possession.

The outer tower of the Ha Ta gate also disappeared in flames and smoke during those stormy days, while that of the Ch'i Hua Mên was destroyed by the Japanese on their entry. After the foreign soldiers took charge of Peking the city gates were never closed at all, the dependence for security being not upon the wall but upon the guards and the sentries at the outposts.

The first instinct of the Occidental on taking possession of a Chinese city is to provide facile means of ingress and egress. The Chinese seldom make gates except in the middle of the walls on each face of the city, to the great inconvenience of traffic and with a waste of time utterly intolerable to Westerners. Peking had not been occupied three days before the hole already mentioned had been blown through the walls into the Imperial City, at the head of the canal above the British Lega-

RUINS OF CHIEN MÊN GATE

CHIEN MÊN GATE, PEKING

THE PUNISHMENT OF PEKING 523

tion, and this has ever since been an important thoroughfare. At a point more than half-way up the east face of the same wall another slit was cut also, wide enough to admit of the passage of carts, saving many hours of time in crossing the city. But the greatest innovation of all was at the southwest corner of the Tartar City, where the British dug a tunnel quite through the entire outer wall, making an arch, securely boarded in, and labeled in Chinese "English Gate." It has a barricade on the outside and on the inside, and has become indispensable to foreigners, although the Chinese will doubtless hasten to close it up when they have the power. The cutting thus laboriously drilled through the tough concrete, on which dynamite is said to have made but a faint impression, gave an interesting exhibition of the internal anatomy of the fourteen and a quarter miles of this vast protecting rampart, which after all failed to protect.

During the spring there was witnessed the remarkable spectacle of the demolition by the Royal Engineers of the south-western tower at the corner of the wall of the northern city, that its timbers might be employed for the rehabilitated railway to Tientsin. It will be remembered by those who have ever visited the Capital of China that each face of these towers has eight and forty little windows each provided with the board shutter on which is painted the picture of the mouth of a cannon—a not inapt symbol of the general defences of Peking.

Directly in front of the Temple of Heaven was the new terminus of the Tientsin and Peking Railway, formerly at Ma Chia P'u, a mile or two outside the southern city. A huge breach was made in the wall of the southern city, through which the trains enter, reminding the traveller of old York in England—an innovation for which, but for the Boxers, we might have waited long. In front of the station stretched a long row of electric lights, the plant of which was rescued from the Summer Palace by the British, and was now for the first time made useful.

The carts and wagons which cluster about the station on arrival of the trains were kept from overrunning the platform by a long line of stone posts with a familiar look. One face read " Southwest boundary Wang Family," and the next " Northeast boundary Chang Family." They came from the corners of cemeteries in the country, the practical and unsentimental Occidental soldier finding the removal of these landmarks the easiest way to accomplish his end.

The original terminus of the Lu-Han Railway, one of the first enterprises of this sort undertaken by the Chinese Government, was placed at Lu Kuo Ch'iao, on the Yung Ting (or Hun) river, so as to be at a safe distance from the Capital. During the military occupation it appeared to be a suitable opportunity to extend the line directly to Peking, no questions being likely to be asked. This was accordingly done, and a hole was blown in the west wall of the southern city, and the rails laid near the dividing wall between the cities and parallel with it. The station was fixed just outside the Ch'ien Mên.

The British military authorities, on the other hand, determined upon a line to the Peiho at T'ung Chou, which was at once begun on the same facile terms. The embankment passes through the enceinte of the Ha Ta gate, to a station just outside the water gate through which the British relieving force entered the city; from the Ha Ta gate eastward it passes under the wall in a direct line, through a breach in the wall of the southern city.

Thus T'ung Chou, which cut off its own hope by refusing the railway when it was first projected, may yet through its agency be raised, as it were, from the dead.

The plan of the Allies in this and numerous other improvements appears to be to introduce practical ameliorations of existing conditions which may have to be defended by pressure for a few years, after which it is hoped that the Chinese will so thoroughly appreciate them that there will be no call for a return to the previous conditions.

Let it not be supposed that because Western modes of transportation are increasingly employed, Asia is suddenly to be hustled into the abandonment of its past and of its traditions. Perhaps the best symbol of that past and its traditions is the patient, slow, but sure-footed camel, who has always abounded in Peking streets, " a prince in winter, a beggar in summer," with bits of hair here and there clinging to his almost bare hide. The long lines which used to be seen loaded with tea for Russia have disappeared, but droves of them are still bringing coal from the western hills as of yore. It is a Chinese adage that when the camel carries despatches, whatever may be said of his speed, he is at least sure. Attentive contemplation of their apparently expressionless visage may reveal the ground-plan of a sly half-wink, as if the leader of the long line of deliberate creatures were calmly ruminating thus: "Ah! I perceive that you believe you could get on and not use me. Ah! you were wrong, as you shall see; for I am strong, I can wait long; here I belong; long after you and yours are gone, here I shall be."

The numerous jinrikishas which had begun to form so prominent a feature in Peking, and which were so utterly extinguished by the siege and its concomitants, again became all-pervasive, forming a useful link in the not too abundant facilities for locomotion. Carts once more began to ply for hire, at rates somewhat advanced above those of former days, and the streets, including the few which had been metaled, after being badly worn by the heavy army and other traffic, were repaired, although but superficially, if at all, by the military authorities.

In ordinary times the dust is partly laid by throwing on the roads all the waste water of the city, but for many months this was altogether pretermitted, and the result was such depths of loose, friable soil as passed all previous experience, which was already sufficiently painful. The whole winter may be said to have been one semi-continuous dust-storm, reducing life to its lowest terms, although the climate is not in itself objectionable.

Under the military government of the city, Peking was lighted at night as it had never been before, in many places every house being required to maintain a lamp at the door. Even on the walls of the Imperial City, and in places where heretofore there had usually reigned Cimmerian darkness, small kerosene lamps shone clear, enabling the traveller to see his way with sufficient distinctness. Even the smaller alleys were thus lit to some extent, and in the larger streets, as outside the Ch'ien Mên, the effect was not unlike that of a Western row of street lamps. The military also endeavoured to teach the Chinese how to keep their streets and alleys clean, an art never previously acquired in the capital of China. Had the occupation of the city been prolonged, there ought to have been a marked improvement in its sanitation as a whole; but that the Chinese themselves will ever adopt and enforce regulations like these is too much to expect. As the saying goes, "When the windlass stops, the garden-beds dry up."

THE PUNISHMENT OF PEKING

The huge piles of lime which during the siege were so conspicuous in readiness for the repair of the Peking highways, were absorbed by military or by private individuals, who will doubtless never again find such material so conveniently provided. A huge combination of capital had a " corner " on all the lime-kilns in the Western Hills region, as well as on all the brick-kilns, and expected to realize great sums when rebuilding once set in.

The siege barricades were everywhere entirely removed, and the British Legation was soon put into its normal trim and tidy condition. But the wall at the extreme end of the north stables was left as the relieving forces found it, battered by the incessant impact of bullets, shot, and shell, the whole surmounted by a damaged lookout, surmounted by decaying sand-bags, while beneath on the outer face of the wall are printed in bold capitals the significant words: " LEST WE FORGET."

The disposition of the refuse from the cavalry stables appeared to have been a perplexing problem. It was ill solved by making huge winrows in the spacious broadways in front of the Imperial City on the south, forming a perpetual Gehenna, where lean and mangy dogs during the bitter winter weather reposed in peace and security on the warm and reeking manure piles. One of the military eccentricities was the renaming of all the Peking streets, one being " Gaselee Road," another " Stewart Road," etc., so that when an American soldier informed one that his barracks were at " the corner of Ave. A and 5th St." in the southern city, it was necessary to study a new map.

The presence of so many foreigners in the Capital rendered the pursuit of philological researches both easy and fascinating. One of the more recent arrivals wished to know why the Chinese were always saying "Quite so," and what they meant by it. It turned out to be merely a reflection of the impatient foreigner, whose most imperious demand is *k'uai-tsou* (go on fast.) Still another thoughtful observer noticed the singular fact that the Chinese appeared familiar with one of the most doubtful of French novelists, and frequently spoke his name —"Zola," *tsou-la* (gone)!

The one phrase of pure and unadulterated Pekingese which is more certain to be heard than any other, is the expression "*Pukou pên'rh*"—meaning that the sum of money supposed to have been mentioned is less than the article cost. It is said that "poko" is a Filipino word, meaning "a little," and it was soon introduced into Pekingese as a new slang phrase with a wide range of meaning. A defective postage-stamp was "*pukou pên'rh*," and so was a lad who failed to win a race with his fellow, or a lamp chimney with a flaw.

The city in which all foreigners were but lately stormed at with shot and shell, now began to display posters in Chinese informing the natives at what places schools might be found where English, French, Russian, or Japanese could be learned. The walls of the entrances to the Forbidden city bore huge hand-bills notifying the whereabouts of the "Y. M. C. A. Reading, Writing, and Coffee Rooms," while on West Legation street might be observed the announcement printed in neat capitals: "The work-shop in which any iron-work are proposed." French and German advertisements everywhere abounded, and the main street of the southern city bristled with notifications in every leading European language, as well as in Japanese; they were of every variety, from a barber's shop with its colored pole, to the peremptory announcement at the railway station in front of

STREET PANORAMA, PEKING

Y. M. C. A. HEADQUARTERS, PEKING

the Temple of Heaven: " No Admittance Except on Business."

The Winter Palace, within the innermost recesses of what the troops have dubbed " The Sacred City," was visited during the winter by many thousand persons, military and civil, and later by a stream of tourists, and while all of its buildings may not have been entered, the greater part of them are now as familiar to us as the palaces at Versailles, and have been photographed times without number. It has been well known that from the very first opening of these apartments to the select circle, the curios and bric-a-brac began to disappear, until, ere weeks had passed, nothing portable was left in sight, and but little of any kind which would be worth carrying away. It is supposed that much still remains within the storehouses and treasuries with which the residences of princes and the Imperial family are amply provided; but for the exclusive and haughty Manchus who have so long ruled China, it is difficult to regard their abodes as other than hopelessly defiled by the contamination of the Barbarian for so many moons.

There were left the foreign musical instruments, an organ, a baby-organ, and a piano, all horribly out of tune, together with a pile of books in the Emperor's library, some silk-covered mattresses on the divans (stuffed with cotton), and the usual worthless bric-a-brac of the Chinese mansion, all that is really valuable having been removed to some other sphere of usefulness. Some time ago there was the huge brass (or bronze?) elephant with his preposterous accompaniments of a train, but like the real animals in the city he seems to have gone the way of the rest, and perhaps some time when a visitor's vest-pockets had an unusual bulge, it was owing to this two foot monstrosity tucked carelessly away inside!

As the restrictions upon entering became more stringent, the number of doors closed up with a long typewritten set of rules and regulation multiplied, until there were many places, once easy of access, closed to all comers. And the public was politely requested not to kick the Chinese attendants because they declined to open doors which they were forbidden to unlock. This caution was not unnecessary, as the demeanour of the military portion of the visitors frequently demonstrated. They are used to being minded without question, and to have a " heathen Chinee " refuse to do what they told him was intolerable.

On the whole the more minute and reiterated inspection of the " Palaces " was disappointing. We knew all the while that they must be much the same as other Chinese elegant dwellings, yet we had a secret hope that it would prove otherwise. To begin with, courts in the Winter Palace are surprisingly small in area, and one is not without a feeling of pity for an Empress and an Emperor who should have to put up with much smaller breathing-places between their dwellings than some of their humbler subjects. Why the palaces were laid out on such a scrimped pattern is as unaccountable as the like phenomenon in the village hamlet, where the land, being worth absolutely nothing at all, is treated as if it were the corner-lot of a city, and must not be wasted. Taking into account the far ampler accommodations of the buildings used as headquarters by Count von Waldersee and the German officers, it is easy to see why they should have gradually displaced in favour the others in the more " Forbidden City " itself.

This " Western Court " (Hsi Yuan), which has long been the city home of the Empress Dowager and the Emperor, is situated to the west of the main Forbidden

THE PUNISHMENT OF PEKING 531

City, to which it forms a species of annex. The abode of the former (called Ying T'ai) was the handsomest building in Peking, with rich black-wood carving adapted to entrance the eye (and to hold the dust) in an unusual degree. In the adjacent courts there were theatres, lotus-ponds, and endless pavilions, while at the south-western angle there was a stretch of what is probably the most extensive and elaborate rock-work in China, so skilfully concealing the relatively small areas of the enclosure that the general effect was that of intricate labyrinths, though the whole tract is but a few rods in width.

Still further east is the palace of the Emperor (Nan Hai Tzu) in which for many months he was confined upon an island in gilded misery, daily sitting on the terrace on the southern side overlooking the lake, and vainly longing for a turn in the wheel of Fortune, which, when at last it came, by no means brought the relief expected.

On the night of the 17th of April the Ying T'ai Palace of the Empress Dowager was largely destroyed by a fierce fire, which was so rapid in its spread that the Commander-in-Chief of all the Armies was rescued through a window, while his Chief of Staff, Gen. von Schwartzhoff, who returned to his room to save valuable papers, was burned to death immediately. It is altogether likely that these, and similar disasters, are largely if not entirely due to the careless manner in which Westerners introduced their huge stoves into the fragile structures designed to be heated only by braziers, or at most by coal fires under the brick floor. The first step taken by the Occidental is to build brick partitions, and to wall in the verandas, and the next is to set up his stoves with pipes of all sizes, made of the most imperfect materials, protruding through the flimsy wooden lattice-work at all heights and angles. The Chinese servants, in the effort to suit their masters and keep the fires always hot, stuff the stoves to the top with fuel, and then leave the stove door open to prevent too rapid combustion. With such antecedents the consequences experienced are almost inevitable.

From the Nan Hai Tzu to the Ying T'ai, and northward along additional lotus-ponds, extended the line of the toy railway built for the delectation of His Majesty, where he was wont to ride in the carriages pushed by coolies so as to insure immunity from railway accidents. For the accommodation of the handsomely furnished cars elaborate sheds had been built, but the vehicles had long been entirely exposed to the weather, and during the rains and snows had not only parted with their elegant varnish, but likewise with every scrap of plush and velvet trimmings. A string of open freight cars was daily employed for removing the manure from the stables of the German cavalry.

The hitherto inaccessible Coal Hill became greatly appreciated by the Chinese as a recreation park, for which it was much frequented. At its eastern side near the base is pointed out the gnarled and stunted pine-tree on which the last Emperor of the native Ming Dynasty hung himself in 1644, when he saw that the Manchus had entered his Capital and seized his Empire.

In the beautiful Iho Park, within the inclosure known as the "Summer Palace," or Wan Shou Shan, several miles northwest of Peking, the Empress spent much of her time, and it was here that she was visited by her favourites in the official ranks, bringing word of everything said and done outside. These spacious and beautiful grounds, known as the Mountain of Ten Thousand Ages, were in 1860 visited by the besom of destruction as a penalty for the

COAL HILL, CHINESE SERVING GERMAN OFFICERS

SUMMER PALACE FROM THE LAKE

THE PUNISHMENT OF PEKING

treachery of the Imperial Court in capturing and torturing Sir Harry Parkes and others while protected by a flag of truce. Within recent years the buildings have been restored to something of their pristine beauty, and re-stocked with those elegant adornments inseparable from Oriental luxury.

It is a strange fate which has overtaken this pleasure park that, at the expiration of just forty years from the former destruction, it should once more fall into the hands of the Barbarians, and, while not this time reduced to absolute ruins, should yet be unmercifully looted. Even the huge Buddhas were toppled over with violence to get at their true inwardness, and the looters have often been rewarded by securing old Chinese treasury notes dating back to the middle of the fourteenth century.

The crowning Temple to the Five Hundred Buddhas, on the crest of the hill, which almost alone escaped the devastation of 1860, has now been less fortunate, for in some unexplained manner a fire was started in it, and though its structure was too massive to fall, its walls are blackened and cracked from the effects of the intense heat.

From the lake at the base of the hill upon which this Temple stands to the summit, stretched a splendid suite of apartments, which when inspected by civilians were found to be scenes of wreck and ruin. The rooms were littered with broken fragments of carved partitions, and pieces of immense plate-glass windows, while prisms of chandeliers and broken bulbs of electric lights strewed the floors. That portion of this palace assigned to British care was carefully guarded and kept in fair condition, while all bric-a-brac still remaining was removed to a place of safety and securely guarded.

The fate of the Imperial palaces in falling into the

hands of the invader was matched by that of the abodes of the Princes, Dukes, and other nobility, all of which were promptly pitched upon, as a " military necessity," for headquarters. The former palace of Prince Ch'un in the southwest corner of the city in which the present Emperor was born (and which therefore had to be given up as a residence and rebuilt as a family temple) was occupied by Gen. Stewart. Among its unique features was a model of a Chinese junk made with great fidelity in details, but built on a foundation of brick and stone in an artificial pond, where the occupants might go and imagine themselves on a voyage. This was employed by the British as a small-pox hospital!

A still more surprising curiosity, however, was a model of a small steam-boat likewise on a rock-work basis in another pond, in which were decks, upper and lower, steering-wheel, cabin with complete set of berths, each state-room with a foreign lock, etc., etc., all complete. This proved a most useful mine to the carpenters in refitting the Fu for foreign use, and all the cabin flooring, the locks, gangways, and the like, were unceremoniously transferred to the rooms of the General and his staff.

At another palace in the neighbourhood there was supposed to be treasure buried, which the officers tried in vain to discover. At length a representative of the owner succeeded through Li Hung Chang in getting a pass for men and carts to go by night and remove whatever was concealed, the British officer being politely requested to shift his bed (temporarily) while the jars of ingots buried beneath were being exhumed!

XXIX

THE CAPITAL IN TRANSFORMATION

ASIDE from the residences of the nobility, countless dwellings of those whose names are known all over China were open to inspection, and with the inspection commenced what was practically a transformation. A particularly desolate place of this sort on an alley opening on the Ha Ta street was pointed out as belonging to Wêng T'ung Ho, formerly tutor of the Emperor. The Austrian contingent took possession of the house of Ch'ung Li (Governor of the Nine Gates of Peking)—a very attractive place not at all like the typical Fu and quite neat and clean. When the late owner sent over to ask for a fur garment as the winter was coming on, they genially replied that they had none to spare!

By an arrangement with the Italians, the T'ung Chou Christians and their shepherds occupied the premises known as the Chao Kung Fu, north of the Tung Hua gate, and close to the Imperial City wall. This place was owned by someone who had an eye to the picturesque, and built a very pretty two-storied building facing east and west, called the " Ying Ch'un Lou," or " Chamber to Welcome Spring." An enemy at Court promptly denounced the audacity of erecting such a structure which should command a view of the Imperial City, and the Empress Dowager saw her opportunity and fined the unhappy welcomer of the Spring one hundred thousand taels. As he was unable to raise more than forty thousand taels, the Empress kindly confiscated his place for the remainder, and gave it to her own younger brother, whose son was living in it when the troubles came on. The owners were very willing to have foreigners in occupation, as their premises were thus safe from further pillage than they had already undergone from the Italians, and they have now been put in good order again at some expense. A considerable Christian community is lodged in numerous houses all around. The hours by day and night are sounded by a watchman on the large 500-pound bell of the North China College at T'ung Chou, which was stolen by the Boxers when the place was burnt, carried to a village and buried, and later rose from the dead and was brought to Peking. This bell and three or four bunches of keys are all that now remain visible of that institution of learning, aside from low rows of brickbats on its former site, and numerous pits.

After the occupation of the premises by the T'ung Chou station, Mr. Tewksbury, its indefatigable manager-in-chief, employed the chamber mentioned above as a printing-office, whence have issued, together with much else, numerous copies of the tonic-sol-fa hymn-books to replace those destroyed last year. One of the rooms consists of five expansive divisions, and appeared to be foreordained for a chapel, which it has become. It is now filled every Sunday with several hundred Christians, and the Duke and Duchess who formerly lived there regularly attended the morning worship. During the winter the premises, through Prince Su as middleman, were leased to the Mission for two years at a fair price, payment beginning at the signing of the Protocol in January. At the back of the room used as a chapel hung a large tablet draped with white silk, as the Chinese symbol of mourning, and across its front were hung, against a background

THE CAPITAL IN TRANSFORMATION 537

of blue cloth, tags of silk containing the names of those members of the T'ung Chou church who gave their lives in witness of their faith. The list, though far from complete, embraced the names of forty-four men, forty-six women, and forty children.

The Missions of the American Presbyterians and of the American Methodists were each lodged in the residences of the gentry, with full approbation of the owners, who would otherwise have lost everything left in these dwellings. The latter Mission required accommodations for the students of the Peking University, and for the hundred or more school-girls who had been successfully carried through the siege, but for whom a secure domicile was imperative.

The experiences of the London Mission refugees were so unique that a few paragraphs may well be devoted to them as strikingly illustrating the exigencies of the time.

On account of the absence of the male members of the Mission, Miss Georgina Smith found herself in charge of about 200 destitute refugees who had no food and no means of getting any. The compound next to the London Mission on the southeast was vacant, having been owned and occupied by a Manchu family active in the Boxer outrage, who had promoted the destruction of the mission buildings and later walled in a portion of the land for their own use. Now they justly feared punishment and had all fled, and the authorities, legation and military, handed over this place to Miss Smith with all which it contained.

She had no money and could get none, but she issued tickets for a certain amount of grain, redeemable on demand at the neighbouring shops just resuming business. The latter preferred the orders to ready money as they were liable at any moment to be robbed by the Russian soldiers, against whom Miss Smith was provided with a written protection signed by the General, which was framed and in constant requisition.

The furniture of the premises was left untouched, and funds were raised in the only practicable way by the sale of the furs and other clothing of the establishment. All the converts were set to work and the proceeds thrown into a common fund, a plan which worked surprisingly well. Contracts were taken for making mattresses, quilts, and horse-cloths for the British troops, and then for the Germans. Later another contract was taken to furnish hay for the Indian horses, and finally to undertake the scavenging of the German section of the city, thus providing full employment for all. Preachers, teachers, hospital-dispensers, and all others received a uniform allowance of about sixpence a day.

When German rule replaced that of the Russians the whole district would have been impartially occupied and incidentally looted but for the prompt action of Miss Smith, who offered to provide the Germans with furniture for barracks, officers' rooms, etc., on condition that the matter should be left entirely in her hands, and no soldiers allowed to enter the homes of the people. On these terms the non-Christian Chinese in the neighbourhood gladly collected all that was required, and countless families were saved from spoliation.

The authorities with the aid of the Christians sought out some of the chief Boxers and dealt with them, while others through intermediaries offered to make restitution or compensation for the injuries which they had inflicted on Christian families, and in this way provision was made for widows and orphans. In recognition of her distinguished services Miss Smith was presented with six pairs

THE CAPITAL IN TRANSFORMATION   539

of the gorgeous "Myriad People Canopy," the highest popular honour in China, and not often bestowed.

Attentive consideration of an instance like this makes it strikingly evident how much may be accomplished by one resolute and resourceful Western woman, and how hopeless it would be to judge of such conditions and the steps required to meet them without full and accurate acquaintance with the facts.

The Government of China has always been conducted through the agency of the six Boards, of War, Rites, Works, Revenue, Civil Office, and Punishments, mostly situated on a street named after one of the most important—the Board of War. At the wide doors concealing the arcana of this Chinese official life, foreigners have for the most part hitherto gazed from afar. Every one of these Boards was promptly occupied by the military, as well as several other Government Bureaus in the vicinity, some of which were destroyed during the occupation, and others, like the Board of Revenue, burned somewhat later.

The Board of Works and the Board of War fell to the British as headquarters of an Indian regiment, the tall and dusky warriors of the hill tribes of the Indian frontier making themselves at home in the ample apartments at their disposal. The thrifty Japanese contrived to get the west side of this same street redistributed so as to come within their lines, and then sent a caravan of mules working day and night for a long period, and carried off from the Board of Revenue treasury a sum reported to be at least three million taels, in silver ingots. This same Oriental race, who appeared to know much more about Peking than the Pekingese themselves, promptly fastened their talons on all the principal

Imperial granaries, and are said to have gained possession of rice to the value of several million dollars—their indemnity being thus automatically paid with no diplomatic pressure whatever, or any consent asked of any "Power."

Perhaps one of the most characteristic structures in China is that of the Board of Punishments. All the Boards are situated almost in a block just west of the British Legation, but this stands by itself to the west of the dividing street of the city. You know when you get to it, because you seem to be going into a basement as you alight from your cart and look down into the main entrance, which is several feet below the average level of the road. If your visit is in summer, you will see a huge pond in the first courtyard, and the same repeated in every other. If you enquire of one of the attendants, remaining after the Empress took her flight and somebody liberated all the hundreds of prisoners then confined there, to what height the water really comes when it is highest, he raises his hand to about the level of his neck, "To here." "But," you observe, "then there must be water in all the side-rooms, which you see are on a still lower plane" "Of course," he replies simply.

Scattered about the court were parts of the Complete Laws of China, at present much more conspicuous in Peking by their absence than otherwise, and records of cases innumerable, now gone to the region which Carlyle compendiously referred to as "the mud-gods."

The prisons proper, of which there are perhaps twenty or twenty-four (or perhaps forty-eight, it does not matter), are all just alike, old buildings with brick walls, with thick wooden gratings to the windows, which a European prisoner would whittle in two with a pocket-knife in fifteen minutes, and within, two-inch planks laid on

THE CAPITAL IN TRANSFORMATION 541

piles of loose bricks. Copies of the "Peking Gazette" were at first (just after the siege) as thick here as the leaves in Vallombrosa (or thereabouts), and that was far the best place to get complete files at that time, when all others had omitted to "take in" the "oldest daily paper in the world." Later the place was used as an International prison for a select lot of criminals, or alleged criminals, who had not been condemned by the military, and were sent to the Chinese to be tried by their own officers.

In the spacious Carriage Park adjoining the British Legation on the west, which was such a thorn in the side of the besieged, there are several large halls for the storage of the Imperial furnishings.

The British relief corps had no sooner occupied the Legation than a hole was blown in the Carriage Park wall by means of dynamite, and the swarthy Pathans and Beluchis filed into the large pastures thus placed at their disposal. It did not take long to run out of doors the lacquered red and yellow Imperial equipages, sedan-chairs, wedding-chairs (including the one used when the Emperor was married), and elephant-carriages of an eccentric and peculiar construction, where they were afterwards exposed to the vicissitudes of the hot August sun and the pouring rains.

Mountains of paraphernalia were found in every building—silk cushions, satin pillows, gorgeous harnesses and trappings of every description and of no description at all. Mule-loads of this elegant rubbish were brought into the Legation for sale by auction, or perhaps for transmission to the distant Isle of the Ocean whence came the "fierce and untamable Barbarian" (as the British used to be termed in Chinese despatches). Both in the expansive grounds of the Carriage Park and in the far larger ones of the Temple of Heaven, parks of artillery stood serenely awaiting fresh orders, the mules meantime trampling in the mire hundreds of moth-eaten official hats made of felt, and furlongs of once elegant and costly silk coverings of bridal chairs and palanquins. The tall weeds, undisturbed for no one can say how long by the hand of man or the hoof of beast, rapidly disappeared, and the entire spectacle was one adapted to make Celestials weep.

The destruction of the Hanlin Yuan has been described in connection with the narrative of the siege, but a few additional details deserve mention. The principal literary monument of the most ancient people in the world was obliterated in an afternoon, and the wooden stereotype plates of the most valuable works became a prey to the flames, or were used in building barricades, or as kindling by the British marines. Priceless literary treasures were tumbled into the lotus-ponds, wet with the floods of water used to extinguish the fires, and later buried after they had begun to rot, to diminish the disagreeable odour. Expensive camphor-wood cases containing the rare and unique Encyclopædia of Yung Lê were filled with earth to form a part of the ramparts for defence, while the innumerable volumes comprising this great thesaurus were dispersed in every direction, probably to every library in Europe, as well as to innumerable private collections. Not a few of the volumes were thrown into the common heap to mold and to be buried like the rest.

Thousands of Hanlin essays lay about the premises, the sport of every breeze, serving as fire-wood for the troops. Odd volumes of choice works furnished the waste-paper of the entire Legation for nearly two months; they were found in the kitchens, used by the coolies as pads for carrying bricks on their shoulders, and lay in piles in the

THE CAPITAL IN TRANSFORMATION 543

outer streets to be ground into tatters under the wheels of passing carts when traffic was once more resumed.

Of the varied forms of Nemesis connected with the uprising against foreigners in China, the fate of the ancient and famous Hanlin takes perhaps the foremost place. Out of twenty or twenty-five halls, but two remained and a few months later every trace of these had been removed from the Hanlin premises, which are now a part of the British Legation grounds. On the northern side a high wall has been put up, with scientific loopholes concealed in its upper part, and protection for gunners in arched recesses at the base, while a clear space is left in front to make a surprise impossible.

Within three minutes walk of the British Legation stands an old yamen known as the Li Fan Yuan, which had to do with Mongolian affairs. During the siege it was barricaded and loopholed, and served as one of the numerous points from which to attack the Legations, being directly across the main road from the northern end of the Su Wang Fu, and but a few rods distant. When the siege was over the buildings were found to be in ruins, and some sales of loot were conducted there by the Italians, but otherwise the place was completely abandoned.

During the winter this ancient Government Bureau was fitted up as an International Club, at the rear of which it was possible for members to order meals in parties or singly, while a large room was devoted to the indispensable bar. In the front building there was a large room supplied with the latest British and Continental periodicals. The most recent telegrams were posted upon a daily bulletin, and on a large placard were registered the names of about five hundred members of the Club—mostly the military officers of the eight different nations represented in Peking, whose flags floated serenely from as many staffs at the entrance.

The part which the Tsung Li Yamen, or Foreign Office, has taken in the relations between China and the West is well known. It has been an Oriental circumlocution office, not to transact but to prevent the transaction of business. It was itself an epitome of the double-dealing, shuffling, and treacherous policy which has marked the course of China's intercourse with her " Sister Nations." A just fate has overtaken it, for while guarded by a party of Japanese soldiers, the various interpreters of the Legations went on a set day and unitedly sealed each the bureau containing the records of the correspondence with his own country, so that they are in the safe custody of all the Powers, while not accessible to any one solely—least of all to the Chinese. Surely the humiliation of a great Empire could scarcely go lower than this.

On the first of May these records were restored to the custody of the Chinese officials appointed to take them over, but one of the terms of settlement between China and the Powers involves the abolition of the Yamen as a Bureau—the only fit manner of dealing with this cumbrous and exasperating piece of Oriental machinery.

The questions with regard to the survival of the records of Chinese yamens and other public offices in Peking, is naturally one of much interest to the Chinese themselves. From repeated and diversified inquiries one seems justified in inferring that as a rule there is nothing whatever left of the documents of any of the six Boards, or of the public offices of any sort with the exception of the Tsung Li Yamen.

Among the numerous offices for preparing the materials for future histories, are two historiographers'

TARTAR WALL, LOCATION OF ASTRONOMICAL OBSERVATORY

THE CAPITAL IN TRANSFORMATION 545

bureaus, the one belonging to the State and called the Kuo Shih Kuan, which is situated in the Imperial City, inside the Tung Hua Mên. The records of the Emperor's sayings and doings were kept in the Ch'i Chü Chu which was located, as we are told, within the limits of the Hanlin Courts. When the latter were attacked, the records were prudently moved to the Kuo Shih Kuan for safe keeping. A Chinese teacher who visited the place, ascertained its present condition. He reported that it was closed, but that the contents have long since been scattered to the winds of heaven. During the anarchy following upon the occupation of Peking, whoever had a mind to do so visited the place and carried off whatever he chose for waste paper, and although there may be some parts of the archives remaining, nothing is said to be complete, and all might as well be lacking.

On the night of the 4th of June, 1901, a building called the Wu Ying Tien in the southwest corner of the Forbidden City was destroyed by a fire, the origin of which was disputed. It was a Throne Hall, or Imperial Pavilion, and its contents were archives of State, edicts, records, books, and blocks of governmental works, and attached to it were the Recording Office and the office of one of the Grand Secretaries. It was the final act in a long series of conflagrations and destruction, the ultimate effect of which can not fail to be far-reaching.

The Astronomical Observatory situated on the eastern wall of the city, and containing the ancient and wonderful products of the genius of the early Jesuits in China, Verbiest and Schall, was speedily dismantled by the French and the Germans, every one of the instruments being removed to the French or German Legations, and in the process the needless incidental damage was so great that the whole place was left a wreck. The Chinese looters were not long in following those from abroad, and the iron railings which once enclosed the terrace were broken off in mere wantonness, and many of them stolen —as why should they not be, since the place was ruined? It is a perfectly just reflection that this vandalism of Continental troops, under orders from their highest military authorities, is far less excusable than the attack of the savages under Tung Fu Hsiang on the Hanlin Yuan, for that was done under strong excitement, and this deliberately and against the protests of a large part of the civilized world.

The Examination Grounds display the same reckless destruction. The cells for the students (a little less than 8,500 in number) open in front, with a roof slanting backward, supported on two or three small poles. Other woodwork there is none. Yet in order to secure this trifle of material for kindling, hundreds of the stalls were pulled down, as well as the buildings at the entrance.

It should be mentioned that the foreign troops in urgent need of firewood during a cold winter, demolished indiscriminately whatever buildings were most convenient— yamens, old granaries, and temples. It was reported that by the time the winter was over, hardly any temples remained in the city of T'ung Chou.

The headquarters of the American troops during the military occupation of Peking were in the Temple of Agriculture, a spacious series of enclosures in the southern part of the Chinese city. One of the main halls was employed as a hospital, and another as a supply depôt for the commissariat, displaying long rows of hams, cases of tobacco, boxes of army beans, and barrels of beef.

One of the side halls became a reading-room, and others were hospital wards. Another had been used for the storage of the gilded and lacquered specimens of

THE CAPITAL IN TRANSFORMATION 547

agricultural implements, the plough, the seed-drill, the harrow, the brush-harrow, the spade, the broom, the pitchfork, and smaller utensils such as baskets and broad hats. All of these were unceremoniously hustled into the open air, and some of the smaller articles furnished convenient fuel for the 9th and 14th Regiments of U. S. Infantry.

The officers for whose headquarters the main halls were used had no sooner taken possession, than they began to have holes cut in the venerable walls and large plate-glass windows inserted, a proceeding which must have appeared to the shades of the divinities worshipped as an additional profanation and humiliation.

The marble altar where the Emperor worships old legendary Shên Nung was a convenient place for the cavalry horses to be left in charge of the nearest coolie, and the choice spot of earth which the Emperor is supposed to cultivate with his own hand every successive spring, as an example to the tillers of the soil all over the Empire, was quite indistinguishable amid the dense growth of omnipresent weeds.

Across the wide street opposite the Temple of Agriculture is the vast area, at least a mile on each face, inclosing the Temple of Heaven. For many years it was absolutely inaccessible to foreigners, and even during the minority of the present Emperor it was difficult to set one's foot inside. Now there is not a single Chinese anywhere to be seen, the keepers having been all driven away by the British when they took possession immediately on reaching Peking. One can drive his cart quite up to the lofty terrace leading to the triple cerulean domes denoting the threefold heaven. Each gate was sentried by a swarthy Sikh soldier—the personification of the domination of a greater empire than that of Rome in its best days—who merely glanced at you as you passed or asked unintelligible questions in Hindustani, and made a respectful salaam when he was informed in several European languages, as well as in Chinese, that you were unable to catch the drift of his observations.

The door to the great circular building devoted to the ancestral tablets of the Manchu dynasty stands wide open. It contained a huge tablet on the northern side, to Imperial Heaven, and eight cases—four on a side—to the eight Emperors who have thus far reigned during the past two hundred and fifty-six years. Every one of the eight cases, with heavy carved doors, has been broken open, and every one of the eight tablets to the deified ancestors has been taken away by British officers for transmission to the British Museum—an act of almost justifiable reprisal for Chinese treatment of the foreign cemetery.

The Emperor's Hall of Fasting was used as the headquarters of the British army in this part of the city, and every day was partly filled with many cart-loads of loot —silks, furs, silver and jade ornaments, embroidered clothing, and the like. This was daily forwarded to the British Legation, and sold at auction for the benefit of the army, to be soon replaced by as much more. The personal apartments of the Emperor in the rear served as the bedrooms of the officers, who looked mildly surprised when the circumstance was communicated to them at their dinner, and merely gave an inquiring glance, as much as to say, " Well, what of it, don't you know? "

The seventh section of the Peace Conditions imposed by the Powers upon China provided for defences around the Legations and for the removal of all Chinese buildings from their vicinity. The " Legation Area " was construed to embrace at least all the territory within a rectangle bounded on the south by the wall of the city,

TEMPLE OF AGRICULTURE, PEKING
AMERICAN HEADQUARTERS

ENTRANCE, TEMPLE OF AGRICULTURE,
AMERICAN HEADQUARTERS

THE CAPITAL IN TRANSFORMATION

on the north by the wall of the Imperial city, on the east by the Ha Ta street, and on the west by the median line of the city, leading to the Ch'ien Mên; but that part lying north of Legation street, and west of the Board of War street will probably be excluded as superfluous. Within this broad tract, measuring more than a mile in length by perhaps half a mile in breadth, the most revolutionary changes at once began, such as the demolition of dwellings, yamens, and temples, and the general rehabilitation of the old Legations, with the most liberal additions.

Opposite the Austrian Legation stood a green-tiled building which contained the Tablets of the pre-Imperial Ancestors of the founders of the Manchu Dynasty. This comes within the territory demanded for the Legations, and will be removed, the efforts of the Chinese and Manchus to save it having proved abortive. Its removal is in itself a fit outcome of the Manchu effort to end all relations with the rest of the civilized world by destroying its representatives.

The Japanese take in the Su Wang Fu, to which they have a strong claim, while the Italians, the French, and the Austrians, in like manner will cover a large part of the fighting area of the siege, absorbing the site of the Imperial Maritime Customs, the Imperial Mint, and the unfinished Chinese Bank.

The abolition of the immemorial buildings belonging to several of the six Boards was vainly resisted by the Chinese, who will be helpless in the presence of the new fortresses commanding the Imperial palaces. It is a bitter humiliation, but one which the Court of Peking richly deserves.

That Court was itself the great contriver and executor of the crime against all nations in Peking, and some of its agents have suffered a fit penalty. The provincial Treasurer of Chihli, Ting Yung, whom a Military Commission held at Pao Ting Fu in October adjudged guilty of the death of the fifteen British and Americans killed near that city, was there beheaded, together with others of lesser importance. During the winter two other officials of high rank were handed by the Allies over to the Chinese authorities to be beheaded in Peking, Ch'i Hsiu, and the son of Hsü T'ung, Hsü Ch'eng Yu.

No Chinese had more to do with promoting the attack upon foreigners than Li Ping Hêng, former Governor of Shantung, and subsequently the active agent of the Empress Dowager. He either died or committed suicide, and was subsequently bewailed at his home in Chang Tê Fu, Honan.

Imperial Decrees ordered and subsequently certified to the death of Prince Chuang (who was allowed to strangle himself), of Yü Hsien, the most infamous of them all, under whose personal superintendence forty-five foreigners were hewn down at his yamen in T'ai Yuan Fu, of Chao Shu Ch'iao, Ying Nien, and others of less notoriety. Kang I, another important factor in the Boxer rising, was reported to have died in southern Shansi. Since there was no foreign witness of these deaths or executions the evidence of their reality has been regarded by many as inadequate, but there seems little reason to suppose that any of these officials will ever again figure in Chinese affairs. There is a long list of those who might well have been included, but if all were named who are guilty it would be hard to make a beginning and still harder to know where to stop.

The experiences of the Chinese Court in the second enforced flight of the Empress Dowager within forty years, have a peculiar interest for one who pursues this strange story to its conclusion. The following notes of

THE CAPITAL IN TRANSFORMATION 551

some of its incidents are quoted from an interesting article by Miss Luella Miner, in the " Century Magazine," the collator being a progressive Chinese who, together with his relatives, suffered much bitterness from his friendship for foreigners, and regard for Western learning. It is morally certain that the Empress Dowager had been deceived into a belief that foreign troops were either not near Peking, or would be unable to enter it, otherwise her delay in effecting her flight is utterly inexplicable.

" On the 14th of August the sound of rifles and cannon was heard incessantly throughout the day, and it was rumoured that foreigners and native Christians were sneaking up from T'ung Chou and attacking one of the eastern gates. Toward evening it was noised abroad that a great company of Mohammedans, in most peculiar costume, had entered the city and encamped in the Temple of Heaven. Not till the next day was it generally known in the city that Peking had been captured by the ' foreign devils ' and that the so-called Mohammedans were Indian troops under British officers. That Tuesday afternoon, soon after the Rajputs and Sikhs had entered the British Legation, General Ma was summoned to the Palace, and commanded to await the Imperial chariot at the northern gate of the Forbidden City. Toward evening the American troops captured the Ch'ien Gate, and sent shot and shell against the southern gate of the Imperial City. The Empress Dowager wept, and together with the Emperor, the Empress, and the heir apparent, burned incense in the palace and prayed to Heaven. Kang I entered the palace and with great earnestness urged them to seek a refuge from the blast of the enemy. An edict was issued ordering all the princes and ministers to follow in the Imperial retinue.

" Early on the morning of August 15th, the allies attacked both the southern and eastern gates of the Imperial City, whereupon the high Ministers hastened to the Ning Shou Palace to see the Empress Dowager; but before they entered the palace a eunuch met them with the intelligence that the Empress Dowager and the Emperor had already fled, having heard a false rumour of a revolution.

"From the 14th of June, when the Empress Dowager returned to the city palaces, she had simply twisted her hair in a knot and worn the common dress of the people. The morning when she took her flight it was in this guise. The Empress Dowager, the Emperor, the Empress, and the heir apparent, each rode in a separate cart, the Empress Dowager having Duke Lan's private cart, from which she had the red side-awnings removed. They left the city by the Tê Shêng Gate on the north side, General Ma escorting them. The Chinese report that the favourite concubine, "Pearl," was strangled and thrown in a well. Of the Princes, nobles and high Ministers, about thirty were in their retinue; Prince Tuan, Prince Chuang, Duke Lan, and Kang I being of the number.

"The first night the royal fugitives lodged at Kuan Shih, a little village containing a Mohammedan inn, about thirty miles north of Peking. At this point they obtained mule litters,—palanquins borne by poles on the backs of mules, one in front and one behind. The Empress Dowager lay down in her litter all day, eating very little. The next night they lodged at Ch'a Tao, a place just outside the inner arm of the Great Wall, about fifty miles northwest of Peking. The District Magistrate did not know of the arrival of the chariot, and had made no preparation for their entertainment, so there was nothing for the Imperial table but a few grains of corn, while the retinue all had a hungry look. The District Magistrate had only one sedan-chair, in which the Empress Dowager rode from this point, while the Emperor and the Empress still rode in the mule-litters.

"On the 17th of August they arrived at Huai Lai. When they left the capital in haste and confusion, they were simply clad in summer raiment. After going through the Pass, the weather became suddenly cold, so they stayed in the Pure-True Temple of Huai Lai for two days to make their winter clothing.

"On the 20th of August they arrived at Hsüan Hua (twenty miles from Kalgan). From this point three Vermilion Pencil edicts were dispatched, one giving the causes which led to the flight of the Imperial family, the Emperor blaming himself for lack of intelligence in his use of men as officials, and blaming his Ministers for not using to the utmost the talents with which they were endued by Heaven. A second edict commanded the Ministers to follow the court to T'ai Yuan Fu, while another remitted the taxes of the region through which they had passed. They stayed five days at Hsüan Hua.

"From Hsüan Hua they went to Ta T'ung (near the northeastern boundary of Shansi), where they stayed two days. In going from there to T'ai Yuan Fu they passed through Tien Chên. This place had already been looted by rebels, so that shops and markets were all empty. Just as the District Magistrate was in great confusion and dismay, having nothing to lay his hand to, it was announced that the holy chariot had suddenly arrived. Crazy with grief and fear he drank poison and died. So, when the Imperial party arrived they found only an empty city, and that night supped on a few drops of soup. They then sent the Imperial butler, a eunuch, back to Peking to purchase provisions and other necessities.

"When the chariot, the retinue, and the Eight Banner

(Manchu) soldiers arrived at T'ai Yuan Fu, over three hundred soldiers were sent back to Peking, under the command of General Tê, with only four taels apiece for pay, and later over three hundred men were sent back under Prince Su, each man receiving five taels. Of the high Ministers, only Kang I, Wang Wên Shao, and Chao Shu Chiao were left in the Imperial retinue, though there were several lesser Ministers.

"Toward the end of September the earnest plea of the Emperor for a return to Peking seemed likely to win the day. The provincial Treasurer of Pao Ting Fu telegraphed that the allies were about to make an attack on Pao Ting Fu, followed by an invasion of Shansi, so again the wish of the Empress Dowager prevailed, and the course of empire took its way westward. It is almost as far from T'ai Yuan Fu to Hsi An Fu as from Peking to T'ai Yuan Fu, so now it seems as if the Empress Dowager had burned her bridges behind her. In this ancient capital of the Empire she means to stand at bay."

It seems likely to be the strange fate of this woman, after directly authorizing the commission of perhaps the greatest crime against the intercourse of nations in the whole history of the human race, to be restored to her usurped throne, and to undisputed power, with no criticism upon her conduct in the past, and no guarantee as to her behaviour in the future.

Whatever her fate or that of the Empire which she did so much to ruin, one of the most picturesque scenes of modern times will continue to be the Punishment of Peking. The city has been turned inside out, like the fingers of a glove, but whose hand shall ultimately fill it remains still to be settled.

XXX

THE RUIN OF T'UNG CHOU

THE city of T'ung Chou, twelves miles east of Peking, is situated at the head of navigation of the Peiho, or North River. The plain upon which Peking is built, while thickly populated, does not afford sufficient supplies for the use of a large city, and every year enormous quantities of tribute rice from the central provinces pass through this river port on their way to the capital.

The very name of the city denotes that it is the town by which traffic penetrates to Peking ("t'ung" signifying "to pass through"). From T'ung Chou to Peking a broad stone road on a high level was constructed centuries ago, but this has fallen into complete disrepair, so as to furnish at once a monument of the capacity and the incapacity of the rulers of the Empire. Parallel with this great stone road, of which countless foreign travellers have had heart-breaking (and back-breaking) experiences, a canal leads to the Tung Pien Gate of Peking, at the junction of the northern or Tartar City with the southern or Chinese City. Five blocks interrupt the passage of boats, the cargoes requiring as many reshiftings, but to the patient Chinese this is an altogether minor matter.

Contrary to the erroneous impression prevailing in Western lands, Chinese cities may be said to be built with an invariable irregularity for geomantic purposes, but few city walls even in China have such a devious outline as that of T'ung Chou. This is because it consists of two cities, an old and a new, the latter added many hundred years ago on the western side of the former one, apparently for the purpose of including within its spacious and devious circuit an Imperial Granary, long since fallen into ruin.

Owing to the composite structure of the city, T'ung Chou enjoys the unusual (perhaps the unique) distinction of having two south gates, but the principal suburbs are outside of the east and the west gates, although that on the north, in the vicinity of the handsome and striking old pagoda, is also of considerable size.

What the population of T'ung Chou may have been no one can say with certainty, but there is good reason to suppose that since foreigners have known it there have been perhaps between fifty and seventy thousand persons in and about the city. The arrival of the grain-boats from Tientsin, as well as those bringing the tribute direct from Shantung, was an annual event of capital importance to the whole population, for a large part of the people got their living directly from this nourishing stream of rice. This rice which had formerly been brought in junks by sea, and within recent years in steamers from the south, was trans-shipped at Tientsin to special boats which ultimately discharged their cargo on mats spread upon the bank of the canal leading to Peiho, a short distance below. After being measured and sacked, it was carried to the granaries, thence passing through the intricate and tortuous channels established by Chinese precedent before reaching its final destination. Armies of huge brawny coolies were to be seen shouldering the clumsy sacks weighing perhaps consider-

THE RUIN OF T'UNG CHOU

ably over 200 pounds avoirdupois, and in this manner thousands of laborers found employment.

Next to the excitement caused by the annual arrival of the tribute grain, was that occasioned by the various Literary Examinations in Peking, especially that for the second degree of "Selected Men" (Chü Jên). For a period of several weeks, when the river was alive with boats and boatmen, innkeepers, carters, wheelbarrowmen, merchants, and coolies, as well as many others in T'ung Chou, reaped a rich harvest. At such times the prices of boats and carts would mount to extravagant figures, for the traveller from a distance was completely at the mercy of the local sharks, each one of whom took care to get a liberal bite. Aside from these special causes of prosperity the steady stream of official and unofficial travellers, merchants, and traders, and the handling of the merchandise passing through for Peking, particularly the large and important item of foreign freight, upon which it was easy to collect the most exorbitant charges, made the carrying of goods and passengers a lucrative specialty of this gateway of the Capital.

For about a third of a century, or since 1866, T'ung Chou has been a station of the American Board Mission, beginning with small premises in the center of the city, and later extending to others further west. Within the past ten years they have embraced also an extensive area some distance beyond the south-west corner of the city. Within the city walls were located a dispensary and hospitals, for both men and women, a theological seminary, schools for boys and girls, as well as four dwelling-houses and numerous other buildings. Outside the city was the North China College of the American Board, together with four dwelling-houses occupied by the faculty of that institution; there were also adjacent premises, where were the beginnings of an industrial plant.

It is important to observe that, from the first, the relations of the people of T'ung Chou with the foreigners living among them had been one of ideal friendliness. There had not only never been a riot, but no disturbance of any sort had broken the uniform harmony. The influence of the long years of work in the hospital and dispensary had been wide-spread. The College was recognized by the people and by the local scholars as an honour to the city. Intercourse with the officials had always been friendly, and sometimes cordial. That the foreigners were well known and trusted, the following instance will show.

When the Allied Forces attacked Peking, in October, 1860, the city of T'ung Chou took occasion to capitulate on its own account, offering to furnish the foreign troops whatever was required in the line of supplies, on the condition that the city itself should not be harmed,—an arrangement which was carried into effect.

During the progress of the war between China and Japan, when it was feared that Peking must fall a prey to the invader, Dr. Sheffield, the President of the College, was approached, with a view to ascertaining whether in the event of the arrival of the Japanese he would undertake to go out and meet them, and make such terms as would secure the integrity of the city. When it was learned that he was willing to assume the undertaking, upon a set day a guard of five hundred soldiers was sent to their residences to escort Dr. Sheffield and Dr. Goodrich to the military headquarters. There they were received with the salute of cannon, reserved for officers of the rank of Governors-General, and were introduced to an audience with several high officials, all of whom

NORTH CHINA COLLEGE, T'UNG CHOU

treated the foreigners with the highest respect, and were greatly relieved at the prospect of intervention at a crisis of peculiar difficulty. While the later movements of the Japanese did not call for the execution of this service, the fact that it was asked and promised, and especially the gaudy concomitants of the explosion of so much powder and the marching of so large a force of soldiers in honour of two foreigners, tended to surround them with a blaze of glory, the effects of which were not evanescent.

For more than ten years previous to the building of the railway between Tientsin and Peking, such a work had been not only projected, but approved by Imperial Edict. Upon one occasion, when it seemed about to materialize, Dr. Sheffield was visited by one of the gentry of the city, whose first movement was to perform the kotow. Subsequently he arose to explain that he was praying to be saved from the terrors of an invasion of his ancestral grave-yard by the iron road of the fire-wheel-carts, which would disturb the slumbers of his forefathers, and bring swift and irreparable ruin upon the whole family. It was no doubt difficult for him to comprehend, and still more to believe, Dr. Sheffield's statement that this entire business from first to last was in the hands of the Government, and that private Americans living in T'ung Chou had absolutely no connection with it.

After many false starts and countless set-backs, the building of the line from Tientsin actually began to take shape after the close of the war with Japan. At a previous period, when it was regarded as certain to materialize, Chinese speculators took pains to lay hold of large tracts of land in the vicinity of the city, where the railway station was likely to be. The people of T'ung Chou were in an agony of apprehension lest the geomantic fortunes of their city be overwhelmed with disaster, and the trade ruined by the new and dreaded innovations now not merely threatened, but certain to come upon them. They had left no means untried, no stone unturned to avert this calamity, but in vain.

At their very extremity one more device was thought of, which was their last hope. The difficulty with the innumerable protests which had been made was, that some yet more influential counter-memorial always took the wind out of T'ung Chou sails, and left them in a worse position than before. It was by bribing the Censors in Peking that an influential memorial against the proposed line was secured, pointing out its dangers for T'ung Chou, and the undesirability of antagonizing the people of that city. There was a popular impression that one of the Princes was also induced to interest himself in the matter, and that it was owing to his influence that the course of the railway was turned toward the west, around the great Hunting Park, known as the "Nan Hai Tzu," where it passed through a region destitute of any towns of importance. While it would receive no local traffic, there would at least be no opposition. At all events, although the evil could not be altogether prevented, it was at least driven to so great a distance that it would no more disturb the peace of the denizens of the City of Penetration.

There was a brief period during which these hopes seemed to have been completely accomplished. Everything went on as it had always done, and fear was banished. But in the spring of 1897 it began to be noticed that the usual number of travellers did not visit the city, *en route* to Peking, and that the boat traffic fell off in an unexampled manner. This happened to be the year for the triennial examinations in Peking, when, as mentioned, T'ung Chou expects a plenteous harvest. But only a fraction of the students came by the river as they had hitherto invariably done, for the fire-wheel cart had just begun its regular trips, and the curiosity of the travelling public to see it and to experience the sensation of "rapid transit," brought such a multitude of passengers that the means of transportation were much more than exhausted. The vans were all filled, and so were the freight cars; even the platform cars used for hauling gravel had to be pressed into service.

The railway was a triumphant success from the start, but poor T'ung Chou wept in secret (and in public) places over the loss of its passenger traffic. Business was no longer done as before. The inns were largely unoccupied, the stores sold but little, building and repairing stopped at once; the carters and donkey-boys, constituting a by no means insignificant portion of the active life of the city, had nothing to do. Venders of food on the street found a small and a diminishing market. The barbers would tell their customers, as they gossiped over the dressing of their queues, that from the largest firm in the place down to the peripatetic seller of ankle-ties not a soul but was suffering from the locomotor ataxia which had attacked every form of business. In short the place was beginning to die, and the people were likely to die with it.

This was bad, but worse was in prospect. The numerous important families who farmed the tribute grain business of T'ung Chou had good reason to fear that their innumerable perquisites, derived from the transportation, the storing, and the handling of the rice, would soon be cut off. It had been discovered that galvanized iron box-cars had proved a complete protection to the great quantities of tea formerly shipped from Tientsin *via* T'ung Chou for Russia, much of which used to be stolen *en route* by broaching the packages on the river. A memorial to the Emperor already quoted had long since suggested the sending of the Imperial supplies by the same route, on the ground that "it would put a stop to stealing by the crews of the boats." It would also put a period to the subsistence of a large part of the T'ung Chou people, as they clearly foresaw.

But as their earnest prayer had been granted and as the peril had not invaded their grave-yards, and as the new road was built for the Emperor himself, it did not appear that there was anything to be done about the matter, unless it might be to repent in dust and ashes, which the whole city appeared to do. From the merchant in his large and unfrequented shop to the manure-gatherer and the beggar, all alike would tell you of the decay of business and the fact that it was no longer possible to make a living. A score or more of large firms were said to have removed bodily from the eastern suburbs of the city to Peking, to regain their trade which had left them, and in some of the streets grass was literally growing where it had never been before noticed.

The northern part of China is the land of dust-storms. On some sunshiny day it is noticed that the rays of the sun appear to be less powerful than usual. Presently they are obscured. No cloud is to be seen, but a dull haze of a dark brown hue becomes more and more pervasive, until the dust settles down quietly from above, or, if the wind has arisen, arrives in swirls speedily enveloping everything, so that on the worst occasions it may be necessary to light the lamps in the middle of the day. No one knows whence the dust comes, why it comes at some times and not at others, or why it comes at all. It is simply an indisputable and an influential fact.

Not unlike the dust-storm of the quiet type, was the arrival of the Boxer movement at T'ung Chou. "Like a spirit it came in the van of the storm."

The writer reached that city on the 17th of May by boat from Shantung, with a guard of three soldiers, who were regarded with surprise by all foreigners and most Chinese, as an unwonted and a superfluous luxury of travel. The river route was quiet, and so was that by land. T'ung Chou was quiet also, although there were rumours that trouble was brewing in the east suburb. It was afterward known that the Boxer virus had been brought by men who came in boats from Tientsin, or perhaps Tu Liu, a noted Boxer head-quarters on the Grand Canal eighteen miles south by water, and afterwards nearly destroyed by foreign troops. The training was recommended as useful for protection of one's person, one's home and family, and one's village. It had no elements of hostility to foreigners, and was so simple that even children could learn it, as was soon demonstrated.

Occasionally some of the ladies going about as usual in their sedan-chairs or otherwise noticed demonstrations which attracted their attention. Once a man capered in front of the chair and made motions as if to cut off his head, and the by-standers laughed. In about ten days the rumours grew more alarming, but were vague, indefinable, and could not be verified.

The movement had no sooner begun to make headway than a beggar was seized who had been to the foreign hospital for treatment of the itch, where he had been given a sulphur ointment. This was held to be a deadly drug designed for use in the poisoning of wells. An elaborate examination was held by the Chou Magistrate, at which the charge was solemnly declared to be not proven, but it had the effect of inflaming the minds of the people, already wrought upon by the rumours of what had been done, or was to be done elsewhere, in the way of driving out all the foreign devils.

The culmination of this movement has already been described in connection with the account of the flight of the party of Americans from T'ung Chou to Peking, on the 8th of June. A notification was sent to the officials that the premises were turned over to their care, and on the following day the college was burned and looted by the troops themselves, as well as the dwelling houses and every building connected with the place. On the day following, the same ruin fell on the property in the city, where a large street chapel was approaching completion. So complete was the wreck that it was not only possible to ride a horse over the site of two-story buildings but it was difficult even to identify the sites themselves.

The telegraph office and the Imperial post-office were likewise destroyed. The post-master (a Christian) had a series of the most dramatic adventures in the escape to Peking, where he turned over his accounts in full, and then barely made his escape to the south, arriving eventually in safety at Shanghai. Shen Taotai was imprisoned in his own yamen, the sport of the Boxers, and was at length enabled to fly, being plundered *en route* of all his possessions, his yamen being one of the first places looted. Such was the terrorism of the Boxer movement that it may be said that the whole population of the city went into it, willingly or otherwise, with a heartiness wonderful and instructive to behold. If there were any who protested, their voices must have been drowned in the general madness. Their only tangible grievance was the railway which had destroyed their traffic, and to right this wrong T'ung Chou committed suicide!

The Chou Magistrate was especially hateful and hypocritical, endeavouring to get evidence against the foreigners through the incriminating testimony of the beggar arrested with his colored itch-ointment; failing in this he had the yamen-runner who made the arrest beaten eight hundred blows, for the real reason that the proof was incomplete. When the hospital was pulled down he had the skeleton found in Dr. Ingram's laboratory ostentatiously hung up in the front hall of the yamen, where it was exhibited to every one as a positive and visible demonstration of the truth of all the charges previously insinuated against the Westerners. When the College was pillaged the Taotai ordered the Chou Magistrate to take the articles of value and put them into the treasury, but the latter purposely did nothing, and allowed everything to be either looted or destroyed.

The Intendant of the Grain Yamen, named Ch'ang Ts'ui, was really the head of the T'ung Chou Boxers, and the most incriminating documents were found in his premises when they were occupied by United States soldiers. A few months later large bundles of these papers with complete lists of the Boxer leaders, the memoranda of their camps, rations, and followers, and much other like information, were captured by the British, and sent to Mr. Tewksbury to be overhauled and annotated.

A few paragraphs from the graphic account of a Chinese "Refugee" on his flight south, may serve to give an insight into the condition of this city after the foreigners had escaped. He arrived on the 21st of June and saw a boisterous crowd entering the city gates, while others fired off three volleys from their guns as a sign that some Christian had been killed, after being dragged to the bank of the canal, where the bodies of the slain were thrown to prevent the infection of the country with an epidemic.

These volleys were heard many times a day, and indicated the terrible slaughter in progress, for about one hundred and fifty of the Protestant Christians of that station in city and country lost their lives in this reign of terror.

When the Boxers had gathered sufficient headway, they demanded an interview with the Taotai, intending to kill him. He, however, resolutely refused to see them. The Boxer mob began threatening to break down the yamen doors, when the other subordinate officials, although out of sympathy with him, came to his rescue and saved his life, the Boxers being persuaded to accept ten "shoes" of sycee (taels 500) in lieu of the Taotai's head. It was also agreed that he was not to appear outside his yamen upon any pretext, else he would be killed. They further compelled him to give them a written Commission empowering the Boxers to keep order in T'ung Chou and its dependencies, to punish all traitors found by them, to demand money and food whenever necessary, and to decapitate all who threatened the city.

On the 22nd of June, the Imperial Decree having arrived authorizing the destruction of the Legations, the Boxer banners had prefixed to the characters "Support the Dynasty; Exterminate Foreigners," the additional words: "By Imperial Command." The result of this was to make the Boxer desperadoes absolutely supreme, and from the 26th of June onwards the city was under their sole control.

It is worth noting that after the arrival of Li Hung Chang, the Chou Magistrate, under whom all this took place, was restored to his office (without protest from the Ministers), and it was with him that the T'ung Chou missionaries were obliged to negotiate for indemnities for the native Christians who had been pillaged through the connivance of this very man, now ostentatiously friendly and complaisant.

The embarrassments attending a readjustment of the old relations was aptly expressed by the prefect who was appointed to confer with the missionaries as to the indemnities for the Christians, and the punishments which should be thought sufficient to atone for so many cruel and unprovoked murders. "If you are to take those really responsible," he observed, "you must begin with the Empress Dowager and go right down, for we were all in it,"—an accurate and a compendious summary of the general situation.

Within a few days after the Japanese had taken the city, several tons of powder stored in a small building on a section of the northern wall were blown up, by Indian troops as is supposed by some, but with the result of a terrific explosion which not only destroyed its authors, but the city itself for more than a quarter of a mile in either direction. The ruin and desolation within this area was more complete than in any other region in northern China. The whole tract seemed to have been tossed in a blanket, so great was the force of the concussion. The temple to the god of war, a prominent landmark in T'ung Chou, was left in fragments, its skeleton standing, but the remaining timbers lying or leaning at every angle. The roof also was gone, but amid the debris three figures of the late divinities might be seen standing erect, as if striving to appear unconcerned at what had befallen their abode. The city was parcelled out among the various detachments, and while the Japanese, had they been in sole control, might have carried out their promises, as it was, not many hours had elapsed before T'ung Chou was looted and burned. From the centre of the city eastward to the east gate, scarcely a shop remained on what was once the great thoroughfare, and on the main street connecting this with the north gate not a single shop or dwelling remained standing. Nearly all the large places of business were destroyed, and the devastation in the eastern suburb, which is long and populous, was only less complete. The western suburb escaped being burned, and to a large extent the northern also, but the latter was occupied by the French and the Russians, from whom the people suffered unspeakably.

A correspondent entering the city tried to find a house which had not been looted in which to spend the night, and where he hoped to secure a bedquilt. He did indeed find three in succession in the same building, but each one contained a dead Chinese woman, who had evidently been first outraged and then cut open, and covered with her own bedding! The miseries of the people for leagues about T'ung Chou and for all the following month, from the brutalities of the foreign soldiers, will never be known.

A month after the capture of the city the apparent population, aside from the attendants upon the foreign troops, amounted to but a few hundreds of persons. One might walk for miles even in the western part of the city, where the buildings had not been extensively burned, and see no sign of life in any court-yard other than those occupied by the Japanese,—with the exception of the troops of starving dogs. Carts and rikshas were to be seen tumbled into a pond, and covered with green slime. Some of the largest shops had been looted but not burned, and within was still a large quantity of furniture which there was no one to use. Only the account-books left scattered in the street indicated what firm had gone to wreck, while on the dead-wall opposite smiled the felicitous saying: "Great Joy on Issuing from the Door."

On the north back street where the foreigners had lived,

THE RUIN OF T'UNG CHOU

and where some of their neighbours had joyfully hastened to plunder their goods, might now be seen in Japanese, French, and English the announcement: "This people is belonged to Japanese entirely 5th regiment." "No admittance to enter this house," was common, and in some districts every door had "Japan" over it, with the motto overhead in Chinese (left over from the last New Year's posting) "Imperial Grace; Family Happiness."

In the destruction of the dwellings of the foreigners, all the adjacent houses had been destroyed also. Not a shop was open, not a vender to be seen, not a cup of hot water nor an egg to be bought, but throughout nineteen-twentieths of the long city desolation reigned supreme, while the Japanese flag waved over the granaries holding what was left of the tribute rice, which had been the life-blood both of T'ung Chou and of Peking. On the river-bank, where in the autumn of the year trade was wont to be brisk, there was indeed a busy scene, but it was not the grain-fleet from Tientsin, nor the cargo-boats with tea for Russia, but the Japanese, British, French, Russian, and American transports crowding the otherwise unvexed waters of the canal leading to the Peiho. Not a boat arrived or departed but under military orders, and every boatman was impressed under inexorable—but mildly despotic—martial law.

In a particularly impassable mud-hole (probably dating from the Yuan Dynasty) one might come on the strange spectacle of a party of Sikhs engaged in making out of the roof-timbers of a Chinese house a species of bridge, covered with doors, shutters, and other wood-work, on a foundation of huge bundles of ripe sorghum cut from the fields with the grain attached. The military road, of which this bridge formed a minute section, passed directly over deep trenches where the walls of the grounds of the North China College had lately stood. When it was destroyed the Boxers or the joyful neighbours hastened to plant its land with Indian corn, and by the time the troops arrived in the autumn this was just ripe enough to feed the animals of the members of the mission who halted there to inspect the ruins.

Over the whole twelve miles between T'ung Chou and Peking one might pass and repass, and never see a human being, nor find at any of the countless tea-houses and inns along the route a single opportunity to purchase a mouthful of food, or even to water the animals. Unusually luxuriant crops were standing absolutely untouched, or if, as happened later, the heads of the grain were cut off, it was done swiftly and furtively, and with scouts looking both ways to detect the presence of foreign troops on that much travelled military road. Many of the soldiers took a keen delight in shooting every human being in sight who looked like a " heathen Chinese," and the result was a broad belt of practically depopulated territory, where any one could pillage the empty houses with comparative impunity, except for the all pervading fear of the sudden appearance of the dreaded polyglot foreign troops. Each of them represented a hasty and a bitter nation, marching through the breadth of the land to possess the dwelling-places that were not theirs, whose horses were swifter than the leopards, and more fierce than the evening wolves, their horsemen spreading themselves and coming from far.

Many weary months was this heavy burden to be borne, with many nameless horrors upon which we do not venture to touch. And all this—and more—was a part of The Punishment of T'ung Chou.

XXXI

TIENTSIN AFTER THE SIEGE

THE city of Tientsin is the natural gateway for the provinces of Chihli and Shansi, as well as for parts of Shantung and Honan, and of Manchuria and Mongolia. In its relations with foreigners there is much which is instructive, and which in view of the history of the past year throws light upon the action and interaction of causes in a manner well adapted to rivet attention.

The Tientsin men have a reputation for violence, especially in speech, and all over China are dreaded as quarrelsome and obstreperous. In some places in the central provinces the inns have a standing notice: "No Tientsin men admitted." When the Taku forts were captured in 1860 Tientsin capitulated on its own account, and furnished the foreign troops with all the provisions and other supplies needed, at remunerative rates, soon learning how to make out of a military occupation a mine of wealth. But the people of Tientsin from the first moment of their acquaintance with foreigners down to the present time have had no love for them. At the very beginning of their knowledge of the barbarians a new nickname was employed to designate them, by allusion to their hair, and they were called "*Maotzu.*" There has never been a time when any foreigner passing through the streets or suburbs of this inhospitable city might not at any moment hear himself saluted by infants scarcely able to walk alone, reinforced by children of both sexes and all ages, with a taunting chorus of *"Mao! mao! mao! mao!"* as long as he was within hearing.

The Tientsin massacre of 1870 has already been mentioned among the instances in which the mob element was encouraged by the literati and not discouraged by the officials, and its result was the loss of twenty foreign lives. The French were the principal sufferers in this outbreak, but by an unfortunate coincidence their overwhelming defeat by Germany in that year made the tardy settlement with China in every way unsatisfactory. Had the Tientsin riot been properly punished, it is morally certain that many important events in the subsequent relations between China and the West would have been different.

But though France failed to secure adequate reparation for the wrong done to all foreigners, according to the belief of the Chinese themselves the city and region could not escape the vengeance of Heaven. The surrounding country is low and flat, and for many successive years it was inundated in a way to cause terrible misery to an enormous number of people. Refugees by the thousand, and even by the ten thousand in years of heavy floods or wide-spread famine, flocked to this metropolis, where they were huddled together in great mat-sheds, or allowed to crowd into huts plastered with mud, so low that an adult could not sit upright; there, with no other furniture than a broken iron kettle and a rice-bowl or two, the occupants lay piled together like the puppies of a litter, kept from freezing in the terrible blasts of winter only by a few handfuls of straw on the bare ground, their ragged clothes, and fragments of gunny-bags.

The population of Tientsin has been estimated at a million, or in that vicinity, but this is almost certainly too high a figure. The city itself is small, and the suburbs while crowded are narrow and straggling. But within the past two decades the increase has been marked. The water traffic centreing here is enormous, and there are miles upon miles of boats, laid up in winter, but intensely active during all other seasons.

The great growth in the commercial prosperity of Tientsin is wholly due to the advent of foreign trade, which had advanced with giant strides. Lord Charles Beresford found that the amount of duty collected in 1897 amounted to about £139,000, a gain in nine years of nearly 65 per cent; while the total value of all the exports and imports in the same year was about £9,232,030, being an increase in ten years of 99 per cent.

No shrewder people than the Chinese are to be found upon this planet—or perhaps any other. They have never had the smallest difficulty in perceiving that the phenomenal prosperity of the "Open Ports" springs from foreign trade, and they are ready enough in every one of them, as well in British possessions like Hongkong, Singapore, and Penang, to put themselves under the rule of the outer Barbarian. But this is not to say that they love him, or even like him, because they do not. Of the innate antipathy between the Chinese and foreigners Tientsin is an excellent, because an indisputable example. What harm had ever come to the people of Tientsin from the Settlements, where the Occidentals lived, and in which they have expended annually a sum equal to the revenues of a kingdom, all of which fell into the hands of the Chinese? There was, indeed, in the details of the intercourse much to be regretted, and something might be said to show that the Chinese had a grievance, but on the whole their treatment we believe to have been conspicuously fair and just.

The rise of the Boxer movement was far to the south of Tientsin, and appeared to wake little responsive echo in that turbulent metropolis—a fact which excited the surprise of many old " China hands." Even in the early months of 1900 very little if any unusual excitement was visible, and absolutely no sign of a great popular rising. A few anticipatory Boxer enthusiasts who paraded the streets to beguile the people were promptly arrested, severely punished, and put in the wooden collar; when the ferment apparently disappeared.

Yü Lu, the Governor General of Chihli, like most other high officers everywhere in China at that time, was a Manchu. There is always much difficulty in ascertaining what a Chinese (or a Manchu) official means by what he says, or by the proclamations which he issues, but there certainly appeared to be strong circumstantial evidence that His Excellency was not then friendly to the Boxer enterprise. Gen. Mei, the commander of the provincial troops, was actively fighting and destroying them in large companies, which could not have been the case had Yü Lu desired to stop him, as the Governor of Shantung (Yü Hsien) did with his military officers. At all events there was an apparent effort to put the Boxers down, and some of the proclamations had a ring of severe earnestness and firm purpose. A little later all this was changed by the undoubted approval of the Boxers by the Court, and definite orders from Peking to patronize and to utilize them.

It was noted as a singular and on the whole an unaccountable fact that this city, which one would have expected to be the head-centre and distributing point of all maleficent anti-foreign virus, was not actually captured by the Boxers until long after they had been operating in Pao Ting Fu, Cho Chou, and T'ung Chou. In the country districts within an hundred miles they were already violent by the middle of May, and Christian refugees were pouring into the missionary compounds at the foreign settlement in anticipation of a storm which they well knew would be unprecedented.

The correspondence afterward discovered in the yamen of the Governor General showed conclusively the complicity of that official with his subordinates in Pao Ting Fu (under instructions from Peking), in feeding and patronizing the Boxers. The events which took place along the line of the Lu-Han railway, and especially the destruction of the machine shops and engines on the 28th of May at Fêng T'ai, and later the stations on the Peking line, made a profound impression at Tientsin, which was already throbbing with excitement.

The escape of a large party of Belgian engineers from Pao Ting Fu has already been mentioned, and added to the tension of feeling. They had left that city on twelve boats for Tientsin with an escort and an interpreter. They were abandoned and betrayed on the river, lost their way, became separated, and several of them disappeared. Twenty-six of them formed a square with the women inside and made direct for Tientsin, travelling as well as they could, being ill clad, ill shod, and without food, and obliged to drink from pools and streams as they could. Five of this party, almost delirious with suffering and excitement, became separated from the others, two of them arriving in Tientsin by themselves. A rescue party of twenty-five mounted volunteers and ten men on foot bravely went out to bring in the refugees; the former missed them by going around the city, but the others brought them into the settlement much more dead than alive, and for a time they were totally unable to give any account of themselves. One man was shot in the leg, and had besides seven wounds in the shoulder and head; one of the ladies was shot through the shoulder, and others had wounds of various descriptions.

The Chinese in the city, as well as the settlement, with few exceptions were convinced that the Boxers could do all that they claimed—and more. They could resist swords, were impervious to bullets, could emit fire at will, and could fly. The foreigners, on the other hand, were much too self-confident. The very same correspondent who reported the adventures and sufferings of the engineers, remarked on the 3rd of June that "there is no reason whatever for anxiety about Tientsin." The people of the native city were almost crazed with excitement. Many houses were found smeared with blood, and this was laid to the door of the Christians, while incendiaries and robbers saw in the general disorder a rich harvest time.

On the evening of June 14th (one day later than the similar outbreak in Peking) the Boxers began operations, and from the second story of high buildings their proceedings could be watched. Three chapels inside the city were set on fire, and many of the adjacent buildings were involved in the conflagration.

It was probably not anticipated by those who exerted themselves to destroy foreigners by shooting at them from buildings on the land adjacent to the French settlement, that within a few weeks their property would be confiscated and in some cases sold to the very ones whom the late owners had diligently endeavoured to kill; nor did the short-sighted Chinese who surreptitiously attacked their employers foresee that it would not be long before it would not be safe for them to go about the streets of their own city, and that after nine o'clock at night no Chinese would be allowed abroad on the foreign

AMERICAN BOARD MISSION, TIENTSIN

AMERICAN BOARD MISSION, TIENTSIN, AFTER THE SIEGE

TIENTSIN AFTER THE SIEGE 577

concessions, except jinrikisha men actually drawing a foreign passenger.

There is no doubt that the Chinese armies under command of General Nieh and others fought with a desperation for which nothing in the war with Japan afforded any parallel. The official report of Yü Lu published in the " Peking Gazette " of June 25th and subsequent dates, is an interesting document. He mentions that the troops and the Boxers are in coöperation, and that the latter were willing to offer their services freely and had fully demonstrated their patriotism. Their numbers actually present at Tientsin, can not, he says, be less than 30,000, and " they regard the burning of churches and the killing of foreigners as their profession." So did His Excellency, for in the papers captured at his yamen there is an entry of one hundred taels as having been paid as a reward for the heads of two foreigners!

The net result of all this Boxerism and of the sacrifice of so many Chinese soldiers in numerous engagements was that the Chinese troops were utterly routed (even where they might have made a formidable stand outside and beyond the walls), and the city left a prey to its foes.

Military government at once began, and so likewise did destruction and pillage. When the whole field had been surveyed the destruction of life and of property was found to have been enormous. Of the former it is impossible to speak with definiteness, but of the latter there were everywhere visible proofs. The south gate which the Japanese blew open, and at which they entered, had its tower totally destroyed, and a temple within the southeastern quarter, used as an arsenal, was the scene of a great explosion. Between the south gate and the central drum-tower many of the houses and shops were burned, and between this tower and the north gate nothing was left standing on either side of the street. From the drum-tower to the west gate the ruin was not quite so universal, while east of the drum-tower except in the vicinity of a mission church there was not much devastation.

Outside the north gate, the narrow street extending to the iron bridge leading to the yamen of the Governor General for display of its wares and for the extent of its trade, was perhaps one of the finest in all China. Between the Boxers, the Chinese soldiers, and the local ruffians whose habit was first to loot and then to burn, this long row of business houses was almost entirely obliterated, involving losses amounting doubtless to tens of millions of taels. For many days the principal occupation of many soldiers, and civilians also, was the garnering of the rich crop of looted silver from the innumerable places where it was to be found, and whence it was carried off by the wheel-barrow load and the cart load. It was a standard story that when the attention of a soldier was called to the fact that he had dropped one or two "shoes" (each worth about $70 Mexican), he would reply; "Never mind, you pick them up—I have all I want!" The treasure found in the various yamens must have been enough to furnish a mint.

The fate of these yamens was interesting as a part of the general retribution. That of the Governor General which for twenty-two years had been occupied by Li Hung Chang (a large part of it accidentally destroyed by fire during the winter), became the headquarters of a "Tientsin Provisional Government," established by the military authorities, when it was found that there were insuperable objections to conceding the request of the Russians that Tientsin should be turned over to that Power alone. This Provisional Government was constituted by the appointment of a British, a Russian, a Japanese, and later a German, Colonel to act as Commissioners, the number being subsequently increased to six, assisted by the necessary staff for the execution of the functions of policing and controlling so large a city and so important a centre.

As soon as Tientsin was taken every Chinese official, civil as well as military, promptly disappeared, and most of them suffered extreme "bitterness" on the flight southward, being systematically pillaged by the Chinese at all points of their long journey, so that they were in many cases reduced to absolute penury. The yamen of the Customs Taotai (one of the most important in the city) was occupied by the Japanese; that of the Prefect by the French; while those of the District Magistrate, of the Salt Commissioner, and of the Brigadier General, were reduced to complete ruin. Thus an incidental outcome of the plan of the officials to combine the Boxers and the Chinese troops to drive the foreigners into the sea, was that within sixty days of the beginning of serious operations officials, Boxers, and Chinese soldiers had absolutely disappeared from the scene, leaving the hated foreigner in undisputed charge of everything everywhere.

The fort near the Governor General's yamen from which the settlement had been viciously attacked, was soon taken by the Japanese, who posted a small guard over it, other troops occupying the numerous forts in the immediate vicinity. Numbers of new and unused Krupp guns were captured in the neighbourhood of the city, showing the utter demoralization which seized the Chinese soldiers when once it had set in.

The city had no sooner been occupied than the British and other officers pressed on to the river outside the north gate to seize the junks, cargo-boats, and house-boats for military transports, in consequence of which thereafter not a boat could stir nor a boatman peep except with military consent. Every craft of every sort either had the label of some "outside country" painted upon it— British 87, U. S. Transport 63, etc.,—or flew a flag with the mystic symbol "T. P. G.," showing that it was registered and licensed by the Tientsin Provisional Government, as were the carts, barrows, rikshas, "and also much cattle."

The rice tribute came to an abrupt period, and all the extensive supplies on hand were soon looked after by some of the military, who were at once omnipresent and omnipotent. The long mountain ranges of salt stocked up on the left bank of the Peiho, had over them a Russian flag at one end, and a French flag at the other, and for the next year or so no salt-boats left for the interior, where the people got on as they could.

At the New Year season, when the Chinese most delight in the promiscuous and unrestrained explosion of innumerable bunches of fire-crackers, proclamations were issued in Tientsin (as well as in the other cities under foreign military rule) positively forbidding anything of the kind on pain of arrest and punishment. Few of the hitherto universally posted ornamental and flowery inscriptions over doorways, and on the door-posts, were to be seen, and such was the terror inspired by the foreign soldiers that even formal bows on the streets (said to be forbidden by the Japanese police) had to be wholly pretermitted. It was not considered altogether safe to perform these indispensable ceremonies even in the privacy of one's own court-yard, where even women were said to be sometimes arrested for indulging in the inevitable gambling appropriate to the period of national relaxation. Under these strange and bitter conditions many Chinese were heard plaintively to exclaim that it would have been better not to have any New Year at all!

A year ago the word "*yang*" (foreign) was everywhere so odious that even the innocent Mohammedans who sold "*yang jou*" (sheep-meat, a word with the same sound but different meaning), were attacked on that account. Everything foreign was taboo, or if indispensable was dubbed with a new name. Foreign drilling must be called "fine cloth" or "wide cloth," foreign rifles "knobbed-guns," foreign matches "quick-fire," and the like. But now Chinese were everywhere to be met, dressed in foreign hats, coats, trousers, and boots (and in winter even in hitherto unprecedented mittens and gloves), the cast-off property of soldiers and civilians. All classes learned the military salute with more or less inaccuracy, the smallest children ostentatiously performing it before every passer by, and old beggar women carefully shaded one eye under the impression that they were thus punctiliously observing the foreign proprieties while soliciting a "foreign cash."

The fate of the materials which were especially depended upon for the destruction of the hated foreigner is an apt illustration of the miscarriage of plans which seem to their promoters the best laid in the world. The Arsenal in the southeastern corner of the city was found stocked with weapons of the most miscellaneous nature, all of which were taken over by the Provisional Government and issued to whatever foreigner presented a request for them as a defence to his life and property. Lead from this Arsenal and elsewhere was collected by the Provisional Government, melted into 200 pound bars, and shipped to Shanghai in large quantities, the proceeds going to swell the handsome revenues which were presently pouring into the coffers of that energetic corporation, which with conspicuous success undertook many branches of administration hitherto distributed among a score or more of yamens, or left altogether undone.

The right to excavate and remove the remains of the Arsenal at Hsiku partly destroyed by Admiral Seymour's party was sold at auction, the purchaser unearthing vast lava-flows of lead and other metal melted in the general combustion, to the enrichment of the foreigner and the impoverishment of the Chinese Government.

For two months after the siege the people of Tientsin, many of whom had fled to villages at a distance, were afraid to return, but by degrees the city began to look less deserted, and the Taku road which passes through the foreign settlement began to assume something of its wonted activity. Numerically considered, the destruction of dwellings in the city itself was a small matter when compared with that in the environs. The densely crowded main street running through the French concession, upon which were most of the Chinese shops dealing in foreign goods, was totally destroyed, not a single building left standing. Some of them were burned by the foreigners during the siege to prevent them from being used as forts to attack the foreign houses, and then the shops were looted by whomever could get there first. Large tracts of the French concession were burned in the same way, for since so much was being destroyed it would be convenient to have the whole area laid out anew, and no questions asked.

On the east of the river around the railway station, where the fighting was most furious, not a Chinese dwelling was left, nor for a long distance in any direction. The villages along the river between Tientsin and Taku have likewise been destroyed, and the same was true on every side of the city, but in varying degrees. This extensive diminution in the number of houses, resulted in great inconvenience and discomfort, and, when the cold weather came on, in unspeakable misery. Extravagant rents were demanded for the meanest huts; even more serious than the lack of an abode was the difficulty of buying food and the scarcity of fuel, for the rains had been deficient, and the crops, such as they were, had been neglected.

Prices were at a preposterous figure, while wages, owing to the irrational standard set by the military, seemed to promise sudden riches, forty cents being paid for the labor of a short day, instead of twenty as heretofore. Cash ceased to be the topic of conversation, as it had been since the creation of all things, and all the talk was of "*mao*" (dimes), and "*yüan*" (dollars). But this fictitious prosperity had its outcome in the fact that instead of one's buying for cash—a tenth of a cent—as a unit, almost nothing was to be had for less than ten cents, so that in terms of food and clothes no one was much better off than before.

To these evils due to a violation of the laws of political economy, were added others arising primarily from a contempt for the laws of nations. China had defied the world, and the world was upon her. With such a polyglot force of troops it was next to impossible to keep them in order, and as a matter of fact it was not done. Some of the Russian, the French, the Indian, and the German troops distinguished themselves as high-way robbers, plundering the Chinese of their money, their goods, and their clothing, and this in broad daylight and in public places.

Military raids into the regions about Tientsin were made in all directions, and although it is impossible to get at the facts it is certain that the three shortest of the Ten Commandments were constantly violated on an extensive scale, and with no redress for "the heathen Chinese." Every individual coolie must have a label sewed to his coat, or he might be commandeered by an urgent military officer for his particular job, perhaps being paid good wages, and perhaps at the end being dismissed with a kick. Lest their badges be stolen from them for the protection of others, some of the Chinese had brass plates clamped to their arms, and many poor fellows after working hard all day on their way to their hovels had the results of their toil snatched from them by a French trooper from Algiers, or a German from Kiaochou.

The native scoundrels who had lately been drawing rations from the Governor General as "patriotic Boxers," had thrown away their red girdles, and while the looting season lasted gave themselves to that industry with a single eye and with both hands earnestly. If however, one continued poor, he mingled with the crowd and offered his services as a policeman of the Provisional Government, where he might levy black-mail indiscriminately, since there was no one to testify to his past record. Now and then, as a result of too great temerity one such lost his head, but this was regarded as a mere incident in the ordinary line of risks, and had no deterring effect upon others.

The professional rowdies and blacklegs of Tientsin, as the fruit of their prudent exertions at the moment of destiny, are now rich and prosperous, while those who were formerly well-to-do are either in exile or in poverty. As one outcome of this inversion of the social order, the poor being suddenly rich and the rich becoming poor, the numerous and important charities of Tientsin were largely dried up at the fountain-head. The soup-kitchens which usually flourish were sought in vain, and although there are still a few benevolent gentry who would gladly do something for those in distress, their inadequate resources are, in classical language, but " a cup of water to put out a fire in a cart-load of fuel."

Whatever the excellences of the Tientsin Provisional Government, which within a certain radius were many, it entirely failed in the first principle of good administration, that the work should be done through the Chinese themselves. Li Hung Chang indeed appointed a District Magistrate, a Prefect, and a territorial Taotai, not one of whom was allowed by the six military " kings " who held the actual authority to open an office in the city, even if he could set foot in it with safety. The last named official, who is a man of weight and dignity in the Chinese scale of rank, ought to ride in a chair, and appear in his robes of office, but he was ordered out of Tientsin as if his arrival were an impertinence, and was not even allowed to have a place of business anywhere within the county limits. When he called upon the " kings " he dared not appear in his proper costume, but only in undress clothing, being rightly assured that they would never know the difference.

The whole Chinese system of government is one of graded and interrelated responsibility. By their wanton acts of violence the Chinese at Tientsin put an end to their own rule, and that which took its place was at best limited, inadequate, and irresponsible. The incessant raids of the military drove away the officials in wide tracts of country, over which there was no government of any kind. Bands of pirates who usually rob watercraft and hide up the inaccessible creeks and bays, now ranged the country as mounted thieves. Their only and inappeasable cry was for " silver." If that were not forthcoming, the poor wretch who was attacked might be tied by the queue to a beam in his own house and slowly roasted over a fire of fuel. This is termed " sitting on the lotus flower." Or he might be forced into a framework of telegraph-wire heated red-hot, which is called " riding on the fire-wheel cart," until he should pay the sum demanded. When complaint was made to the Provisional Government, the very natural reply was received that they had at present (although later it was otherwise) no jurisdiction beyond the outer rampart of Tientsin—all the rest was a No-man's land dedicated to misrule and to primeval chaos!

The great eastern arsenal, from which the attacks upon the settlement were so fierce and persistent, was captured by the Russians on the 27th of June, and although largely destroyed as a work-shop for weapons, became an excellent Russian hospital. The western arsenal, in the " Treaty Temple," was a complete wreck, and all its machinery was sold to private speculators by the Provisional Government, and was stacked up in a melancholy row next to the foreign cemetery on the British Concession. The huge bell presented by the Krupp Company to the Chinese Government long years ago, was in turn presented by the Provisional Government to the Tientsin British Municipal Council, where it hangs in the Public Gardens, and is expected to give the settlement its much-needed standard of time. Could the military humiliation of Tientsin go deeper than this?

The land lying between Tientsin city and the settlements had gradually increased in value to the extent of many hundred *per cent,* and as much of it was dotted with graves it was not to be had at any price. Not many months after the capture of the city the French Consul General issued a circular notifying the public that that

RUINS OF ROMAN CATHOLIC CATHEDRAL, TIENTSIN

ARSENAL, TIENTSIN

TIENTSIN AFTER THE SIEGE 587

office "did not recognize" the validity of any Chinese deeds drawn before the 17th of June (the date of the capture of the Taku forts), and that within specified and expansive limits all land had now by this fiat become the property of the French Municipal Council, any previous deeds requiring to be registered at the Consulate. In pursuance of this act of annexation the ruins of Chinese houses were leveled, broad boulevards laid out in desirable directions, and all plaints of Chinese owners for compensation answered with a shrug of the shoulders. As much of this land had swarmed with dwellings, the hardship to innocent owners was great and remediless, and presently these unfortunate individuals found themselves required to pay a tax of several dollars a month for the right to continue in temporary occupation of their own houses! These additions to the French territory extended from the settlement, north to the river, and thence west to the rampart enclosing the city. Upon a large part of this it is announced that in future no Chinese will be allowed to live.

Immediately adjoining this is the Japanese quarter, embracing the whole battlefield of July 13th, and extending to the south wall of the city, and east and west from the Peiho to the mud rampart. The densely crowded houses had almost all been destroyed, and over the ruins of every door was posted a sign in Japanese and Chinese: "This house reserved for Japanese troops."

Along the whole frontage of their extensive addition they demolished all buildings, dwellings, shops, yamens and temples with the rest, and opened a wide street along the water front, which the Provisional Government continued the whole distance to the Grand Canal, and to the Iron Bridge opposite the yamen of the Governor General. Innumerable Chinese shops and dens thus disappeared.

The boulevard which replaces the narrow and tortuous alleys is macadamized and wholesome—but it is by no means certain that the late Chinese occupants are entirely happy.

In continuation of this new avenue it was decided by the Provisional Government to make a roadway entirely around the city, but this could only be accomplished by the removal of the city wall. A contract for this work was given out to a Chinese, who, during the winter months hired armies of the poor, thus having the melancholy satisfaction of assisting in destroying the defences of the city which had so recently felt the need of them. Multitudes of "squatters" along the city wall were thereby dislodged and had no place to go, and such was the number of homeless wretches in the bitter months of the winter, that every temple was choked with them, and they filled even the jail of the yamen of the District Magistrate, an official for whom there was now no yamen and no use. The whole city wall was levelled, the city moat filled up, and adjacent dwellings demolished, all to make a long esplanade, sixty or more feet wide, encircling Tientsin, looking to the probable introduction of an electric road to accommodate the steadily growing and hitherto unmanageable traffic.

A proceeding so revolutionary could not take place without exciting the most bitter opposition from the gentry and the people, who sent repeated and urgent memorials to Li Hung Chang against it, pleading piteously in the figurative language of the Orient that a Chinese city without walls is like a woman without her nether garments! Li quashed their petitions with the curt remark that the wall was old and of no protective value, and the work went on apace to its completion. In the meantime the official surveyor of the Provisional Government was set at work to map out the whole region, and to mark out a street of uniform width from the north to the south gate, remorselessly cutting off several feet from each shop-front for the advantage of that hitherto disregarded entity, the Public. The extensive ponds and holes in different corners of the city are all to be filled up, and the land offered for sale, and as every situation is incomparably more accessible than before, the ultimate convenience will be great, while the actual owners may perhaps be heavy losers.

The mountains of bricks from the facing of the city wall were exposed for sale, and now form the enclosing walls and the pavements of foreign premises on the settlements, whose owners a few months since were shot at and bombarded by soldiers posted on that same city wall and perhaps treading on these very bricks. Throughout all the streets and alleys of Tientsin, and the other cities similarly governed, the houses are all numbered with Arabic figures, and many of the streets have been renamed, especially by the Japanese, who appear to regard their settlement as merely an addition to the Islands of Nippon.

Below the mud rampart so often mentioned, the Germans, by the same simple formula now exclusively employed, have annexed a large tract which has become an integral part of the German Empire. Across the Peiho on the east, the same facile plan has been followed by Belgium, by Russia (whose miles of addition included the railway station, and brought two Empires to the very verge of war), and by Italy and Austria. Each of these nations has now broad areas dignified by the satirical designations of " Concessions," but which might rather be styled " Aggressions."

All the " Powers " (except China) are now accommodated with a commodious water-front, nearly the whole distance from the junction of the Grand Canal and the Peiho being appropriated in this way, with the prospect of larger demands for the "hinterlands" of each section in the future.

The foreign settlements of Tientsin have been turned into a camp, and its principal buildings occupied for military purposes. The Gordon Municipal Hall was a British, and the Union Church an Italian hospital. The Japanese took the building of the Y. M. C. A.; the Temperance Hall was filled with Sikhs, the Tientsin University with Germans, the Chinese Military and Medical School with French. All nations, all races, were on perpetual exhibition. One might see everywhere the sturdy little Japanese; the coarse-featured, stocky Russian; the somewhat undersized Frenchman (perhaps a company of Zouaves from Algiers in flaming scarlet trousers of astonishing size and shape); the burly young German; the stout Britisher of the Royal Welsh Fusiliers; the lithe American; together with a motley flow of tall and swart Sikhs, Pathans, Beluchis, and Rajputs, as well as the Chinese organized into the British First Regiment of Wei Hai Wei; here and there an Austrian, Italians decorated with huge tufts of feathers on their hats, and occasionally the shrewd white-turbaned Parsee.

To deal with the problem of the commissariat for all this mixed multitude was a mighty task.

In the dead of night one might detect the deep tones of the bells hung to the neck of long strings of camels loaded with stores for Peking, a mode of transportation not seen in Tientsin for decades, and only employed while the railway was undergoing its slow repairs. The streets were choked with interminable processions of British pack animals, lines of the capacious Studebaker American

FIRST BRITISH-CHINESE REGIMENT, WEI HAI WEI

RUSSIAN TROOPS EN ROUTE TO PEKING

TIENTSIN AFTER THE SIEGE

army wagon, the clumsy forage carts of the Russians, German vehicles bought from the Dutch and made in Java, and the trig little trucks of the Japanese. The big humped Indian buffalo drew a light framework supporting a water-barrel for the Mohammedan troops, and long lines of all descriptions of wheeled drays or carts struggled at the hydrants, or at the hose-pipes furnishing distilled water.

The enterprising Cantonese, who owned most of the Chinese stores dealing in foreign goods, being regarded by the Tientsinese as practically foreigners, were either driven away or killed, and their possessions impartially looted. The "Tientsin Road" on the French settlement, formerly filled with these shops from end to end, was totally destroyed, and their places taken by French barracks. The Temple of the "Purple Bamboo Grove" (Tzu Chu Lin) which gave its name to the settlement, was wholly demolished and burned, its site being heaped with the timbers of wrecked buildings. The once stylish Victoria Road was lined with patient Chinese squatting in attendance upon stands (if that can be called a "stand" which is merely a cloth spread upon the ground), displaying a stock of pears, eggs, turnips, and the odds and ends saved or plundered from the wreck of the numerous stores dealing in foreign goods—candles, lamps, chimneys, towels, socks, mirrors, pictures, and all the miscellaneous wares found in Chinese shops, each "stand" a small department store in itself.

New places of business burst forth in unexpected spots. A gate-house suddenly developed a glass-window on the side to the street with the legend: "Exchange to Money," for the coin was most confusing. Counterfeit dollars and fractional currency abounded, so that one was afraid to take any change at all. The city which hated foreigners and their speech began to be full of signs in English, Japanese, French, and German, perhaps informing the passer-by that " Japan Wishky are sold here," or that the proprietor was prepared, for a consideration, to " Makee tattoo in the skin."

It is a melancholy fact that it was the worst phase of Occidental civilization which was displayed most widely and conspicuously to the Chinese, and that they were given the very best reason to suppose that the principal object of every " ocean man " was to find a place in which to drink.

The entire lower end of the Taku Road was filled with saloons and disreputable resorts of every variety, where roistering crowds of foreign soldiers from all the great countries of the world nightly met, and drank, and fought. Privates and officers, the latter too in considerable numbers, were shot and killed during the winter in quarrels between different contingents of the " China Expeditionary Force," and more than once the French and the Americans, the British and the French, or the Russians and the British, seemed to be on the point of open hostilities, with no greater cause than some private bar room dispute or a national feud growing out of hotly reciprocated taunts and flings.

All this, however, belongs to an exceptional and a transitional state. Tientsin is undergoing a great transformation. It is sure to be in the future far more than hitherto a vast commercial distributing depot, its river deepened and straightened, the navigation improved, and the intractable Taku bar brought under effective control. It will be a great manufacturing, railway, and educational centre, and before the twentieth century is well under way will enjoy a prosperity unthought of in the past, which will make the year of the Boxer rising seem in retrospect like a troubled dream.

And all this it will owe to the far-sightedness, energy, persistence, and skill of the foreigners for whom in the closing year of the nineteenth century the Chinese Government and the Chinese people had no other wish than to kill them all.

XXXII

FOREIGNERS IN THE INTERIOR

TO describe in detail the experiences of the great number of foreigners who were scattered all over the interior of an Empire far larger than the whole of Europe, would of itself require a volume. All that can here be attempted is such a rapid survey as to make clear that the Boxer movement was in no sense a " rebellion," which it soon became the interest of the Government itself and especially of its Ministers abroad to represent it to be, but a deliberately planned and comprehensive attempt to exterminate foreigners wherever found.

That there were edicts issued from the Central Government in Peking to different and distant parts of the Empire ordering the immediate massacre of all foreigners, is certain. The evidence is of a varied and convincing nature. Intelligence of such a Decree was brought to missionaries and others by friends in the yamens, by friendly telegraph operators, and by officials—some of them of high rank—in at least three provinces and in numerous places hundreds of miles apart, almost simultaneously. Twice at least the original dispatch was seen by foreigners, and its phraseology is indelibly engraved on the memories of those who were stunned by the appalling and unexampled words: *" Fêng Yang-jên pi sha, yang-jên t'ui hui chi sha,"* " Whenever you meet foreigners you must kill them, and if they attempt to escape they must still immediately be killed."

It has been generally believed that the two Ministers of the Tsung Li Yamen who were executed during the progress of the siege in Peking, Hsü Ching Ch'êng, and Yüan Ch'ang, admitted that they had altered the character for "kill," into another meaning "protect" (*pao*), and this is said to have been affirmed by the son of one of them, and assigned as a reason for their decapitation. This point remains in some obscurity, for several different reasons. As a matter of fact the dispatch was not altered within the numerous regions where it most seriously affected foreigners, and in the case of Imperial Edicts it is thought incredible that any one should dare to take such a step at once fatal and futile. It was of course convenient both for the Governors General and Governors who refused to obey this Decree and later for the Chinese Government itself to assume that it was "spurious," a legal fiction which has been consistently maintained, and will doubtless remain as the standard explanation among the Chinese, and among many foreigners. The theory in that case is that Prince Tuan was "a usurper," and that his clique gained possession of the seals of State, and for a time put the real "Government" under duress.

It is a Chinese maxim that "an officer depends upon his seal,"—losing that he loses his office too, and having the seal he *ex officio* is the person to whom the seal belongs. Prince Tuan was put in power by the deliberate act of the Empress Dowager herself for a definite purpose, and there seems to be no evidence that his acts were either disavowed by her, or in any way objectionable to her until their consequences became so. After that, the adoption of the theory of "spurious Decrees" was inevitable, and has been definitely fixed by an Edict, as from the Emperor, ordering the collection of all the Decrees issued after the siege of the Legations began, that their genuineness might be officially denied, so as to put an end to their citation as acts of "the Government of China." But it should be distinctly recognized that such disavowal has no real bearing upon historic facts, and can in no way undo the irreparable past.

In this connection peculiar interest attaches to the accompanying note from Sir Robert Hart, Inspector-General of the Chinese Imperial Maritime Customs:

"PEKING 18*th June,* 1901.
"DEAR DR. SMITH:
"It would be interesting to get a really reliable Chinese account of Palace doings—and Peking doings—during 1900: As it is, we are all guessing and inferring and putting this and that together, but we have not got at the facts yet! It's all a question with no finality in it—*you* may put down your pen, but every new touch will bring a new picture to the eye that looks through the kaleidoscope of history—and the *Aurora Borealis* of circumstance will change unceasingly.
"Truly yours,
"ROBERT HART."

While the Empress Dowager may not have had personal knowledge of every Decree put forth in her name, it is morally certain that without her general sanction none of them could have been issued. That she was kept misinformed of the actual conditions is altogether likely, and nothing is more probable, if not indeed certain, than that the decisive and irrevocable step was taken in one of those paroxysms of fury to which all Chinese and Man-

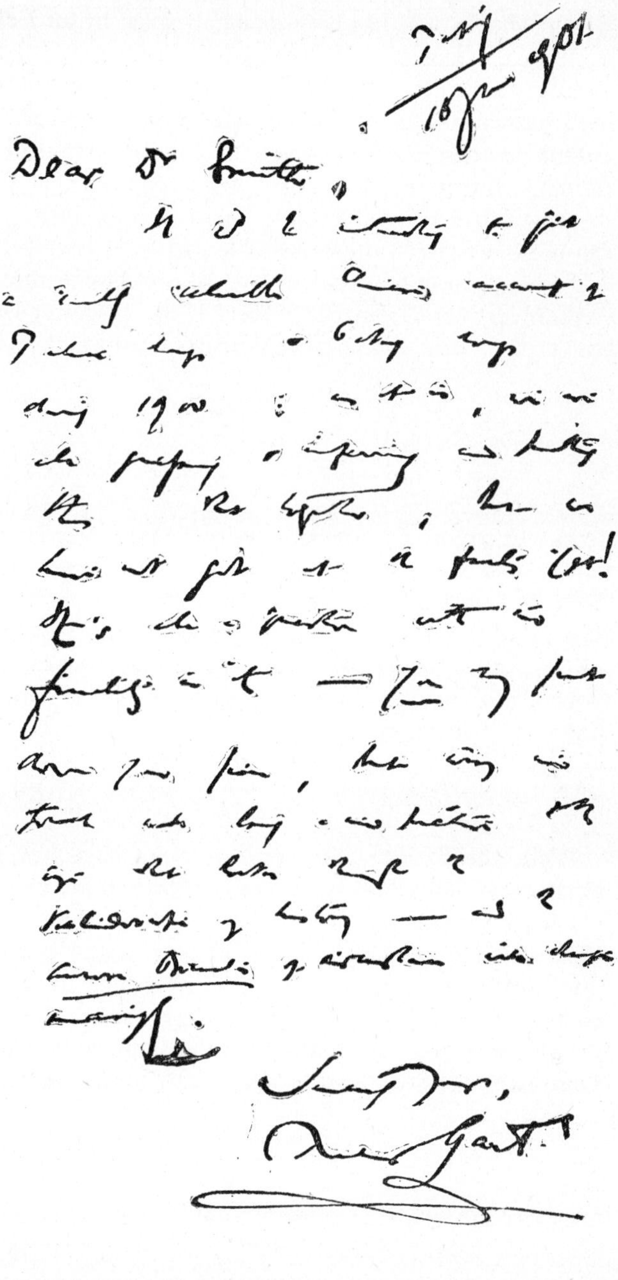
Dear Dr Smith,

chus, high and low, the latter quite as much as the former, are perpetually liable.

That this act was itself caused by a piece of intelligence received just before the decision was taken, which exerted a powerful influence on the mind of the Empress Dowager, has been often and confidently affirmed, and is in itself so natural an explanation of her sudden anger that, while it is impossible at present to prove it, there is yet sufficient evidence to adopt it as an hypothesis. It must be premised that it had long been the habit of the Court to have translations made from the foreign journals in China for palace perusal, many of which must have been particularly unpleasant reading.

The story is that on the 19th of June an unknown official in Shanghai sent to the Grand Council in Peking a telegram embodying the substance of something which had there appeared. What that article was is not known, but that there were editorials printed at that time which would have been likely to produce such effects is indisputable. Of that type is the following paragraph, which appeared in the leading journal of the Far East, the "North China Daily News," on the morning of June 19th, 1900.

"The Empress Dowager is reaping the whirlwind with a vengeance, and it is very doubtful whether she will stay in Peking to gather the harvest. . . . Instead of having one or two Powers to pacify, China is at war with all the Great Powers at once, and she is at war by the choice of the Empress Dowager and her gang. . . . Whatever happens, this gang, if it does not go of its own accord, must be driven out of Peking. It is to be hoped that it will be possible to get out the Emperor Kuang Hsü and replace him on the throne. Meantime, it should be made perfectly clear that it is the Empress Dowager who has undertaken the present war, and that we are not fighting China, but the usurping Government at Peking."

This newspaper, which has for a sub-title "The Supreme Court and Consular Gazette," might very naturally pass among the Chinese for what is remote enough from its real character, the organ of the British Government and its official spokesman, although the smallest acquaintance with the facts would show any reader that it was the almost incessant critic of the acts of that Government.

The Relief Expedition under Admiral Seymour had been already ten days on its way from Tientsin to Peking. Should it succeed in entering the city this was to be its program, and no faltering for sentimental reasons was to be allowed: "The Empress Dowager was to be deposed,"—the mere suggestion of which had brought about the *coup d'etat* of 1898. "Hell has no fury like a woman scorned"—and the rest we know.

Attention has been repeatedly called in these pages to the fact that the greatest hostility to foreigners in China arose among the Manchus, rather than the Chinese. In the Grand Council the former were represented as being practically unanimous in favour of defying the world, while the latter offered strenuous albeit unavailing objections. The leading officials at the bottom of the movement, with a few prominent exceptions, were Manchus. Among the singular phenomena of this strange time was the frankness with which Chinese Ministers abroad expressed themselves in regard to the policy of the Government at home, in marked contrast to the usual caution of all Chinese officials in refusing to commit themselves. Press reports of utterances of this sort on the part of the Minister to Great Britain (Lo Feng Lu), the Minister to France, and the Minister to the United States (Wu Ting Fang), agreed in thus fixing the responsibility for the invasion of the laws of nations on a Manchu clique.

The substance of a few sentences from an interview with the first named, as published in the October (1900) number of "Crampton's Magazine" (English), clearly illustrates this point. "The enlightened part of the population," he says, "including all the Chinese Viceroys and Governors, condemn the Boxer movement, and have no sympathy with it. But with the Manchu Governors and Viceroys the case is different. They get their posts without rigorous examination tests, and are on this account less educated. No educated Chinese would believe, for instance, that foreign rifles would prove harmless in battle. I should never have supposed that a Manchu mandarin could believe such a statement. It has been a revelation to me, I confess. If there is to be a free competition of talents, there can no longer be a class monopoly of the high offices of the Empire. The Manchus are all conservative, while the Chinese are more liberal."

After explaining how Confucius can be interpreted as in favour of some check upon unlimited authority, he expresses the opinion that there would be no justice in the demand for implicit obedience if the man at the helm of State would go madly in support of a Boxer movement so as to endanger the destiny of four hundred millions of people who are quite innocent. He closes with these significant words: "I hope that financial, educational, and judicial reforms will be introduced after this crisis is over, and I would even say—as a representative of my country as well as of my Government—that I hope the Powers will insist upon reforms."

The Chinese Ship-of-State under its Manchu Pilots was thus launched upon its dangerous course down unknown rapids, and the shock was distinctly felt in every part of the huge craft, from the southern top of the province of Kuangtung to the banks of the Amur River in the distant north, and from the sea-board to the confines of Turkestan. No such evidence of the unity of the Chinese Empire has ever been witnessed.

It was of the greatest importance to the Government that there should be practical unanimity of action throughout the Empire, as well as in the Peking Grand Council, and to make sure of it a Decree was issued on the 26th of June, addressed to twenty-four Governors General, Governors, Military and Naval officials, in the following terms:

"We yesterday announced to Li Hung Chang, Li Ping Hêng, Liu K'un Yi, and Chang Chih Tung, the facts that it is equally difficult to repress or to soothe the feud of the society men against the converts, and that hostilities were first resorted to by the Powers.

"The reluctance of you Viceroys and Governors, after considering the position and estimating your strength, to provoke foreign enmity lightly, may well be the policy of tried Ministers consulting the interests of their State. But unfortunately, in the present case, the Boxer bands have spread over the whole capital, and their numbers are not less than several hundred thousand. From soldiers and people up to princely and ducal palaces, alike comes one cry of hatred of the foreign religion: the two can not exist together. Repression meant intestine trouble and the utter ruin of the people. The only course, therefore, was to turn the movement to account, while slowly devising reformation. The warning in your memorial not to endanger the State by believing their heretical talk, leaves out of account the helpless position in which the Court is placed.

"Did you Viceroys and Governors realize how great is

the crisis in the capital you would surely be unable to eat and sleep in peace, and would be so anxious to do your duty that you could never think of making one-sided representations. The present state of things is one in which the incitement and pressure of providential opportunity and human affairs have combined to make war inevitable. Do not any of you longer hesitate and look on, but with all speed provide troops and supplies, and vigourously protect the territories; for any remissness you shall be called to account."

That any Chinese officials, after a warning such as this, should have hesitated to obey the express and repeated commands of the Court, would seem to have been in itself virtual rebellion, especially as it was not the cue of those in authority to claim or to admit that the Empress Dowager was in any sense a "usurper."

The outcome of this unexampled situation was that Chang Chih Tung, Governor General of the provinces of Hupei and Hunan, Liu K'un Yi, Governor General of the "River Provinces," and Yuan Shih K'ai, Governor of Shantung, entered into an agreement with one another and with the representatives of foreign Powers that order should be maintained within their territories upon certain specified conditions, of which the absence as far as possible of foreign gun-boats formed a part. While refusing to relinquish her treaty rights, Great Britain was anxious to do everything in her power to strengthen the hands of these Chinese officials who were "loyal," if not to the reckless Manchu rulers, at least to the best interests of China itself.

It was most fortunate that the welfare of Great Britain was represented at Shanghai by Mr. Pelham L. Warren, as Acting Consul General, and later as Acting British

Minister, and at Hankow by Mr. E. H. Frazer, whose activity and energy were constantly exercised for the general behoof. At the suggestion of Mr. Warren, an arrangement was made by which the British Government took the unusual step of loaning Chang Chih Tung the sum of £75,000 for ten years at 4½ per cent, on the security of the unpledged likin revenue of his provinces. Mr. Warren pointed out (Aug. 9th) to Lord Salisbury that it was "most important to strengthen the Viceroys in their present position, for if they were overthrown the result would be a rising, the suppression of which would involve the expenditure of much time and the employment of large forces, and this would inevitably be followed by the partition of China. The firm position of the Viceroys," he adds, "has for the time checked the plans of the Peking Government for a general uprising against foreigners, which but for this would certainly have been carried out."

The policy of Yuan Shih K'ai in Shantung, where the Boxer movement had its origin, was very unpopular, and it is said that his own life was in constant danger, a special guard of a thousand of his men—the best drilled soldiers in China—being stationed at his yamen gates with machine-guns to prevent any demonstrations. Many months later, when it was perceived that it was only the foresight and firmness of Governor Yuan which had prevented Shantung from being over-run by foreign troops as the adjacent province of Chihli had been, the popular feeling changed materially; but in the summer of 1900 the outlook was a dark one.

Another official to whom perhaps the most credit of all is due—considering that he is a Manchu—was Tuan Fang, then Acting Governor of Shensi. His firmness prevented the development of the Boxer bacillus in the province, and in the face of the decree of extermination already quoted he used the utmost diligence in protecting all foreigners, not only within his jurisdiction but also in sections contiguous to it, without that punctilious reverence for boundary lines which generally characterizes Chinese officials. He specially dispatched strong escorts for all foreigners leaving Shensi, and gave express orders that the soldiers should not return until their charges had been actually turned over to the troops of Chang Chih Tung sent to meet them, wherever that might happen to be. On the long routes thus traversed from Hsi An Fu to the comparative quiet of Hupei, there were times when but for such protection the travellers would have been attacked by large armed bands, and might easily have been destroyed. As it was, all the foreigners both in Shensi and in Kansu escaped across the mountains of Hankow, with no loss of life.

In the adjoining province of Honan, while there was no actual massacre, there were terrible hardships, and marvellous escapes. The officials and the people were more hostile than in Shensi, yet there were some notable exceptions.

In Shantung, thanks to the protection of Governor Yuan Shih K'ai, there was not only no foreigner killed during the troubled season of anxiety and flight, but comparatively little of the suffering elsewhere so common. The American Consul at Chefoo, Mr. John Fowler, (assisted by the Rev. George Cornwell and others), displayed the greatest energy and resourcefulness in this time of emergency, at his own risk chartering, by the kind aid of the Japanese Consul, a small Japanese steamer at several hundred dollars a day. This made repeated

PEI TAI HO WATERING PLACE, FROM WHICH FOREIGNERS WERE RESCUED BY CONSUL FOWLER

FOREIGNERS IN THE INTERIOR 605

trips to Yang Chia K'ou, at the mouth of an artificial canal terminating near Chi Nan Fu, by which and other means more than two hundred and sixty foreigners were brought safely out of the province.

The firm stand taken by the triumvirate of high Chinese officials previously mentioned, saved the central and the southern provinces from becoming inoculated with the virus so fatal farther north, but it did not and could not prevent isolated manifestations of hostile feeling in the intensely anti-foreign coast provinces, as well as in the interior. Early in the summer there was serious danger in Yünnan, where the French had been active, but from whence they were compelled to retire. There were hostile demonstrations in Kuangtung, resulting in much loss of mission property, and these continued at intervals for a year or more. Fukien was excited, though not to the danger point; and it became necessary to remove all foreigners from the isolated port of Wên Chou farther up the coast.

On the 22nd of July a ghastly tragedy occurred in K'ü Chou Fu in western Chêkiang, by which Mr. and Mrs. Thompson, and two sons, Miss Desmond, Miss Sherwood, and Miss Manchester, of that city, and Mr. and Mrs. Ward and infant, with Miss Thirgood, stationed at Ch'ang Shan, were all killed with the utmost cruelty. The movement among the people by which these missionaries of the China Inland Mission lost their lives, is believed to have had no direct connection with the Boxer rising, but was a local rebellion, in which the District Magistrate was himself killed while endeavouring to quell it.

Although there was no actual outbreak in the remote province of Szechuan in south-western China, it was considered advisable to remove all the foreign residents from that province, and from the other interior stations of all inland provinces, to the ports.

There is no reasonable doubt that the Boxer rising had been planned to come to a crisis in the eighth moon, for occult reasons connected with the intercalary eighth month of that year, already mentioned in a previous chapter; but, like a time-fuse which could not be regulated, it exploded prematurely in the month of May, at least twelve weeks in advance of schedule time.

Some of the phenomena connected with this sudden development were entirely new in the long experience of foreigners in China. In Mukden, the capital of Manchuria, for example, the relations between the Protestant missionaries and the officials had been of the most friendly character. The Military Governor had assured the Presbyterian missionaries, who were holding their annual sessions during the early part of June, that no safer place could be found than where they were. Yet within the space of less than a week the whole atmosphere had changed, and the extreme of friendliness on the part of officials and people was replaced by suspicion and hostility. The Governor would return no answer to communications of urgent importance, and it was evident that the temperature had been artificially altered from Peking. The Protestants escaped just in time to Newchwang, their property being destroyed by a mob on the 30th of June, and the Roman Catholic Cathedral being burned and sacked (July 2nd) and all its inmates roasted or butchered.

Places in which heretofore there had never been any open hostility to Occidentals were suddenly turned into hot-beds of fanatical fury against everything foreign, the people stopping at no atrocities until their purposes were

FOREIGNERS IN THE INTERIOR 607

accomplished. The passions of the Chinese appeared to be kindled, as fires are lighted by stray sparks falling in dry prairie grass, automatically and with no previous preparation of any sort. This occurred not in cities only, but in the most remote and inaccessible mountain hamlets, as well as on the crowded plains and on the Mongolian steppes. After all reasonable explanations of this fact have been offered, it must be admitted that there is a residuum of mystery in these terrible explosions, resembling those of contact mines, without perceptible antecedent causes.

The foreigners north of Mukden scattered through Manchuria were able to escape by the friendly help of the Russians to Harpin, or other places of relative security.

There had long been serious friction between the Chinese and Manchu population of Manchuria and the numerous Russian troops sent to guard the new railways. To what extent this had gone it was difficult to judge, owing to the constitutional reticence of the Russian press. The Russian Empire was suddenly electrified by the announcement that, on the 14th of July, the steamers on the Amur River had been fired upon at the Chinese town of Aigun by Chinese officers who affirmed that they were acting under orders, one Russian officer being killed and six men wounded. The next day unexpectedly and with no warning the Russian town of Blagovestchensk across the river was bombarded by a Chinese battery, three Russians being killed and six wounded.

The reprisals on the part of the Russians for this breach of faith, under the misconstrued orders from St. Petersburg, were of a terrible nature, involving the massacre of many thousand Chinese, men, women and children, whose bodies filled the Amur, as certified by the testimony of several independent and unprejudiced travellers, themselves eye-witnesses of the devastation. In the following September the British Legation in St. Petersburg called the attention of Lord Salisbury to the report in a Russian paper of a formal thanksgiving service held on the ashes of the Chinese town of Sakalin, now renamed Ilinsky, in the presence of the authorities, the army, an English officer, and a large crowd of people. The priest said: "Now is the cross raised on the bank of the Amur which yesterday was Chinese. Mouravieff foretold that sooner or later this bank would be ours." It was added that "in a beautiful speech Gen. Grisbsky congratulated the victorious troops!" In reply to the remonstrance of the British Minister to Russia, Sir Charles Scott, Count Lamsdorf explained that the Government had only just heard of this incident, and that it was an unauthorized act of the military at too great a distance from the central Government to be in touch with its views.

Meantime Russian troops were pouring into Manchuria in immense numbers, and the Russian Government was able to give the most satisfactory assurances to all the Powers in regard to her intentions to turn over Manchuria to the Chinese, as Sancho Panza definitely promised Don Quixote that he would perform the necessary self-flagellations on behalf of the Lady Dulcinea del Toboso "just as soon as ever I have a mind to do so."

Next to ordering the attack by the regular Chinese armies on the Legations, the most fatuous act of the Chinese Government in the summer of 1900 was its assault upon Russia, to the threatened dismemberment of the Chinese Empire, and the exposure of "the open door" to unknown perils in the future.

In the province of Chihli there were many Protestant

and far more numerous Roman Catholic stations, from which if the foreigners escaped at all, it was with difficulty. The sea-side resort of Pei Tai Ho, one hundred and fifty miles from Tientsin, near the Shan Hai Kuan railway, was soon isolated, and its residents were removed to a British vessel, the various establishments being promptly looted by the local villagers without the aid of Boxers or soldiers.

From T'ang Shan to Shan Hai Kuan the railway was defended by the Cantonese and others employed in the mines, and there might be seen the singular spectacle of an Imperial railway operated by the workmen for their own convenience and safety, the coal mines being likewise kept from injury, until the advent of the Russians, who impartially plundered all property public and private.

From Pao Ting Fu to Ting Chou the Lu-Han railway was kept in operation for the transport of Chinese troops.

The London Mission station of Ts'ang Chou on the Grand Canal was destroyed, but thanks to a friendly official its occupants escaped overland to a small sea-port, and thence to Taku. Those living at Hsiao Chang, farther to the southwest, another station of the same mission, fled to the village of P'ang Chuang in Shantung and thence to the coast.

It was the strange fortune of the last named mission station, after having been threatened for more than a year, to escape at last absolutely untouched and even unentered, being, with the exception of defended treaty-ports and one or two minor instances, perhaps the only case of this sort in all the vast stretch from the Yellow River to the Amur. The temper of most of the people was friendly, the reputation and influence of the hospital and dispensary wide-spread, but the rancourous fury of the Boxers thirsting for loot was held in check only by a timely agreement between one of the native pastors and a Boxer leader, by which, in consideration of a "feast" and a horse to boot, the place was not to be attacked.

The residents of Kalgan, American and Russian, escaped across the interminable deserts of Urga and Kiakhta, with great hardships and many wonderful deliverances from seemingly insurmountable perils.

The China Inland missionaries in Shun Tê Fu were for a time in great danger. They were driven out of their city, but after wandering in the mountains were escorted a part of the way to Shansi, whence they were turned back by an official just in time to save their lives, and at last found refuge in the great Cathedral at Chêng Ting Fu. Owing to the prudent and inflexible determination of the civil and military authorities not to open the city gates, this was not attacked at all. Here the Roman Catholic Bishop, three priests, five nuns, and a party of refugee Belgian railway engineers were protected until rescued by Chinese and later by the French troops about the middle of October.

The adventures of the Greens and Miss Gregg, who were at Huai Lu Hsien at the entrance to the Ku Kuan pass, were of the most terribly dramatic character, and furnish material for a small volume. They endured everything, hunger, nakedness, peril and sword, and their escape at all is a standing miracle. The fate of Dr. Taylor, Dr. and Mrs. Hodge, Mr. and Mrs. Simcox, and three children, of the American Presbyterian Mission; of Mr. Pitkin, Miss Morrill and Miss Gould, of the American Board, and of Mr. and Mrs. Bagnall and daughter, and Mr. William Cooper, of the China Inland Mission, at Pao Ting Fu was still more tragic.

CORNER OF CITY WALL, PAO TING FU, DESTROYED BY ALLIED TROOPS IN PUNISHMENT FOR MASSACRE

FOREIGNERS IN THE INTERIOR

By the connivance of the officials, civil and military, they were all killed. The former party were burned alive in their dwelling by a mob on the last day of June, and the two latter parties were shot, stabbed, or beheaded, on the first day of July.

In penalty for this great crime a mixed Military Commission sitting in that city in the following October, after full investigation recommended that the Provincial Treasurer Ting Yuan be beheaded, together with Kuei Hêng, the Tartar official of the city, and Lieut. Colonel of the cavalry camp, near the China Inland Mission, to which Mr. Bagnall and his family with Mr. Cooper fled, only to be betrayed to the Boxers and slain. This sentence was approved by Gen. Gaselee and Count von Waldersee, and was carried into execution. Several of the temples principally used by the Boxers as their headquarters were also blown up, the most important being that of the city-god, and the Ch'i Shêng An, in the southeastern part of the city, where the prisoners had been examined at the Boxer altar. All the towers of the city gates were destroyed, and the corner of the city wall was also blown away for a distance of several yards, to leave a brand upon the provincial capital which had witnessed such official crimes.

But it was in the province of Shansi and the adjacent regions of Mongolia that the most terrible fruits of the Boxer rising against foreigners were produced. This was mainly due to the presence there of the founder and patron of the Great Sword Society, Yü Hsien, so often previously referred to, who had taken his seat as Governor when the nets for extermination began to be spread.

It has already been mentioned that so rapid was the spread of the anti-foreign rising that, by the time danger had become certain, it was sometimes too late to escape.

Many of the missionaries, especially in the northern part of Shansi, were Swedes, with but an imperfect acquaintance with China, and with only infrequent communication with the coast. Others, both British and Americans, who had been long in the country, had become accustomed to being rioted, and regarded this as but one of the extended series of outbreaks of which they had had abundant experience in the past. Many of them could not make up their minds to desert their native Christians, and nobly preferred to die with them, rather than to consult their own safety only.

Friends at the ports exhausted every effort to convey information of the apparent conditions to those known to be in danger, but events moved so rapidly that it was impossible alike for those at a distance and those nearest the storm-centre to determine with certainty what it was best to do.

The danger of the missionaries, great as it was, was less than that of other foreigners unable to speak the language, and in regard to whom nothing was known by the Chinese who saw them pass. Capt. Watts Jones, a brave officer of the British Royal Engineers, was barbarously murdered west of Kalgan. Mr. Saunders, one of the members of the China Inland Mission whose party endured the most terrible sufferings before they escaped from Shansi through hostile Honan to Hankow, at one place saved his life only by proving that he was not the railway prospector who had been through the country some time previously, disturbing the repose of the Earth Dragon, spoiling the fêng-shui, and preventing rain, thus bringing on the terrible drought which was destroying the whole land.

It will be seen from an appended table that the total number of Protestant workers murdered during the whole

Boxer disturbances was one hundred and thirty-six adults, and fifty-three children, of whom more than eighty-four per cent were killed either in Shansi or the adjacent regions of Mongolia. The story of a few of these terrible experiences can be recapitulated only in the merest outline.*

On the 29th of June, the Swedish Union in association with the Christian Missionary Alliance, experienced a fearful tragedy at So P'ing Fu, in northern Shansi, when ten of its members were killed at one time. Six members of the China Inland Mission were slain at Ta T'ung Fu at about the same date. At T'ai Ku Hsien, on the 31st of July, Rev. D. H. Clapp and wife, Rev. Geo. L. Williams, Rev. F. W. Davis, Miss Rowena Bird, and Miss Mary Partridge, all of the American Board Mission, were killed, and their heads are supposed to have been sent to T'ai Yuan Fu.

There were numerous other atrocities in other cities, but nowhere anything equal to the terrible spectacle at T'ai Yuan Fu on the 9th of July, the account of which we have from an unwilling witness,—a Baptist convert whose story has been confirmed from other sources. He saw the foreign pastors and their wives and children, the Roman Catholic priests and nuns, and several Chinese Christians, taken to the Governor's yamen. Hearing that they were to be killed, he vainly endeavoured to get out of the crowd, but was borne along by it, and witnessed the massacre.

* Partial accounts of some of the experiences of the members of the largest of the Protestant Missions in China, may be found in "Martyred Missionaries of the China Inland Mission, With a Record of the Perils and Sufferings of Some who Escaped." It is a volume of more than three hundred pages, filled with tales of touching pathos, a story of which any branch of the Christian Church in any country and in any age might well be proud.

"The first to be led forth was Mr. Farthing (English Baptist). His wife clung to him, but he gently put her aside, and going in front of the soldiers knelt down without saying a word, and his head was struck off by one blow of the executioner's knife. He was quickly followed by Mr. Hoddle, and Mr. Beynon, Drs. Lovitt and Wilson, each of whom was beheaded by one blow of the executioner. Then the Governor, Yü Hsien, grew impatient and told his body-guard, all of whom carried heavy swords with long handles, to help kill the others. Mr. Stokes, Mr. Simpson, and Mr. Whitehouse were next killed, the last by one blow only, the other two by several.

"When the men were finished the ladies were taken. Mrs. Farthing had hold of the hands of her children who clung to her, but the soldiers parted them, and with one blow beheaded their mother. The executioner beheaded all the children and did it skillfully, needing only one blow, but the soldiers were clumsy, and some of the ladies suffered several cuts before death. Mrs. Lovitt was wearing her spectacles and held the hand of her little boy, even when she was killed. She spoke to the people, saying 'We all came to China to bring you the good news of the salvation by Jesus Christ; we have done you no harm, only good, why do you treat us so?' A soldier took off her spectacles before beheading her, which needed two blows.

"When the Protestants had been killed, the Roman Catholics were led forward. The Bishop, an old man with a long white beard, asked the Governor why he was doing this wicked deed. I did not hear the Governor give him any answer, but he drew his sword and cut the Bishop across the face one heavy stroke; blood poured down his white beard, and he was beheaded.

"The priests and nuns quickly followed him in death.

Then Mr. Pigott and his party were led from the district jail which is close by. He was still hand-cuffed, and so was Mr. Robinson. He preached to the people till the very last, when he was beheaded with one blow. Mr. Robinson suffered death very calmly. Mrs. Pigott held the hand of her son, even when she was beheaded, and he was killed immediately after her. The ladies and two girls were also quickly killed.

" On that day forty-five foreigners were beheaded in all, thirty-three Protestants and twelve Roman Catholics. A number of native Christians were killed also. The bodies of all were left where they fell till the next morning, as it was evening before the work was finished. During the night they had been stripped of their clothing, rings, and watches. The next day they were removed to a place inside the great south gate, except some of the heads, which were placed in cages on the gates of the city wall. All were surprised at the firmness and quietness of the foreigners, none of whom except two or three of the children cried, or made any noise."

Yü Hsien was Governor of Shansi for but a few months, yet such was the fatal spell thrown over the people of that hitherto friendly province by the known approbation of the Imperial Court, that when he left the city he was escorted by thousands of the people, who had prepared wine and refreshments along the road-side for miles, his " boots of honour " were taken off and hung in the city gate to commemorate his virtues, and as if this were insufficient, a stone tablet was erected in the south suburb to glorify his achievements in clearing the province of the hated foreigners.

It was almost universally recognized at the entry of the foreign forces into northern China that the honour of the five countries represented among those officially butchered at this time (Great Britain, the United States, France, Italy, and Holland) as well as the safety of all future residents of Shansi, required that an indelible brand should be affixed to T'ai Yuan Fu, as was done at Pao Ting Fu, and that the yamen of the Governor ought to be destroyed. But in the pressure of other military expeditions all over northern Chihli, this one was omitted, to the extreme surprise of the Chinese, and later to the unalterable conviction on the part of the population of Shansi that their province was totally inaccessible to foreign troops.

Four different parties from the southern portion of Shansi succeeded after terrible sufferings in making their way to Hankow, but some of them died of ill treatment or exhaustion. So far as known it appears that in this part of the province, while nineteen escaped, thirty-five adults and ten children were killed, or died.

One of the most pathetic instances of all was that of a company of ten, composed of Mr. and Mrs. Atwater and two children, Mr. and Mrs. C. W. Price, and daughter, of the American Board Mission, with Mr. and Mrs. Lundgren and Miss Eldred of the China Inland Mission, who were betrayed by the officials of Fên Chou Fu, taken on a pretended journey to the coast, and then killed at the junction of two counties, their bodies being tumbled into a pit near by at the request of the villagers.

While this tragedy was being enacted in this distant province, American cannon were already shelling the Forbidden City in Peking, but it was too late to save the lives of this and other beleaguered bands, some of the members of which were killed more than a month after that event.

The stories of the tragedies connected with those who at last escaped from their tormentors, yet so as by fire, are among the most touching memorials of the Christian Church in any age. Men, women and children were besieged in their own dwellings, and when these had been fired, were speared or stabbed as they endeavoured to escape, or were thrust back into the flames. They were driven forth from their homes as outcasts unfit to live, robbed of their scanty possessions at every turn, until in the blistering heats of June, July and August, they were bareheaded, bare-footed, and in many cases possessed of only the clothing upon their bodies. In repeated instances ladies were left but a single garment, and on more than one occasion a missionary was deprived of every stitch of clothing, standing naked upon the streets of the inhospitable villages of Shansi. One Catholic priest escaped only by being carried a long distance in a coffin.

They were continually not only under that observation without sympathy which Mrs. Browning called torture, but were everywhere, for days and weeks in succession, confronted by mobs, chased from village to village, into mountains, and swamps, obliged to take refuge in abandoned huts, in grave-yards, and often in caves of the earth. They were hunted by armed bands like wild beasts, and when caught were beaten, dragged on the ground,—one of the ladies being purposely run over by a cart to kill her—were tied hand and foot, and carried to Boxer altars that it might be decided by the spirits when, where, and how they should be murdered. Sometimes they were saved because the villagers were afraid to have them killed in their village, sometimes by a timely fall of rain, and again by the instinctive pity of Chinese for the poor suffering children and the agony of their mothers.

Repeated efforts were made to poison them, they were often almost starved, and compelled to subsist on roots and leaves. Some of them were delirious from uncared for wounds, and all were subjected to the continued nervous strain of incessant alarms by day and by night. They were the victims of repeated and deliberate treachery on the part of officials, soldiers, and professed guides. Yet amid the almost all pervading gloom some act of human kindness would lighten their sky. Some officials were most friendly, and would have been still more so had they dared. One such was degraded by the Empress Dowager when she traversed Shansi, for no other reason than his kindness to the destitute foreigners passing through his jurisdiction. In some cases members of the same family were not allowed to see or to care for each other, although almost at the point of death. Is it any wonder that one who escaped remarked that the text most frequently recurring was that which declared that " the tender mercies of the wicked are cruel?"

Who were these that were thus entreated? They were earnest God-fearing men and women who had left all to obey the command of their Master to make known the glad tidings of the Kingdom of Heaven; men and women of irreproachable character and blameless lives; some of them graduates of the best colleges and universities, to whom attractive careers had been opened in the home lands, but upon which they had turned their backs. Many of them had given long years of toil to the relieving of Chinese suffering in dispensary and hospital work.

Many months later the last letters of some who were killed were brought out of their concealment by faithful Christian friends. There is in these missives no note of despair, only the solemnity of those face to face with a terrible death. One father leaves as a legacy to his son the hope that when he shall be twenty-five years of age he may return to China and take up the work which the father could not do.

As long as the Church of God survives upon the earth, the record of the lives and of the deaths of these martyrs will be a precious heritage.

That so many parties, travelling under the conditions which have been imperfectly hinted at, should have passed through hundreds of miles of hostile territory, been seen by hundreds of thousands, and in the aggregate by millions of enemies, many of whom were eager for their death, and yet have escaped to tell their story, is a moral miracle to be accounted for only by the recognition of the restraining hand of God.

The great disproportion between the number of the Roman Catholics killed and that of the Protestants, appears to be due to the greater size of the Roman Catholic flocks, and to the circumstances that in numberless cases they had extensive establishments which they defended with earth ramparts, deep ditches, and rifles or even foreign machine guns. The number of such places successfully defended is at present unknown, but is certainly not a small one, and thus far we happen to have heard of but two instances where these defences failed.

No more illustrious examples of martyrdom can be found than some of those of the Roman Catholic faith. Bishop Hamer of the West Mongolian Mission, nearly thirty-five years in China, was seized while celebrating mass, bound, and marched through the city to be mocked by all that saw him. His hands were cut off while he was counting his beads, and three days later his garments were torn off, he was wrapped in cotton upon which petroleum was poured, and was burned alive. Five thousand Christians were killed, and every church and building in his diocese was destroyed.

In the Jeho district, Father Segers was tied by his hands and feet and carried by a pole, not allowed to speak to his converts, but thrown into a ditch, where he was buried alive. Once he contrived to stand up and his head became visible, when he was struck on the head with a mattock.

Surely if anything is to be learned from the teachings of history, if the saying of Tertullian that the blood of the martyrs is the seed of the Church is a law of unwasting and perennial energy, and if the promises of God are still secure, a religion which has done so much for China, and the heralds of which have suffered so much from the Chinese, has a great work yet to do in the regeneration of that Empire.

MAP OF
SEAT OF BOXER DISTURBANCE
To accompany
CHINA IN CONVULSION
By ARTHUR H. SMITH
SCALE OF MILES

Copyright 1901, Fleming H. Revell Company.
ENGRAVED BY BORMAY & CO., N.Y.

XXXIII

NOTABLE EXPERIENCES

*Canadian Presbyterian Mission, North Honan.**

The trouble which began in Honan during the spring seemed to be local in character, originating in the severe drought from which we had been suffering. Three crops in succession had failed. As early as March there were riots in different places. Some of these were of a serious nature, in which there were conflicts between the people and soldiers, lives being lost on both sides. By the month of June matters became very serious indeed, every day bringing fresh reports of granaries searched and wealthy farmers looted by bands of starving men. The Magistrates stationed small posts of militia at all the market towns, but were unable to preserve peace. They acknowledged their helplessness by refusing to punish any who were accused of stealing grain, saying it was useless to punish starving men, and that those who had lost grain might look upon it as having afforded help to their distressed neighbours.

On June 15th we were startled to receive a telegram from Tientsin saying " Escape south." We also got the news of the murder of two Belgians at Pao Ting Fu. Not having had any reliable news from Tientsin for several weeks, we were ignorant of what was happening there and did not feel like deserting our station without

---

* Prepared at the author's request by the Rev. James A. Slimmon, one of the party.

knowing the reason why we had been advised to do so. We waited on anxiously looking for letters but none came.

Meanwhile we communicated with Mr. Jameson and party of the Peking Syndicate, who had passed through our town on the way to Huai Ch'ing Fu. In reply there came a letter from Mr. C. D. Jameson, saying that he saw no reason for escaping, as he had not had any word from his agent at Tientsin or Peking; and he could rely on their sending word if matters were very serious. But for our comfort he added that if we thought it necessary to go he would place everything he had at our disposal,— arms, money, etc., and the personal services of himself and Messrs. Reid and Fisher.

On June 19th we received word that our friends at Ch'u Wang were besieged by a mob of over a thousand people. This trouble was brought on by a woman who declared she had seen Mrs. MacKenzie at an upper window performing mysterious rites and sweeping the clouds from the sky. Mrs. MacKenzie had been cleaning a window in her new house, and this seen from the outside looked like making passes and motions towards the clouds. The mob gathered round for two or three days, but seemed to be in need of a leader. The official on being appealed to for help promised to send it, but first of all tried to disarm our friends by asking for a loan of any rifles or other arms in their possession. This ingenuous request was politely refused as was also one for a few thousand taels of silver " to purchase arms for the soldiers."

From this time on till the 24th, things began to look more and more threatening. Our bankers refused to pay us any more money, although they had a considerable balance in our favour. We heard of Boxer societies springing up in different towns and gradually coming nearer us, until on the 24th a few Boxer teachers arrived and founded a Boxer school. The motto of this branch was "First kill the foreigners, then annihilate the Manchus."

On June 25th we received word that our friends at Chang Tê Fu and Ch'u Wang had decided to make their escape, and that they were arranging to travel together to Chi Nan Fu, which seemed the best route. Later on they had to abandon this plan, as they found it impossible to hire carts for the trip, could get no escort across the strip of Chihli Province which lies between Honan and Shantung, and had no means of speedy communication with the Governor of Shantung. Our friends had decided on this step because of another telegram which had arrived, saying that the Taku Forts had been taken by the Allied Forces. We knew then that trouble was certain. We sent off messengers, one to ask Mr. Jameson and party to meet us at the Yellow River, another to the Prefect at Wei Hui Fu, and another to the Magistrate at Hsü Hsien. We were afraid of delay in being referred from one Yamen to the other.

We got no help from the Prefect. An escort however was promised by the District Magistrate, and friendly messages were returned. But he refused to take charge of our house, saying that in the present state he could not possibly guarantee protection of our property.

Things were at their very darkest on the 27th. We had got together the few things that we had decided to take with us, but it looked as if we should require to make our escape in the dark, taking no more with us than we might be able to carry ourselves. The carters who had agreed to take us had backed out of their bargains and would not come near us, though we offered four or five times the usual rates. Our servants were panic-stricken, as we heard of one band of desperate characters planning to attack us before we left our premises; and of another band at the other end of the town, formed for the purpose of attacking us after we left.

There was no sleep for us that night; indeed there had not been much for several nights; but this particular one was passed in trying to put courage into our servants, and in spurring on the few friends we had in the town to take active measures on our behalf. We induced one man—our teacher (a literary graduate),—to interview the leaders of one band, and by reasoning, expostulating and threatening, to persuade them to let us go in peace. Another friend performed the same office with the other band. But the argument that weighed most with both was that we had failed to secure carts, and could carry nothing away with us.

Daybreak of the 28th arrived and while we welcomed it as a relief from the terror of the night, we dreaded it as the day on which we should have to set out on our journey without having been able to make proper arrangements for transport. We had sent a messenger to a neighbouring town to secure carts there at any cost, and as he had not yet returned we feared he had failed in his mission. To our great relief, he turned up with four carts while we were pretending to take breakfast. It did not take us long to get our boxes and bedding on board.

And here one of those incidents occurred that force us to believe in a special providence. Just as we were almost ready to mount our carts and face the mob that had gathered around our door, the officer in command of the Militia in our town returned from an expedition against some robbers, bringing prisoners with him. At our request he called on us and we persuaded him to send some of his men to escort us a few miles on our way. This nonplussed the mob who got the impression that the officer had come by arrangement for our special protection. And the fact that he had prisoners with him proved to the rowdies that he did not hold his office in vain.

The whole town was gathered together to see us off, and lined the streets three and four deep on both sides all the way from our house to the town gates; but all passed off quietly and a few miles out our special escort left us to the care of four men who had been provided by our Magistrate. We made our first halt at Wei Hai Fu, and at once sent our cards to both civil and military officials, also to Father Gerrard, who called on us in the course of the evening. We explained the situation to the priest, and invited him to join our party. He replied that he had not power to do so without permission from his bishop, and if the bishop concluded that it was not safe for the priests to remain at their posts, they would all retire to a place already prepared among the hills, where all their converts were armed and could hold out against an army.

The military official arrived just in time to disperse the mob that had gathered round the door of the inn, and was getting beyond the control of our escort. The local soldiers dispersed them and we had peace for the rest of the night. Next day we halted at Hsin Hsiang Hsien for our midday meal. I was well known at this place, and put up at the inn of a man who had been friendly for some years. We had been there about an hour when this innkeeper told us that some Boxers had arrived in the town a day or two before and that some of them had just come to him making inquiries about us, our destination, etc.

We at once sent our card to the official to inform him and ask for protection. The only result was that we were told that the official was not at home, and that our informant was at once sent for by the Yamen people and told to get rid of us at once. We started off fully expecting to be pursued by the Boxers, but reached our inn at night without having heard anything more of them, and from there on "Boxers" seemed to be an unknown term.

Next day, 30th, we reached Yuan Wu Hsien, quite close to the ferry on the Yellow River, where we were to meet Mr. Jameson and party. The official here at once put a strong guard at the door of our inn and thus secured perfect quietness for us inside.

In the evening we were much relieved by the arrival of a mounted messenger from Mr. Jameson, bringing word that he and his party were coming with a large escort, plenty of silver and a few fire-arms.

Next day, Sunday, 1st July, we got to the bank of the Yellow River first and waited two hours for Mr. Jameson. When they arrived we found them dressed in Chinese costume. They had found the people at Wu Chih Hsien—their last halting place—very rude. The Magistrate not only declared he could not protect them unless they put on Chinese clothing, but made them give up much of their luggage. The clothing not only failed as a disguise but seemed to emphasize the fact that they were refugees, and must have been meant by the officials to humiliate them or else as a practical joke, for they certainly looked awkward and clumsy.

Just as we got to the south bank of the river, we saw the Chang Te Fu and Ch'u Wang party arrive on the north bank, so we waited till they came across. We were now a large company—made up as follows: Ch'u Wang party,

Mr. and Mrs. MacKenzie and one child, Dr. and Mrs. Leslie, Misses McIntosh and Dow; Chang Te Fu party, Mr. and Mrs. Goforth and three children, Miss Pyke and Miss Dr. Wallace, Messrs. Griffith and Hood; Hsin Chên party, Mr. and Mrs. Mitchell, Mr. and Mrs. Slimmon and one child; Peking Syndicate party, Messrs. Jameson, Reid and Fisher. The missionaries had only a small escort, but Mr. Jameson's party had a fine escort of mounted men, and a petty court officer who was very useful in making arrangements with officials by the way, about local escorts, inns, etc. Having now the Yellow River between us and the Boxers, we got off bright and early next morning, all in good spirits, with the exception of Mrs. Slimmon, who was beginning to be anxious about her baby, who showed signs of breaking down under the strain of the journey.

Mr. Jameson was inspired with a happy thought this morning and sent a man off on horseback to dispatch a telegram from K'ai Fêng Fu to the British and American Consuls at Hankow, informing them of our whereabouts and asking that help be sent. The messenger had seventy miles to go, seventy miles back, and then to catch up with a party travelling thirty-five miles a day. It was a great undertaking, but Mr. Jameson was not a man to be daunted by difficulties and the feat was accomplished at the expense of the plucky little pony, that died after reaching Fan Ch'êng. The sending of the telegram proved to have been a wise proceeding, as it conveyed to our friends the first intimation that we were alive, and also enabled our Consuls to get Chang Chih Tung to send us much needed help.

The next two days we suffered much from heat, as we were travelling through the loess region. The sun blazing down into the deep roads made them like ovens, and the roads being thirty or forty feet below the level of the country there was no possibility of getting any breeze. On reaching Hsiang Hsien we found Mr. and Mrs. Gracie living in seeming peace and quietness. They were surprised to learn that we were fleeing for our lives and invited Mrs. Slimmon and myself to stay with them for a while, and give our little one a chance to recover. She was by this time very ill indeed and we were sorely tempted to run the risks and accept the invitation. But at midnight Mr. Gracie came to our inn and told us that the converts and friends had strongly advised them to join our party, which they decided to do and would have done, but found it impossible to secure carts. They expected to be able to do so in the course of the day and try to overtake us. Subsequently we learned that they made their escape by way of Chou Chia K'ou to the province of Anhui, having most harrowing experiences by the way.

We were now approaching the Nan Yang Fu district, the only place where we really anticipated any trouble, and our fears proved to be only too well grounded. On the 7th July we arrived at Hsin Tien, thirty li north of Nan Yang city. We had intended halting there for the night, but on our arrival we found it impossible to get accommodations for the whole party. Mr. Jameson, with his usual thoughtfulness for the ladies and children, decided to push on to Nan Yang city, well knowing that it was a most dangerous place at which to halt.

And just here I would like to say that Mr. Jameson and his party nobly fulfilled the promise that they personally, and all they had, would be at our disposal. They not only gave us the best rooms at the inns when there was any choice, but shared their stores with us, giving up their last tins of milk when they learned that our friends

NOTABLE EXPERIENCES 629

had exhausted their own supply. They let us have all the silver we needed, and without this help it would have been impossible for us to get along. Mr. Jameson also proved himself to be a born leader. It was a great relief to leave everything in his hands, knowing that there was no detail of arrangements, such as interviewing Mandarins, getting the daily local escort, securing inns, and the hundred and one little things incidental to such a journey, but were in most capable hands. He never seemed worried or anxious, but had a cheery word of encouragement for each one as he went his daily rounds.

On leaving Yu Chou at daybreak Mr. Goforth's servant took the wrong road and later the other parties got separated from us and went by a different way. This took the large company of ladies and children safely past a procession of rain dancers that we ran into in one of the towns *en route.* Mr. Jameson and his friends were on horseback five hundred yards ahead of our carts, and suddenly found themselves surrounded by an armed body of men two hundred strong, followed by a huge rabble. The rain dancers wore green wreaths on their heads, and were armed with huge swords, being on a pilgrimage to a famous temple to pray for rain. Catching sight of the foreigners they at once surrounded them, crying out " Here are the foreign devils that have chased away the rain." One of the leaders suggested killing them at once, and our friends had a bad ten minutes persuading the crowd that it would be a dangerous thing to try. Meanwhile we came to the fringe of the crowd, and learning that it was a rain procession, we did not stay to make further inquiries but turned hastily up the first lane, which proved to be a *cul de sac,* and our carts stood there with their backs toward the main street effectually screening us from the mob, who passed by quite unaware of the fact that there were foreign women in their midst. Upon getting through the town we found Mr. Jameson and friends filled with the gravest apprehensions for our safety.

We arrived at Nan Yang Fu after dark, and searching the city for quarters had finally to separate and put up in miserably poor inns, but this turned out to our advantage. We approached our inns from the south, thus throwing those off the scent who were expecting us from the north. On trying to see the official we were told he would see us at eight o'clock next morning. This looked ominous. At midnight a messenger arrived from the party at Hsin Tien, saying they were besieged in their inn, and asking for help. We tried to see the Mandarin to get help for our friends, but only succeeded in getting a promise that some runners would be dispatched to put down the disturbance. Mr. Jameson, seeing that it was useless to expect help from the Mandarins, sent back half of his mounted escort.

Some of our servants told us that the Roman Catholics had been besieged in their fortified place four miles away, and that a soldier had been beheaded by the officials, because he had carried out their orders too literally, and in trying to disperse the besiegers had injured one of them; we also learned that plans had been made to kill the whole of our party, and it was for this reason that we had been told to wait till eight o'clock next morning.

Realizing our danger, we at once got our tired animals hitched up again, and got off at three o'clock and travelled to Hsin Yeh Hsien; here some of the mounted men who had been sent back to Hsin Tien to help our friends turned up, and told us what had been taking place. Our friends had been in negotiation with their besiegers, who were demanding a large sum of money. They waited on in their inn till eight o'clock, hoping that assistance would come from us, then despairing of that hope they left their inn, and were surprised to find the town so quiet.

The sigh of relief they gave on reaching the town gate was turned into a gasp of dismay as they passed through and found a mob of several thousand people waiting for them outside. A band of two hundred men lining the road waited till the last cart had passed out of the town and then made a sudden attack on our friends, who jumped off the carts and tried to frighten them off by firing a few revolver shots over their heads. Mrs. Leslie, who was completely prostrated by the fatigue of the journey, was unable to get off her cart, and it was in trying to shield her that Dr. Leslie was seriously injured. Besides a large number of flesh wounds he had his right wrist and right leg cut through to the bone, the large sinews in each case being severed. Mr. Goforth also received bad sword cuts on the head, and two of Mr. Jameson's men who fought bravely received severe wounds, which later proved to be fatal. When our friends got clear of the carts, the mob began at once to break open the boxes and the sight of the loot turned the armed band from their design, thus enabling our friends to make good their escape.

In the course of the day they all found their way back to the main road, managed to get the empty carts, and proceeded on their journey, having lost everything, but thankful to have escaped alive. At daybreak next morning the servant who had lost his way rejoined us. He belonged to Mr. Goforth, so we gave him a shoe of silver and sent him back to meet his party.

We pushed on towards Fan Ch'êng and about midday reached the border of Hupei province to find a fine body of soldiers sent out to meet us from Hsiang Yang Fu, by order of Chang Chih Tung. Our hearts went up in thanksgiving as we realized that here was real and adequate help, and that consequently our dangers were over. Arriving at Fan Ch'êng we found that every provision had been made for our safety and comfort. We waited here for our friends, who arrived on the night of the 10th, in a sad plight indeed, poor Dr. Leslie especially being in a bad case, having had to lie in the bottom of his cart for three days without having his wounds attended to since they had received the first rough dressing by Dr. Jennie Dow, who tore up one of her remaining garments to make bandages for him.

We spent all of the next day providing them with an outfit. Mr. Jameson and his friends were able to supply the gentlemen with underclothing, etc., while the ladies had to be content with a Chinese wardrobe. Our sweet little Eleanore died on the 11th, just nine months old, and while our hearts felt too sore for words, we were so thankful that she had lived until reaching Fan Ch'êng, as we were able to take the body on from there and have it buried in the English cemetery at Hankow.

We travelled down the Han River to that port, and two days out from there were met by a steam-launch sent out by the American Consul to bring us in.

Arriving at Hankow on the 21st we went directly on board a steamer for Shanghai, having been twenty-four days on our journey.

English Baptist Mission, Shansi.

Upon the entrance of Yü Hsien into Shansi as Governor, the Boxers spread rapidly throughout the province. Communication with the coast was cut off in May, so that money supplies were not received. About June 21st Mr. Farthing wrote from T'ai Yuan Fu to Mr. Dixon, at Hsin Chou, that it was known that a telegram had come from the Empress Dowager to destroy all foreigners, and added " If true, I am ready and do not fear; if such be God's will I can even rejoice to die." On reading this, Mr. Dixon said to Mr. Chao, his evangelist, " I feel just the same!"

In the city of Hsin Chou, from June 23-25th, near the mission premises, theatrical performances were given to the god of wealth. A great crowd were present and a clamouring mob formed at the mission gate. Appeal was made to the Magistrate who at first promised a guard, but it failed to appear.

By this time the Edict telegraphed from Peking had become known, as when another request was made, with threat of reporting to the Governor if not granted, the Magistrate replied, " Tell the foreigner he can report to the Emperor if he likes and I shall not fear!"

Reports from country stations of violence of Boxers towards native Christians led to sending a messenger to T'ai Yuan with a letter of consultation to Mr. Farthing. On reaching T'ai Yuan the messenger found some of the missions already destroyed and all abandoned. He hastened back and reported the circumstances. Mr. Dixon comprehended the growing danger, called the mission together and after consultation decided upon flight. There were eight in their party.

Taking food, clothing, and bedding, with some money, they set out in the early morning and travelled thirty li where they rested for a time. While at this point they learned that two hours after they left their homes a proclamation from the Governor had come for the local officials to destroy the foreigners' houses and kill the foreigners. On hearing this they decided to move on at once to the place of hiding which they had chosen.

After leaving the village Mr. Dixon dismissed the faithful evangelist Mr. Chao, who was only persuaded to leave them on the consideration that he might get word to foreign friends and perhaps secure help. It was a sorrowful parting, but in it shone forth the brave spirit of those who were soon to lay down their lives. Mr. Dixon said " If we are all killed and not one escapes there are many more to take our place." Mrs. Dixon spoke of her four children who were to lose a mother's care, but said, " God will surely raise up friends for them."

This same evangelist returned to Shansi in October and learned the rest of the story of this company.

On the evening of that day they reached the village of Liu Chia Shan where the one Christian of the place had his home in a cave, and where they expected to prepare a cave for themselves as a place of refuge and defence.

They lived in this place for twenty days unmolested, when their place of hiding became known to the Boxers who sent a company to arrest them. The villagers fled and the band could not effect their arrest. A few days later a deputy with soldiers went to them and with promises of a safe escort to the coast induced them to return to Hsin Chou. By this time their food supply was exhausted, and they had been five days without food.

On arriving at Hsin Chou they were taken to the yamen. The Magistrate asked how much money they had in the bank, and when told drew it all out and kept it himself.

The missionaries were placed in the common jail where they were kept for sixteen days, receiving only the poorest prison fare. On Aug. 7th, a deputy from Yü Hsien came to see that the Governor's will was carried out.

Two days later they were taken from prison, placed in

four carts and told they were to be taken to the coast. Arriving at the east gate of the city the missionaries were dragged from their carts and stripped of all their clothes. Then both Boxers and soldiers set upon them and literally hacked their heads to pieces. Their bodies were dragged outside the city and left on the banks of a river where they were shamefully treated by villagers near by. Later the head of the literary graduates of the city, who had been friendly to Mr. Dixon, bought mats in which to wrap the bodies and hired men to bury them at the foot of the city wall.

After the massacre the highest military official went to the mission houses, chose the articles which he wanted for himself, and then turned the houses over to the soldiers and the people to loot.

*China Inland Mission, Honan.**

The long continued drought in Honan had produced a restless feeling among the people and made them ripe for mobs and riots. Warning had been sent by missionaries fleeing from the north that it would be better for us at Shê Ch'i Tien to escape at once.

Sunday, July 8th, a large crowd gathered at the close of the service, watching the Christians as they scattered, and although it was dispersed without an outbreak it became evident that we must hasten our preparations for leaving.

The next morning at an early hour the streets were again packed with a mob, evidently intent on mischief. We could not go into the streets, but our boxes were taken over a wall into a neighbour's yard, and we all followed by means of a ladder. Soon after this the mob

* Dr. G. W. Guinness and party.

were battering on our front door. Our teacher, who was pale with apprehension, said "I fear worse than death may happen to you!" The landlord of that house led us to his guest-hall in one corner of which was a ladder leading to a loft. He bade us "go up quickly and keep still!"

There we lay hid, listening to the shouts of the mob and soon to the crash of falling timbers and masonry. The rioting had begun in earnest. The heat was intense and in a little time we heard the crackling of flames, and saw the smoke of our burning homes. Suddenly there were a rush! The mob had traced us over the wall and into the room beneath, where every sound was heard by us. "Kill the foreigners! They must be here! Let us go up the ladder!"

After brisk altercation they were dissuaded from doing so and went away only to return again and again. They got on the roof and stared in through the five windows but we stood between the windows, flat against the wall. Once two boys caught sight of us and spread the news. Back came the crowd but again were bluffed off by the landlord.

So passed the day from 7 A. M. till 8 P. M. when darkness brought relief. One of the ladies had been seriously ill and was very weak. Her month old babe might cry and reveal our whereabouts, when all would be lost. We prayed in silence and the Lord heard and kept the child quiet from dawn till dark. A pot of tea was passed up and then the wearied mother could quench her thirst.

Then the landlord came and said "Don't delay! Follow me!" We descended the ladder, crossed the court and entered a room where grain was stored. A stool was placed on a great basket of grain, from this we clambered through a trap-door to a loft above. The stool was removed, the door shut and all trace of our whereabouts was gone. The room was full of dust and rubbish, but it gave us a safe refuge for four long days.

That first night we left the loft to go to another house where carts were to take us away when the police again appeared at the front gate to search the house. Back we hastened up the ladder and their search was again futile. The next morning rioters came and finished the work of demolishing our house. All day their yells and blows on the house sounded in our ears. Towards night I heard two men piling timbers near our hiding place to burn us out, but they did not fire the house.

Every night new plans for escape were discussed. Every day fresh bands of searchers came to hunt for us. At midday of Thursday our landlord suddenly appeared and said " Fly! they have come with swords to kill you!" In two minutes all had dropped through the trap-door and scaled the wall into the garden of our ruined home and were standing in the blazing sun. Soon a man followed us over the wall, failed to see us, and called back " They are not here!" We were soon safely back in our loft again.

That night came rain and with it a chance to escape to a large business firm, where we were hidden in the strong room in the top of the house. The room was small and dark with one window eighteen inches high. Here we stayed twelve days, guarded by a member of the firm who was armed with gun and sword and sharp, heavy iron pins for throwing.

In the early morning of our last day carts were brought, in which we made our way out of the city and eight *li* down the river where a small boat was in waiting with four men for escort. The boat was searched by customs officials at different barriers twelve times or more, but we were not discovered.

We and our escort lived in the one small cabin thirteen days until we reached Hankow in safety. We paid our escort their well-earned reward and dismissed them. We were ragged and dirty, and in clothing that we had lived in for a month, but we were thankful to have been brought safely through our perils by One who "never forsakes those who trust in Him."

China Inland Mission, Shansi.*

Mr. and Mrs. Ogren had been stationed at Yung Ning in the western part of Shansi only a year. The officials were very friendly, one of them having asked Mr. Ogren privately the right way to pray for rain, as his own prayer had been unavailing. The people had become restless and threatening because of the long drought.

In the middle of June the Boxers came to the city. They rapidly made recruits and soon a guard was sent to protect the mission from them. The official advised Mr. Ogren to take his family away. Their servants began to forsake them.

One day a man went through the streets beating a gong and warning the people away from the wells which the foreigners had poisoned. That day the main spring of the city turned red. The official dared not let Mr. Ogren longer visit him but sent his Secretary by night to consult with them. They at last asked the official to furnish them with funds for their journey, their own supply from the coast being cut off. This he was ready to do; also to take charge of their house.

* Story of Mr. and Mrs. Ogren.

That night while packing, a spy was discovered in a tree of the court watching them. Before daylight the morning of July 13th Mr. and Mrs. Ogren and their little child started in a litter for the Yellow River eighty li away, to go to Hankow. They were provided with a guard, and also with an order from the Magistrate to the official at the river bank to hire a boat for them. On arriving at the river there was a hostile demonstration by the crowd but the official saw them safely off in person. Two soldiers went with them on the boat.

The current was very swift and their frail craft was in constant danger of being wrecked. They went five hundred li, half-way to Tung Kuan, the corner of the province where Shansi, Shensi and Hanan join. At this half-way place they were told that a party of foreigners had been murdered and their bodies thrown into the river only a few days before, and it was probable that this would be their fate if they continued down the river.

They decided to get across the river into Shensi, and soon came to a place where there was an official eighty years old who knew the Yung Ning official and showed them great kindness. He had a farm across the river in Shansi and offered to send them there and let them have food, while they could hide in caves nearby till peace came. While with this old official, a party of soldiers came saying they were sent to drive the foreigners out of the province. Their host gave the soldiers a feast and persuaded them to go away. He soon sent the refugees on their way, with servants to escort them across the river.

It was only ten li distant, but before going half that distance they were set upon by robbers who took all their money, except one hundred cash, and most of their clothing. Reaching the ferry they crossed in the early morning but waited four days to send back to the old official for money. This came and they walked on towards the farm, going slowly, carrying their child. The next day they reached the farm but were not kindly received by the tenants. At first they refused them food but later gave a scanty supply. They were twice visited by robbers, and at last were threatened by the farmer's son, who coveted the hundred taels offered by Yü Hsien for every foreigner's head.

This led them to leave their hiding-place and make their way northward again to return to Yung Ning. The road was very rough, the country sparsely inhabited, but many people were kind, so they could at least get one meal a day and places to sleep.

After several days they came to a branch of the Yellow River which they must ford on foot. An old man led the way through the swift current, and also let them rest at his place that night and the next day. The day after, when nearing a customs barrier, they were set upon by a crowd and later followed by a customs guard who had been ordered to get them out of Shensi. This guard several times seemed on the point of killing them, but finally went with them across the river and then handed them over to the Boxers.

The next morning Mr. Ogren was taken to the Boxer General. Mrs. Ogren could hear his voice for a time pleading for his life, then the sound of the incantations inquiring if their lives were to be spared, then followed a great uproar which she thought to be his death.

Later a man came to take her on, telling her she and her husband were to be sent on to Yung Ning, but she did not believe that the latter was still living. She spent that night in a cave. In the morning while going on they met a Boxer band and her guide disappeared.

The Boxers rushed at her as if about to kill her, but only ordered her to get away, which she did rapidly.

In the afternoon she stopped under the shade of a tree where many women gathered around her. They were very kind and pitiful and gave food for herself and babe. At night she learned that there were Christians across the river. She forded it, being nearly swept away, and then found no friends, only enemies who would only give her water and left her and the child to sleep under the open sky. In the night two Christians stole to her side and led her to a cave, but could do no more for her because of the Boxers.

In the morning she re-crossed the river but was soon seen by Boxers who with drawn swords drove her to a temple. The head-man of the village came out and rescued her, giving her food and some stockings; the next day he sent her on to Ta Ning under guard. The Boxers followed full of fury and were with difficulty restrained from falling upon her. Arriving at Ta Ning she was taken to the common prison. Food and fruit and some money were passed to her through a hole in the door. The keepers were quite kind.

The next morning she was taken to the Magistrate, and made to kneel while she told her story. He became kindly in manner and said her husband was still living and would rejoin her later. She was then led to an inner court where the official's wife wanted to see her. The lady came out on a balcony and threw one hundred cash to her. That night in the midst of the night she heard her husband's voice calling her. She found him speaking through a hole in the door. The next morning they were taken to a comfortable room in the yamen where she was able to dress his wounds, cook some food for him and hear the story of his escape.

When taken to the Boxer General he had first been upbraided for destroying the people with his doctrine and was then given up to the crowd of Boxers. They kicked and beat him cruelly, taunting him with "Pray to your Jesus now!"

They led him to the bank of the river to kill him and there fell on him with spears and swords. Being clumsy with their weapons they inflicted no fatal wounds. He finally jumped into the river and although his hands were bound he struggled across and escaped in the darkness. The next day a Christian farmer helped him with food and money. Learning that his wife was at Ta Ning he worked his way on to that city avoiding notice and evading Boxers until just as he entered the city, when he was chased to the yamen where the official sheltered him. His wounds were severe, on head and neck and shoulders, from sword and spear.

By this time it was the last of August. After two days two donkeys with wooden pack-saddles were furnished them and they were sent on to P'u Hsien. They were attacked by Boxers, but their guard fought them off. From that place they were to have gone on to P'ing Yang, but orders came to send them back to Ta Ning.

This journey was made in great pain and discomfort, no food being given them. Her husband fell into the water when fording a stream, but they at last reached the city. They were again put in prison and given food. At this time the little one grew very ill, but a man brought a cow and they got milk. The vermin in the filthy prison were terrible, and Mr. Ogren grew ill with fever. Their only comfort was prayer.

Here they lived on till early in October, when deliverance came. Orders arrived to suppress the Boxers and send the foreigners to P'ing Yang to be forwarded to the coast. They went part of the way in chairs and part way in mule litters, being forwarded from stage to stage by the officials.

Arriving at P'ing Yang they were most politely received by the officials and sent to a former mission house. It was nearly all in ruins but there were two rooms that could be used. After a few days Mr. Ogren grew worse and died October 15th. The Chinese were kind and assisted in giving burial. Not a few surviving Christians came to sympathize with his widow.

Soon after, the baby boy grew very ill, but again the mother got a cow, and with proper food the child recovered. The latter part of October she was joined by Mr. McKie, Miss Chapman and Miss Way, who with herself were probably the only foreigners who had remained in the province and survived the storm. Early in December a little daughter was born to her and a month later the party were sent under escort south through Shansi, Honan, and Hupei to Hankow, which they reached after about six weeks of travel.

*Kalgan to Kiakhta.**

On June 6th, 1900, the Rev. Mark Williams and the Rev. J. H. Roberts left Peking for Kalgan, returning to that station in haste, to help the Rev. W. P. Sprague and other members of the mission of the American Board against the Boxers. With us went Miss Dr. V. C. Murdock, to do medical work in Kalgan; and Mr. Carl G. Söderborn, whose family were there. Passing through Hsüan Hua Fu, we persuaded Mr. Lundquist and family to go with us, for there were many Boxers in that city.

* Prepared at the request of the author by the Rev. James H. Roberts.

On June 10th we reached Kalgan, and found a howling mob at our gate,—hundreds of men and boys having come to see our houses burned. After a long time, an official sent the mob away, but they returned in the evening, and the danger became so imminent that a shot-gun had to be pointed at the crowd. Most providentially, they yielded to that argument.

In the night we sent away all the Chinese who were with us, and at daybreak we fled to the Yamen of the Manchu General. There were six in our party, including Mrs. Sprague and Miss Engh. We asked to be protected one day, and sent into Mongolia with a guard. In the afternoon a mob gathered in front of the Yamen. The General tried to send us to another part of the city, but we refused to go. At sunset we and our baggage were removed to a little musty house in one corner of the yard, and were locked up—whether for life or death, we did not know—but after midnight we were sent with a guard of many soldiers through the Great Wall into Mongolia.

We found that the Mongols also were Boxers, and there was no place where we could remain. At Hara Oso, fifty miles northwest of Kalgan, we joined Messrs. Larson, Söderborn and Lundquist, with their families, who were living in tents, and preparing to go to Urga. Mr. Sprague went back to Kalgan, and got our money, which was on deposit in a Chinese bank. He brought with him Mr. A. L. Fagerholm, who was vainly trying to reach the coast. Mr. Roberts also went to Kalgan, to get warm clothing for the whole party. We all rejoiced that, when we had to flee for our lives, we found ten camels and nine horses ready for our use.

On June 23rd, under a glorious sunset sky, we started

NOTABLE EXPERIENCES 645

on our long journey. The third day we lost a camel, and the search for it delayed us two days. Meantime messengers came from four Swedish missionaries, who had been attacked by a mob in Fêng Chên and were hurrying to overtake us. Their magistrate, most wonderful to relate, had given them an indemnity of eight hundred taels ($600), and they came to us with large supplies of money and food. The latter was as necessary to us as our camels and horses were to them, and we saw that the loss of the camel was most providential, as without it they could not have overtaken us.

Our party consisted of ten men, seven ladies, six little children, and seven Mongols to care for the animals. At the most we had twenty camels and nineteen horses. At one place we were forbidden to draw water from the well. The King of the Sunit Mongols forbade his people to sell animals to us, and sent soldiers to watch the wells, lest we put poison in them.

Mr. Larson was a splendid leader, a good marksman and horseman, a fluent speaker of Mongolian, and a man of great courage. He had traversed the desert of Gobi twice before. We called him "Moses." We had an armament of one rifle, one shot-gun, and two revolvers, which, under the divine Providence, saved us from attack.

Two ladies and two gentlemen each day formed a Cooking Committee. The other men were a Fuel Committee, the fuel consisting of the dung of animals, dried in the sun and wind. Two large buckets with covers, carried on a camel, contained our precious supply of water. The wells were far apart, and often the water was undrinkable. Once in a few days we killed a sheep and ate mutton, but the meat was little for so many hungry people. Our chief food was thin rice or millet gruel, with gravel in it that cracked our teeth. Once in five or ten days, one would feel satisfied with his dinner.

In the desert, ten days of great heat intensified our thirst. The shade of the six carts, in which the ladies and children rode and slept, was our only relief from the burning sun; and the lack of sleep, due to constant travelling in the night, made existence almost unendurable.

When within one hundred and twenty miles of Urga, we telegraphed to the Russian Consul-General: " Six Americans, seventeen Swedes, going to Urga request protection." His answer, telling us to come right to the Consulate, gave us a new lease of life. Arriving there July 30th, after thirty-eight days (660 miles) from Hara Oso, we had four days of rest.

However, Urga was full of Boxers, and we must move on. Russian passports were given us, to enable us to travel to St. Petersburg; food was bought for our journey; and we started for Kiakhta, the nearest town in Siberia. Mr. O. S. Nästegard, Jr., a Norwegian missionary, who could speak Russian, went with us, and became our " Joshua."

Shortly after leaving Urga, we met three hundred and fifty Cossacks, who had been sent to protect us. In thirteen days we travelled two hundred and ten miles to the border of the two Empires. There the Mongol Mandarin tried to stop us, but the Russian Governor of Kiakhta saved us from his clutches. We rested there two weeks. Many Russians were very kind to us. The infant child of Mr. Söderborn died, and was buried in a Russian cemetery, and even the Priest attended our

Protestant funeral. Money was sent by cable from America for our use, but the robbers, who dogged our steps fourteen days, could not get it, because we took it in letters of credit, to be paid in Irkutsk.

We hired a number of tarantasses—carriages with wooden springs, drawn by three horses driven furiously —and after going five days over prairie and mountains, and through a magnificent forest, we reached Lake Baikal, which we crossed on a small steamer September 1st. The waves on the lake were tremendous. Recovering from sea-sickness, we spent the night sleeping on a railroad station platform. The next morning we reached Irkutsk. Then ten days on the Siberian railway brought us to Moscow. A Government permit granted us a special car, new, clean and commodious. We left our Swedish companions in St. Petersburg, and came *via* Berlin and London to New York, where we arrived November 8th, after travelling more than four months.

It was a special providence that we were driven out of China in the summer, for, exposed as we were to the weather day and night, on the table-land of Mongolia, and in the high latitudes of Siberia, we should have suffered terribly from the cold at any other season. A Russian friend, on hearing about our journey, said: "Your guardian angels have come with you all the way." Not only during our flight, but also afterward, as we have learned of the many deaths of missionaries in China, we have realized that God himself was leading us and fulfilling his gracious promise: "My presence shall go with thee, and I will give thee rest."

The Rev. J. W. Stevenson, Director of the China Inland Mission, compiled the following list of the Protestant Missionaries who were killed, or who died from injuries received during the Boxer uprising of 1899 and 1900; the societies with which they were connected; the provinces in which they were located; and their nationality:

SOCIETY.	Adults.	Children.	Total.
China Inland Mission................	58	21	79
Christian and Missionary Alliance.......	21	15	36
American Board....	13	5	18
English Baptist Mission...............	13	3	16
Shou Yang Mission.......	11	2	13
American Presbyterian, North..........	5	3	8
Scandinavian Alliance Mongolian Mission	5	....	5
Swedish Mongolian Mission...........	3	1	4
Society for the Propagation of the Gospel	3	....	3
British and Foreign Bible Society.......	2	3	5
Unconnected, Mr. A. Hoddle...........	1	....	1
	135	53	188

PROVINCE.			
Shansi and over the Mongolian Border...	113	46	159
Chihli..	13	4	17
Chêkiang............................	8	3	11
Shantung............................	1	....	1
	135	53	188

NATIONALITY.			
British................................	71	29	100
Swedish..	40	16	56
United States.......................	24	8	32
	135	53	188
1901. Rev. J. Stonehouse, London Mission	1	....	1
	136	....	189

List of Roman Catholic Bishops, priests, and nuns killed in 1900:

PROVINCE.	Men.	Women.
Manchuria	10	2
Shansi	5	7
Mongolia	7	....
Chihli	4	....
Hunan	2	....
Peking	7	....
	35	9

N. B.—This list is probably not entirely complete.

XXXIV

CATASTROPHE TO THE NATIVE CHURCH

THE number of Protestant Christians in China at the beginning of the Boxer movement, by which is meant actual members of churches, was estimated to be somewhat more than one hundred thousand. To this should be added three or four times as many more who came under the general name of adherents, denoting those who, while not yet baptized, were either members of families where the leading elements were Christian, or were themselves favorably disposed to the new faith. It is from this class that converts are perpetually recruited. The membership of the Roman Catholics, usually reckoned by families, was several times as numerous, that faith having been in China for many centuries. In each case these Christians were distributed over a large part of the Empire, the number of Protestants in Manchuria being much larger than elsewhere.

While there are among these communities some who are wealthy, or rather in a small way well-to-do, by far the larger number of them come from the farming and the working classes. In China, as in the land of its birth, it has always been true that " to the poor the gospel is preached," and considering the hopes which this faith enkindles, and the barrenness of the average Chinese life, this is not singular.

It is a capital error to suppose that there are in the Chinese churches any considerable number of those who join them from unworthy motives, for what they can get. Of the Protestant churches at least we can speak upon this point from full knowledge. The Chinese are excellent judges of character, and in such a condensed society it is impossible that the main facts with regard to every applicant should not be well and accurately known. Numerous mistakes of judgment must of course be made, but missionaries and natives alike have learned by long experience that eternal vigilance is the price of a church which will not fall apart of its own weight, and the tendency accordingly is continually toward a raising of the standard.

It should be remembered that there are always and everywhere serious risks attending the identification of any one with a body like that of the Christian church in China, and in the face of the inevitable ostracism the advantages are too precarious to be attractive. Those who had joined the Christians from unworthy motives hastened in this last year to cut loose as soon as the dangers of their connection became apparent.

It is important also to bear in mind the fact that in a society like that of China it is inevitable that every Christian should have many enemies. It is a classical saying that on entering a village one should inquire its customs. In China the first and greatest commandment is not to do what others do not do also, for thus only will the whole of the Chinese law and the prophets be fulfilled. But the Chinese Christian is *ex officio* a non-conformist. He objects to ancestral worship, which is the real religion of the Chinese race. He refuses to subscribe to the erection of temples, to the performance of Taoist and Buddhist ceremonies, and to the village theatricals held in honor of some god or goddess.

He is at variance with his family and with his clan

on occasion of every wedding and every funeral, and weddings and funerals constitute a large part of the earthly joys of the barren life of the Chinese. In the incessant and intricate relations with innumerable individuals he will have differences on a great variety of subjects with a great variety of people, and whether he is himself at fault or not, he will have earned the ill-will of many persons. And the Chinese have long memories for grudges and spites, which are not infrequently carried on from generation to generation, each one patiently waiting until his turn shall have come for that revenge so dear to the Chinese, and so strongly inculcated in the Classics.

All persecutions of Christians in China have within them these inevitable elements, but this special one differed from all that had gone before. Those were local and sporadic, often secretly stimulated by the literati, and not infrequently by officials. This one was an emanation direct from the Throne itself. Never had there been such an opportunity as was now afforded to pay off old scores with compound interest.

The social solidarity of China is such that all the parts are more distinctly and exactly representative of the whole than perhaps in any other society in the world. When it is remembered that the Chinese are deeply imbued with a profound respect for all the forms of authority, one gains a faint notion of what an official and especially an Imperial persecution must be in China, far exceeding in its inherent momentum those of ancient Rome. The Chinese mind does not readily entertain the conception of actual resistance to regularly appointed magistrates. Every Chinese is unconsciously something of a fatalist, and when he is commanded by the highest power of which he knows anything to do or to forbear doing certain acts, he naturally regards it as "the Will of Heaven," and bends to the storm. That all Chinese did not behave thus in this universal persecution is itself a phenomenon to be accounted for, and one which shows that some force absolutely new in Chinese history had taken possession of many of the Chinese race.

The officials, some through motives of the deepest hostility to Christianity, and some with a desire to save the lives of their subjects, issued orders to the Christians to recant, sometimes furnishing tickets which should be pasted over their doors, certifying that they were no longer members of "the foreign religion" and were thus entitled to protection. This plan was in accordance with an Imperial Edict, and it is not to be wondered at that many Christians fell into the cunning trap laid for them, especially when, as in Shantung, it was accompanied by the alluring words "temporarily recant." In Manchuria some of the magistrates hit upon the happy plan of requiring the converts merely to step over the figure of a cross drawn upon the ground, which many of them hastened to do, glad to have escaped with no worse test, by no means realizing the significance of what they had done.

In one marked instance in Shantung, two native pastors under great pressure took upon themselves the responsibility and the sin of vicariously recanting on behalf of their whole flock, in order to save their lives. They had not the smallest intention of denying the faith, but nothing else was to be done, they thought, and it was better that two men should incur guilt than that the whole church should do so.

The innumerable varieties of recantation, actual and merely nominal, make the problem of the rehabilitation of the church in the regions where it prevailed a delicate and a serious one. But it should be distinctly recognized that in all but a fraction of cases it was regarded as only a form, an error no doubt due in many cases to inadequate instruction on the part of their leaders. Innumerable instances of absolute refusal to deny the faith under any circumstances, especially among the large Roman Catholic communities, are everywhere reported, but the case is not fully set forth without the distinct avowal that this was by no means the universal rule.

In some regions the threats of the Boxers had been heard for many, many weary months, or perhaps for more than a year. The poor Christian communities had been living the lives of isolated sheep with a day perpetually threatened for the advent of the wolves in force. Is it any wonder that at the last many of them fainted with terror at the actuality so long menacing them, and did whatever seemed to be required to prevent their aged parents from being turned adrift with no home and no food?

Some groups of Christians were pillaged over and over again, while elsewhere there was nothing but rapine and sudden death, the whole storm having passed over in an afternoon, leaving scarcely a living representative of the hated faith. " Destroy Christians root and branch," was often the war-cry, which the Boxers sought to carry into literal effect by killing not only all human beings, but every cat, dog, and chicken belonging to the homes of Christians, cutting down every tree, uprooting flowers, and laying waste the courts and gardens of the ruined houses. In a room occupied by a refugee Christian family, a forlorn little kitten was pointed out to a lady visitor, with the remark: " A whole village was out all night hunting for that cat. They said that it must be found and destroyed or it would bring calamity to the town.

CATASTROPHE TO NATIVE CHURCH 655

It was picked up and sent to relatives at a distance and so escaped."

Never was the prophecy that the foes of a man shall be they of his own house more exactly fulfilled. They were themselves the spies and informants, whose precise knowledge nothing could escape. All human affection, all social sympathies seemed to be dried up at the roots. Daughters drove away their own mothers from their doors, saying "Don't you come in here, or we shall be implicated too—go to your foreign friends, let them look after you." Even the storage of books, or clothing, or any article of furniture was absolutely forbidden under penalty of having the house pulled down or burned. The nearest neighbors were often the ones who invited the Boxers to come, leading them through the village and pointing out every door to Christian courts. Then when the goods were dragged upon the streets and sold for next to nothing, these were the ones who bought them for a trifle, subsequently reviling and taunting the owners, when they crept back to their desolated yards, with the observation that there was no more place for them—their goods were distributed to new owners, and their land had reverted to the village temples!

The cruelties of the persecutors found expression in the most hideous forms. All the barbarities practiced upon foreigners were shared likewise by their followers. Men, women, and children were chopped into pieces and their bodies thrown into running streams to be dispersed beyond power of doing injury. Great numbers were burned alive, and children were flung back into the flames after they had once broken forth. Yet in one case known to the writer a lad who had twice been bound and thrown into the Grand Canal, and had each time succeeded in getting free, was allowed to escape, because it must be " the Will of Heaven." Unusually attractive Christian children were sometimes adopted by the Boxers, or by others, valuable lives being thus saved. Many Christian maidens were sold to a life of odious slavery to be the "wives" of the Boxers who had killed all the other members of their families.

The mutilation of Christians may be said in some regions to have been the rule, not the exception, generally followed by a slow and terrible death. In other cases the joints of the victims were dislocated, and they were left in this maimed condition.

The writer was personally acquainted with a Roman Catholic school teacher who was persecuted by the Boxers, middlemen finally arranging that his life should be spared on payment of a fine of about thirty (Mexican) dollars. His father, however, begrudged the waste of so much money, and together with another son and a nephew tied up the son and his wife in the middle of the night, and killed them with a sword, their little girl being thrown on the ground and stamped to death. Two small boys, however, made their escape. The people of the village, who had no sympathy whatever with Christianity, were so incensed at this inhumanity that they refused to assist in any way at the funeral.

It is worthy of notice that in many places the bitterest animosity extended even to those who had been treated in mission dispensaries, or whose connection with foreigners had been only temporary and casual. In cases where the number of those killed was large, sometimes amounting to quite half of the total membership, there was an additional percentage of those who thus suffered vicariously. There were, on the other hand, some who while not members of the church, nor even probationers, yet refused to renounce its teachings, thus forming an exoteric band of martyrs whose number will never be known.

Attention was early called to the important fact that in many places where the Chinese Church was about to be tested as never before, special strength was afforded them for the coming conflict. In Peking, T'ung Chou, and Tientsin, earnest meetings had recently been held, at which large numbers of the leading members of many churches had been brought near to God, and a similar experience was that of many mission stations in Shansi and Chihli which had been visited by Mr. William Cooper. Numbers of Christians afterwards testified that they had been thus unconsciously fortified for the terrible trials which proved to be so near.

The natural timidity and the clannishness of the Chinese is well known to those who have had intimate relations with them. It has been previously mentioned that both in Tientsin and in Peking the greater part of the servants in every foreign establishment disappeared in a body upon the prospect of danger. It is important to recognize that the reverse was the case with the Christians, not merely where their safety was bound up with that of foreigners, but where they might, but for their fidelity, have easily escaped.

The most impressive instances of this are to be found where the peril to Chinese Christians was greatest, in the province of Shansi, where the Governor had given formal authority to Boxers to kill all Christians, and where any one found writing letters to foreigners was slain without mercy. The foreign letters from those who were martyred in that province, continued in some cases to within a few hours before death and concealed at great risk by their converts, furnish the most ample evidence of the beautiful loyalty of the Christians, and of their fearful trials. In every mission headquarters the first quest was for the mission records, that the names of all the followers of the "foreign religion" might be certainly known. When these were discovered it went ill with the flock.

In repeated instances servants who had been sent away for their own safety returned on the eve of a riot, saying simply: "I heard that you were to be attacked to-night, and I thought that I ought to be here to help you." Many of them voluntarily served as couriers at the imminent risk of their lives, not once or twice, but constantly, and in this way it is known that many were killed. When the missionaries had been robbed of everything, the poor Christians sometimes offered to them their own scanty hordes of silver or cash, saying that it was but right to do something for those to whom they owed so much, "As long as I have anything," said one such, "of course I will share it with you." Many Christians offered to find hiding-places for the foreign pastors and the ladies, at the greatest risk to themselves, and others undertook the yet more difficult office of acting as their travelling stewards during their long and dangerous flight through hostile regions.

Some of the prominent preachers were intrusted by the missionaries with large sums of money, to be sent to whomsoever appeared to be in the greatest need. One of them thus became the steward of about two hundred pounds sterling, which at no little risk to himself he disbursed with great discretion, in such a way as to assist materially many missionaries who had lost everything, and who had no resources. An instance of this sort is of great weight as an aid in estimating the real character of the men who have embraced Christianity, and who are at once its apostles and its proof.

It is to be noted that the reports brought to the coast of the experiences of the foreigners in the interior, while greatly doubted at the time by some, afterwards proved to be exact even in details, and at the same time there was no apparent disposition on the part of those who had helped foreigners under these circumstances to pose as heroes. In a letter brought to light many months after the massacre of the English Baptist missionaries at Hsin Chou, Shansi, was known, it appeared that the Boxers had captured one of the leading Christians and had taken him to the hiding-place of the missionaries that he might witness their death. With the certainty of immediate retribution this Christian uttered a loud cry of warning to his " Pastor," and was immediately himself struck with a spear or sword as a reward.

An evangelist and his family were all dragged from their carts in a Honan village, and their baggage being thought insufficient for loot, they were all, men and women, stripped of all their clothing and left naked in the street.

The manner in which the Christians met these terrible sufferings was a perpetual astonishment to their tormentors. They could not understand what inspired the calm courage of the tall and stalwart Teacher Liu of Fên Chou Fu, who sat calmly in his room fanning himself and awaiting the advent of the Boxers, who killed him instantly; nor that of the Peking deacon who put on his best clothes and went out to meet them joyously, facing death with a smile. Was it any wonder that the Boxers in their superstition cut out the hearts of such people to endeavour by an inspection to ascertain the source of their more than human courage?

The belief that Christians were able to poison wells, and to turn paper images into real foreign soldiers, was practically universal, and accounted for much of the insensate fury of the Chinese against them. The notion also widely prevailed that within three days they would rise from the dead, unless energetic steps were taken to prevent it. It was for this reason that so many were cut in pieces, and burned, in exceptional cases the ashes being passed under stone rollers and dispersed to the winds. The same superstition also accounted for the entirely un-Chinese refusal to allow the bodies of Christians to receive any kind of burial. A convert in Peking several times passed the corpse of his own mother lying in the street where she was struck down, but he dared not touch it.

The question has been often raised as to what the missionaries in China are doing, and what are the results of their work. They have been criticized as "idle and mischievous," but now that the Boxer rising has burst we are told that "they have turned the world upside down." The statement is most literally true. The nature of the totally new energy widely diffused throughout the Chinese Empire may now be clearly perceived. It is one with the life manifested in the Roman Empire in the days briefly described in the Acts of the Apostles, and it is the only force adequate to cope with the gigantic ills of China. This proposition, to those who read the story of the sufferings of the native church in China discriminatingly, will be self-evident, while to others it will remain an idle claim.

The interest of the appended instances of the experiences of Christian Chinese is found not only in the occurrences themselves, but in the fact that these are such cases as have first come to hand, and that it would be possible to duplicate them by the thousand, until the aggregate product would be a series of volumes exceeding

CATASTROPHE TO NATIVE CHURCH 661

in bulk the Encyclopedia Britannica. These narratives need no other comment than a few explanations of technical terms, and bear within themselves the evidences of their fidelity to truth.

Attention has already been called to the fact that the spread of the Boxer movement was largely through young boys who were put under the influence of something like hypnotism, or mesmerism. The proportion of genuine subjects may have been small as compared with the spurious, but the influence of a single genuine case in a superstitious country like China would be great, where education, despite the claim of many influential Chinese, is no bar to the wildest credulity.

In many places, the baneful effects of the movement became manifest to everyone, and often brought the whole Boxer propaganda into discredit. In one instance a lad of fifteen was so filled with the frenzy for murder that he attacked his own parents, an event which filled the villagers with horror, and led to the disbandment of the Boxer camp. Sometimes susceptible children would be so strongly affected with the impulse to perform the Boxer drill that they would go through with it irrespective of time or place. These occurrences made many reflective Chinese dread the unknown influence which they had evoked. When all the phenomena attending the Boxer development are attentively considered, there is reason to believe that many will come to the conclusion that if there is any such phenomenon in this world as "Demon Possession," this was an instance of it.

The frequent expression "Boxer altar," it should be explained, does not refer to a place of worship, a pile of stone, nor even a table, but denotes the organization itself, the band as a whole, with its "Great Elder Brother" as leader, as well as the drill headquarters, and the idol shrines before which tests were made by burning incense or paper. If the latter flamed high the accused was innocent, but if the flame was feeble and deflected he was guilty and must be beheaded at once. The opportunity for fraud in all these ceremonies is obvious.

Among the many singular phenomena connected with the rise and spread of the Boxer sect, nothing seems stranger or more in defiance of Chinese customs and the ideals of long generations than the accompanying organization of the " Hung Têng Chou " or " Red Lantern Light " society. This was composed of young girls between the ages of ten and twenty, just the age when Chinese maidens are most carefully hidden in the seclusion of their homes,—when to go about in the streets would be in defiance of the proprieties, and to be exposed to public gaze would be for rich and poor alike disreputable.

These girls in large companies were taken to the temples, put under the low and vicious men who were the Boxer leaders, and after a certain amount of drill accompanied Boxer bands in their public parades. Their uniform was entirely of red, red cloth about their heads, red shoes on their feet, red banners in their hands. Their training was similar to that given Boxer boys, the repetition of charms by the leader, who was sometimes a man, sometimes a woman,—following this the hypnotic trance, then a frenzy of desire to fight with sword or spear or gun.

The special power said to belong to these girls was to ride upon the clouds and to point out the houses of foreigners or their friends, Christians or others. From the clouds they could kindle a fire that would harm none but those proscribed. From the clouds, too, they could cause the iron battle-ships of the enemy to burn like tinder.

During the weeks when riots and fighting were most violent, towards evening hundreds of ignorant, credulous people would gather outside their villages and watch the sun hastening to the west. The impression upon the retina caused by gazing at its disc, causing a round red spot to appear whenever the eye should turn, was pronounced the magic light of the "Red Lantern," and excited cries of "There are two!" "I see three!" "There are a great many in the north!" would fill the air. Then when the evening clouds gave back the sunset glow, this common sight took on the aspect of the supernatural, and the people would whisper to each other "Truly the power of the Red Lantern is very great! With it we must conquer the foreigners!"

These stories of Chinese persecution may fitly conclude with the citation of a significant testimony in regard to the relative qualities of the Chinese Christians, from a paper read at the Newcastle Church Congress, by the most accomplished lady traveller of the day, Mrs. Isabella Bird Bishop, who began her extended journeying with little or no interest in missions, and who has ended with a sincere devotion to mission activity, after having enjoyed unequalled advantages for learning at first hand what is accomplished by the effort to elevate the men and the women of the East.

"Everywhere small, oft-times very small communities of persons had been formed, who by their abandonment of ancestral worship and idolatrous social customs were subjected to a social ostracism, and who partly in consequence clung together as brethren, with a tenacity similar to that which finds its secular expression in the powerful Chinese organizations known as 'guilds.' These converts live pure and honest lives, they are teachable, greedy of Bible knowledge, generous and self-denying for Christian purposes, and so anxious to preserve the purity of their brotherhood that it would be impossible for such abuses as disfigured the Church at Corinth to find a place in the infant churches of China. Above all, every true convert becomes a missionary, and it is in this spirit of propagandism that the hope of the future lies. After eight and a half years of journeyings among Asiatic peoples, I say unhesitatingly that the raw material out of which the Holy Ghost fashions the Chinese convert, and oft-times the Chinese martyr, is the best stuff in Asia."

XXXV

PERSONAL NARRATIVES

Kao Hsin

KAO HSIN is a graduate of College and Seminary, and has been in charge of the preparatory station school at T'ung Chou. This was closed at mission meeting time and after the meeting he went to his home fifteen li away. In a few days he came back to learn of the condition of things. He found only one man, Mr. Lin, in the city compound, who told him that the missionaries had gone to Peking, and the church members had scattered, and advised him to get his family and follow to Peking.

While they were speaking, a man came from Yung Lê Tien and told them of the murder of the preacher Li Tê Kuei while making his escape with his wife and three of his children. His three older children were pupils in T'ung Chou and Peking schools. Mrs. Li was Kao's own sister. She had pleaded for her baby as it was such a fine boy. The Boxers looked at it and said: "Yes! uncommonly fine! It might be an Emperor some day, it must be killed first." So they dispatched the children, hacking them with swords and burning them. They killed at the same time several church members who were escaping with the helper.

As Mr. Kao was starting back for his home he met a messenger from P'ing Ku Hsien, where Deacon Li Wên

Jung was stationed, forty miles from T'ung Chou. He had come to bring word to the deacon's mother that her son was ill with fever and the invalid wife unable to care for him, and to beg for help. After directing the man to the deacon's mother's home, Mr. Kao went back to Fu Hê, his home.

About dark, the P'ing Ku messenger reappeared saying there was no one to go to the deacon's help. Mr. Kao had told his family about the fate of the Christians at Yung Lê Tien and other places and consulted with them about plans for escape. His mother, an efficient energetic woman, said: "We are all natives of this village and our neighbours will not want to harm us women. You and your nephew go to P'ing Ku where there are no Boxers, and you will be safe yourselves and able to help the sick deacon and his family. We will scatter among our relatives in the village and I will stay and care for the house."

Mr. Kao begged that they all go to Peking, but she thought her plan the safer one. His feelings overcame him and she said: "Don't cry my son! Can we not bear this for Christ? If Jesus saves us we will be reunited. If we are taken we die for Him. Can we not trust Him? Go quickly!"

She prepared them a meal, and at eleven o'clock at night Mr. Kao and his nephew, the eldest son of the murdered helper Li Tê Kuei, set out, a neighbour going with them to bring back word to the mother.

They reached P'ing Ku the next day at noon, and found the deacon's wife in distress at the situation,—her husband ill, and no cart or animals to be hired to take them back to T'ung Chou. She had been praying that God would open the way before them. Mr. Kao advised them to remain as it was quiet there, and if it grew dangerous the mountains were near where they could hide.

The next day was Sunday and the little company of Christians gathered for service. One from a hamlet not far away in the hills consented to let Mrs. Li and the children go to his home, though they had only millet and salt and water to give her. They stole out in the early morning, Mrs. Li walking some distance to meet the donkey sent for her. After seeing her safe in the new hiding place Mr. Kao and the sick husband returned to P'ing Ku where they remained another week.

Conditions grew worse all the time. The evil reports about Christians as poisoning wells and smearing blood on the doors were started in the city. They were threatened with being bound ready for delivery to the Boxers when these should reach the city. A friendly yamen-runner told them these things and advised them to leave, giving the name of friends, one forty and one eighty li away. Mr. Kao and his nephew decided to go. Deacon Li at first remained behind but soon joined his wife and started on his own long wanderings. They were separated from that time on.

The first man mentioned would only give them one meal and sent them on. After going a short distance they were in the mountain gorges with no plain road. Bewildered and knowing not where to go, they stopped and prayed to God to guide, where there was no man to ask. Two crows flew overhead and they asked that they might fly in the direction they ought to take. They flew northeast. This took them back to their unwilling host, whom they begged to escort them a few li. He was afraid and refused, but a caller came in who lived on that very road, and he offered to direct them.

It was cloudy and threatened rain and they begged this

guide to take them to his home for the night. He did so and they had hardly entered the house when the rain fell in torrents. For ten days they remained there working hard for their board. They had said that they were Christians, so that when, soon after, a Boxer altar was started there, the wife of the man was frightened and wanted them to go, giving them money to help them on their way.

The nephew was homesick and begged to return to their home. They started back, but in a few li met Yang Erh, a chair-bearer for a member of the T'ung Chou Mission. He had been to P'ing Ku twice as messenger, but was now fleeing for his own life. He told how he had been pursued by Boxers and had seen them cut down others on the road, and said that neither T'ung Chou nor Tientsin were safe for any Christians.

Mr. Kao and his nephew with Yang Erh turned back to the north-east and went on outside the pass. The wild rumours about Christians were everywhere, and believed by everyone. The rumours said that the Christians smeared blood on the doors, which would make some one in the household go crazy, and kill all the family; that they poisoned wells so that the water would destroy those who drank it; that foreigners were selling sheep-skins and goat-skins and would later turn them all into live sheep and dogs and men. The sheep would hunt people and destroy the crops, the dogs would bite people and make them go mad, but the men were worst of all as they could not be conquered. If these sheep or dogs or men were struck they turned back into sheep-skins or goatskins. The great trade of foreigners in black pig's bristles was said to be for the purpose of performing incantations over them, by which they would turn into evil insects that would fly about and bite like a mosquito, the bite proving fatal. The Boxers claimed that they alone could avert all these evils.

No one was allowed to stay at an inn, as it was said that foreigners hired beggars, fortune-tellers, travelling priests and peddlers to scatter blood and medicine. Every suspicious stranger was searched. If any bottle was found on his person they were sure it was medicine and the man was at once cut to pieces.

It was necessary to appear unconcerned and walk boldly to the crowds or inns as any attempt to avoid notice at once awoke suspicion. They must have a reasonable explanation for their journeying, so they gave as a reason that they were going north in search of a debtor who had owed his uncle a debt to get payment for the same. As they several times got work for a few days in the fields, they could say that they were searching for work on account of drought on the plain. The poppy harvest was ready for the first slashing of the seed-pods, and many came every year to do this work.

At one stage they joined a traveller who proved most kind to them, took them to his village, found work for them with a rich man of the place, cared for Mr. Kao during several days' illness and adopted him and Yang Erh as "sworn brothers" and the nephew as a "dry son." His kindness was the bright spot in the long, sorrowful summer.

While at this man's village, word came of the destruction of everything foreign in Peking except the British Legation and the Cathedral, and with a heavy heart Mr. Kao thought of all his fellow Christians as gone. At last the news of the victories of the Allies in Peking reached them in the mountains and they started back for the plains.

Not far from his old home Kao Hsin met an acquaintance who exclaimed on seeing him, "Why are you here!" "I want to see my home and my family!" "Alas! You have no home to see and your family are all dead, killed by the Boxers." Then the dreadful details were told of how his mother was cut to pieces, all his children but one little deaf girl killed with his wife, all the Christians of the village, with nearly all of their relatives, more than thirty in all, killed in most cruel ways. The aged grandmother, over eighty-four years old, was a mid-wife and nearly all the villagers up to forty years of age had been brought into the world by her—so many begged for her and she was spared. "One old woman and one little girl can do nothing to avenge those killed!" they said contemptuously. They had searched everywhere for Kao Hsin, but said he was a wizard of such power he could burrow in the earth and escape. They feared he would come with an earthquake to destroy them.

Mr. Kao had travelled thirty miles that day and had six more to go. He staggered on almost sleeping as he walked. At last he crawled under a mat shed in which were dead bodies and tried to sleep a little, but was awakened every little while by firing guns and barking dogs. At daylight some Russian soldiers impressing workmen found them and drove them to some boats to unload supplies. There was a motley crowd of coolies, merchants, teachers, rich men, poor men—all kinds in the line. Their burdens were heavy and if they did not handle them just right they were beaten. Kao Hsin felt the lash because he dropped a box too quickly. After a supper he slept on the wet ground with no bedding.

The next day he was harnessed in with some men to drag cannon over the stone road outside the city near to the ruins of the college. One man fell, the wheel ran over his leg and broke it. Another, who thought such a life too bitter to endure, jumped into the moat as they went over the bridge and was drowned. That night they were well fed and given dry clothes. After a little they were better treated, were given three meals a day and paid ten cents besides.

He remained a month in all, thinking the Christians all dead and himself the sole survivor and that the missionaries would all have been sent home. So he made no effort to get away. One day he met a T'ung Chou church member on the streets and learned the good news that many were saved. His presence in T'ung Chou was reported to the Mission in Peking and he was soon passed over to the Americans and sent up to the Capital.

Deacon Li

To find a Christian in a Chinese yamen reminds one of the "saints in Nero's household." Yet it was in such a place that Li Yün Shêng was converted, and it was in pursuing the duties of that place that he led for twelve years a consistent Christian life. He was known as a man faithful to duty, one who took no bribes and shared no "spoils of office." He had the respect of the official in T'ung Chou and of his associates in the yamen. Such a man was a shining mark for the malignity of the Boxers. He had seen the burning of the Mission buildings and boldly denounced the deed. "Your punishment will come," he said, "and these buildings will be restored." When the massacres began, the official at the head of the yamen took Mr. Li under his own protection and found a small, retired room where he was hidden. When the Boxers came to the yamen and demanded the Christian in hiding, they refused to give him up.

At last the Boxers, who had no respect for dignitaries, broke into the yamen and began a search. Mr. Li was taken by the official's command into the apartments of the women. But the Boxers penetrated to that court and soon found their victim. He was dragged out and taken to an altar near by, where they put him to death. His wife was a very timid woman and when she heard of her husband's death she went to a pit of water not far away, leading her little daughter, and the two plunged into the water together.

Deacon Li was buried but the word went around among the Boxers that so zealous a Christian would rise from the dead in a short time, so his body was exhumed and burned to ashes.

The Unknown Martyrs

Among those who died for their faith in this field were many whose names are unknown, but whose steadfastness in the face of death produced so much wonder among the heathen that their stories are being told by those who " were consenting " by looking on silently when they were condemned.

At P'ing Ku Hsien two men were taken to the " Great Elder Brother " of the Boxers for his decision as to which was guilty of following the foreign religion. After repeating his incantations he turned and pointed to one and said " This is one of them ! " The man was led away and killed, the other one was released. He turned away and went off a little distance, then came back to the Boxers. " What are you coming back for? You can go," they said. He replied "Kill me too! I too am one of them!" And they led him to where his friend had died and there killed him.

At the T'ung Chou north gate two boys of thirteen and fourteen years of age were making their escape into the country when the Boxers seized them to question them. These nameless young confessors said boldly "We are of the Jesus Church." When about to be bound they said, "You need not bind us. We will not try to get away. Every step we take to your altar is one step nearer heaven." And they soon joined the victors above.

Deacon Hêng

(As told by himself)

"On returning to Peking from Annual Meeting we found the danger and excitement in the city had greatly increased. A council was held and, soon after, the missionaries and the girls of Bridgman school were removed to the Methodist Mission, while many of the men of the church remained to guard the Mission. On the evening of June 13th, a man came rushing to the chapel saying 'The Boxers have entered the city and are setting fire to the Missions.' I went into the street and could see the smoke of the Methodist street chapel and of the London Mission rising to the south of us. The streets were full of excited people saying 'They will come here next! These will be the next to die!' After a short consultation we decided we could not defend the buildings and could only try to save our lives by flight.

"There were many who saw me and knew me, but I made my way to the north part of the city where I was least known, and as it was dark I hid in a temple near the northwest gate. From there I saw the burning of the two Presbyterian Missions and further south the smoke and flames of our own Mission.

"I rested part of the night but rose at 3 A. M. and went to the Presbyterian Mission, which was still burning, and saw the bodies of those killed during the night, some of them in the burning buildings, some outside in the courts. I went to the An Ting gate, but it was closed not to be opened till noon. After wandering around I came back to the north-east gate. I met several Christians of our own and other Missions, but no one showed signs of recognition. Later we went out through the gate together, each making for his own place of refuge.

"I went to a village eight li away to warn a Christian family living there. They gave me food and I rested for a time, after which I went back to the city by the An Ting gate, which was now open. There were many bodies of the Christians lying along the road, of which I recognized one as a colporteur who had been killed while carrying his books on his back. There were men and women, young and old among them. I then went from one to another of my relatives but none would let me remain. I went to the yamen where I have duties but was told there was no place for me.

"For a day or two I wandered about getting food and shelter as best I could. At last I went to my uncle and he said he would try to get me out of the city safely but could not keep me, as it would surely bring ruin to them all.

"They advised me to shave my head and put on the garments of a Buddhist priest, but I was not willing to wear that garb. Finally they brought me the outfit of a fortune-teller, the mystic character of the 'Book of Changes,' and wrote out for me enough couplets for twenty fortunes. Then my uncle put on his Manchu robes for ceremonial service, gave a suit to me and we rode out of the city as official and attendant. No one challenged me. He went a few miles with me, gave me money for my journey and we separated.

"I went to the village at the north where there were Christians, but found them scattered; went on to another place and found the Boxers were everywhere. I still went north and after a few days reached a valley among the mountains where a large branch of our family lived.

"After waiting two days at an inn and no one appearing, whom I knew, I decided to turn back to the city to learn the fate of our church. I went to a few fairs on the way, spread out my table, told a few fortunes, always watching for familiar faces. At last I met three Christians who told me of the siege of foreigners and Christians at the Legation and North Cathedral. They said we could not go to the city yet,—it was not certain that any one would survive the fierce attack.

"So again I turned north, this time in company with these three. We travelled by twos and stopped at different inns. One of them soon hired out to a farmer and the others found other work, but I was not strong enough to be of any use, so I went to fairs and told fortunes, working my way back to the north to my relatives. Sometimes I was tempted to end my days in a river or to jump from a precipice, but I held back from that sin, feeling that God would care for me or take me to Himself.

"At last I reached again the home of my relatives. There were some sixteen families in the hamlet, all of our clan. I went to the head man, who was the only one of an older generation—an uncle. There were four of my own generation whom I could call 'brothers.' I could not tell them of my being a Christian but did tell them of how Peking was in a state of chaos and ruin, with fighting in the streets and robbers and Boxers everywhere. I had fled for safety and must ask them to give me refuge until the country should become quiet. They consulted together and agreed to share in keeping me. There I remained until after the New Year. They were poor people but they gave me food such as they had and money enough for me to buy a sheep-skin garment and other clothes for winter. I was kept in the house for more than a month by sickness.

"As the weather grew warmer I could wait no longer but turned back to the plain to see if any of our church survived. The roads and inns were full of dispersed soldiers. Several times I told their fortunes and gave them the truth. I told them they could not succeed in fighting foreigners but had been deceived by the Boxers and had better give up being soldiers and go to their homes! They were not angry at this but paid my food and lodging and treated me kindly. I made my way to the city gate where the Japanese were in charge. I could not make myself understood but found my way back to our old street.

"There I saw a notice in foreign letters on the gate, and came inside and found myself in the presence of those whom I had thought dead. The Lord has brought me back. I am far from perfect. The Lord has not done teaching me so He has let me live on to finish His work in me."

Mrs. Li Pên Yuan (Dorcas)

Li Pên Yuan is one of the younger preachers of the American Board Mission, and Dorcas, his wife, is a worthy helpmeet. She was educated in the Bridgman school and is a woman attractive in person and of a lovely Christian character.

On the night when the Missions were burned in Peking Mr. and Mrs. Li were visiting the brother of the former in a distant part of the city. The brother was a preacher of the Presbyterian Mission. As the mob drew near that place they all fled together but after going a little distance the two families separated so as to attract the less attention. Mr. Li found a retired corner in the angle of some house where he left his wife and child while he went on to the great street to look about. She could see him standing at the corner not many rods away when a crowd of Boxers come along. He knew it would not do to run, so followed along as one of the crowd till he could turn aside unnoticed and make his way back to his wife. She had seen him apparently swept along by the crowd, and as a long time elapsed and he did not return she gave him up as lost.

She finally came out from hiding and worked her way slowly back across the city to the American Board Mission, which was burning when she reached it. Wandering about from one place to another she finally sat down in front of a large gate of a strange family and rested till the morning broke. Soon after light a band of Boxers came along and seeing the lonely woman and child marked them with blood-hound instinct as refugee Christians. Just as they stopped in front of Dorcas the gentleman of the place, an entire stranger to her, came out, took in the situation at a glance, and said to the Boxers, "You are mistaken. This is a neighbour of mine!" His word was taken and the mob went on leaving her there.

She told her story to this "good Samaritan" and he

went with her to a village near the eastern city gate where she had relatives living. They found the house destroyed and the people fled. The man who was trying to save her then said they were expecting a visit from a relative named Li, and she must represent that relative to their family and go to his home till some other plan could be made. The women at first received her cordially but after a little, suspicions arose and then she told her story to them. They would not let her remain. The man begged them to keep the little one but they refused that too. As Dorcas left the house he said to his wife, " The one good act of my life you will not let me do! "

She went back near the Mission from one old neighbour to another, none of whom would receive her. She appealed to a police-station, to a man who knew her husband, but he drove her roughly away. Towards night she sat down on some logs near a lumber-yard but was soon told to " move on " and when she said she had no place to go the man pointed down a blind alley and said " You can wait there." There was nothing to wait for but death.

Just then a carter of the Mission came along, saw her and called her by name. She went to his cart and got inside; he quickly dropped the curtain and drove up and down the streets for hours trying to find some place of refuge. At midnight he drove into a cart-stand yard and received permission to keep his cart and mule there for the night. Dorcas spent that night in the cart. The little child of only two years, a bright winsome little one, seemed to know she must keep quiet and did not cry once in the night.

The next morning at earliest dawn they drove away and went to a village where some Christians were known to have taken refuge, and there she remained until word was taken to her husband who came and took her to the

Methodist Mission. They had been separated from Wednesday night till Saturday morning and he had searched all over the city for her.

The T'sai Family

This family is one of the oldest Protestant Christian families in North China, the present head of it, Mr. T'sai Fu Yuan, being of the second generation of Christians. He has been a preacher for nearly twenty years, and their home has been a centre for the church of the Yü Chou region.

By the latter part of June the whole city and region were aflame with the Boxers. Mr. T'sai was in the city with his family. His aged mother, who shared the universal Chinese dread of extinction of the family, saw the approaching crisis and told her son and grandson that they must flee while it was yet possible. After vainly protesting they at last yielded and left the city about the middle of July. They first went to Hsi Hê Ying, where there were other Christians, but found that place still worse than Yü Chou, as the large Catholic Church drew the Boxers to its attack from the whole region around. He then went on to Pai Lu, where he had friends, but soon left them and took refuge in the watch tower of a melon patch, where a Catholic old lady was also in hiding. He remained in this place until he learned of the destruction of his home and the death of all his family except the son who was with him.

The crisis in Yü Chou culminated about the last of July, when a large body of Boxers passed through on their way to attack the Catholic Church of Hsi Hê Ying. At that time a mob surrounded the Mission place and led out the women to a temple near by, locking them within. Then the chapel and homes were looted and burned, after which the crowd scattered, leaving the women in the temple without even a guard. Toward night they were able to escape and went back to their ruined home. They found two small side rooms which had not been destroyed and went into these to prepare some food for themselves.

In a little time some rowdies of the city came to pick up anything that might remain in the ruins and found the women there. They raised the cry and gathered the Boxers again. Some demanded that they all be killed, and some of the baser of the crowd suggested that the young women might be sold to the public houses for a good sum. At this the blind old grandmother raised her voice and said, "We are not that kind! Kill us if you want! We can die!"

The Boxers being on their way to battle did not wish to defile their swords with the blood of women, so led them to the well in the court and threw them in, one after another, burying each with stones and earth as she was cast in. In this way it is thought six perished, though there are rumours that two were carried away and given to a military official.

Pastor Mêng Chi Hsien

Pastor Mêng Chi Hsien was the oldest of the younger body of preachers in the Mission of the American Board, who had been trained from youth in the Mission schools. For eleven years he had been an ordained pastor at Pao Ting Fu. He was a man of strong convictions, of great energy, was a natural leader, beloved and trusted by all.

He and his younger brother, Pastor Mêng Chi Tsêng, attended the Annual Meeting of the Mission at T'ung

PASTOR MENG, A MARTYR OF PAO TING FU

Chou, both taking prominent part in the meetings. While these were in progress, tidings came that the railroad was destroyed and communication with Pao Ting Fu cut off. Mr. Mêng decided to return at once to stand by Mr. Pitkin's side in the perils and perplexities of the hour. He went overland, most of the way on foot. The three devoted missionaries at Pao Ting Fu, Mr. Pitkin, Miss Morrell, and Miss Gould, who were cut off from all hope of escape, were quietly going on with their work for the church.

During the month of June, Mr. Mêng, with other preachers, and returned college students, opened the street chapel daily. They saw the gathering storm and advised the church members to leave the city, helping them to choose places of escape, but these preachers and the Bible-readers deliberately decided to remain at their posts.

They said: " Our missionaries have remained with us, —we will stand by them and live or die together." They could have escaped had they fled. All who went away did escape. They chose to stay, although they saw more clearly than their foreign friends the inevitable results.

One man, a life long friend of Mr. Mêng, said to him, " We have lived together, now we will die together." " No!" said the pastor, " My place is here with our missionaries. I shall stay, but you must take my oldest son and get away. If you escape and he is spared, he will represent me and carry on my work." So the friend took the son, a fine boy of fifteen, and went away. After many dangerous experiences during the summer he brought him safely to Tientsin after the arrival of the Allies.

Friday afternoon of June 27th, Pastor Mêng was at the street-chapel packing books and furniture, preparing to remove from the rented building, as notice to do so had been given by the owner.

Suddenly a company of Boxers came into the chapel, seized him, bound him, and carried him to their altar in a temple in the south-east corner of the city. The first blow had fallen upon the mainstay of the native church. He was beheaded at the altar, his head exposed as that of a criminal, while the body was buried like a pauper's near the city wall.

Nine months later to a day, a great memorial service for the martyred missionaries and Christians was held at Pao Ting Fu, attended by the chief officials of the city and witnessed by thousands of silent spectators. In the stately funeral procession were banners and flags, embroidered catafalques, native musicians, a long line of carts filled with mourning friends, and ahead of all, above thirty memorial banners, more than half of which were to the memory of this noble man. They were no empty show, but gave the last, true estimate of the best men of the city, officials and merchants, guilds and citizens, of the life and character that had been lived in their midst.

Chang Ch'ing Hsiang

Chang Ch'ing Hsiang was a member of the senior class of the North China College, and had returned to Pao Ting Fu at the close of the college year, taking part in the work of the station up to the time when the storm broke upon the Mission.

The night that the elder Pastor Mêng was seized by the Boxers was a sleepless one in the Mission. All felt that they were doomed to death, and it was only a question of time. Towards morning, Ch'ing Hsiang's mother, who was one of the Bible-women, came to him and said:

MISS GOULD OF PAO TING FU AND SCHOOL GIRLS

"There is no need for all to die. You are young and may have many years of work for the Lord. I shall stay and die with Miss Morrell. You must try to escape."

Starting out in the early dawn, he first went to their home to get money and an extra garment, then turned south to a place twenty-five miles away, where there were Christians. Arriving at the town towards night he found the streets alive with Boxers coming in from the country, and knew it was no place of refuge, so turned back to retrace his steps. He was pursued a few li by some villagers who noticed his being a stranger and alone. As night came on it rained heavily, and in the darkness and storm he made his way on the railroad back to his home. His sister met him with the warning to flee at once, as search had been made for him. He had had no sleep for two nights, his limbs were swollen and every step was painful, but his friends led him out a few li and he set his face towards the hills.

He fixed on a town a hundred miles away as his destination, and knowing that single travellers were viewed with suspicion, soon joined some merchants going to that place. After reaching there he decided to go into Shansi, not knowing that it would be entering the tiger's den. He soon joined an official train whose followers were friendly, and with them made the journey all the way to T'ai Yuan Fu. Arriving there he learned that already a large number of missionaries had been killed, and he himself saw a Boxer mob chase down some Catholic Christians.

His money was almost gone, and he turned his face back to Pao Ting Fu, hoping the worst would be over when he should have again made the long journey. After going thirty miles he found that he had taken a branch road to T'ai Ku, and was only ten miles from the city.

His classmate, K'ung Hsiang Hsi lived there, and although not knowing whether he were yet alive, he decided to try to find him. Entering the city he found the missionaries were still living and made his way to the gate. It was very closely guarded as spies had visited them, and his ragged, travel-worn appearance excited suspicion, so that the door was shut in his face.

He finally met his friend and they found a hiding place in a village not far away. After the Mission was destroyed he was again in great peril, and after a hasty visit to his friends, he started to return to Chihli. He soon joined other travellers of his own province and in their company made the long journey out of Shansi safely.

He then turned south to a village where there were Christians, and a good deacon took him in and treated him as a brother. He had journeyed over a thousand miles on foot, had an ulcer on one leg, and his feet were covered with blisters. His clothes were in tatters, and his shoes almost gone. He received the kindest care, his needs were supplied, and he was soon able to join them in the harvest fields and work with them till news came that foreign troops had entered Pao Ting Fu. Then the deacon went with him to keep him company. The friends at Pao Ting Fu received him as one from the dead, having heard repeatedly that he had been killed in Shansi.

His experiences illustrate those of hundreds who wandered from one place of hiding to another, suspected, hunted, in danger every moment of being recognized, not knowing each morning but the new day might be their last. The marvel is that so many were able to escape the constant perils, and survive as witnesses to the providential care of their God.

Mrs. Huo's Story

"When we saw the danger increasing around us,[1] I said to my husband. 'We must not all die. You must go away and hide. They are not so likely to kill me and the children as to kill you. If I am spared you can hunt me up afterwards. If not it will be God's will.' So I baked him some cakes, rolled up his quilt and some clothes, and then had to fairly push him out of the door.

"After the Mission houses were burned the Boxers came and took me and the children to their altar for trial. As we started I begged them to let me say a few words. 'You want to talk *now* do you?' 'If you will let me,—if not I will keep silent.' 'Well, talk ahead!' So I told them how we had lived there many years, how our neighbours all knew we had quarrelled with no one, had offended no one, how my husband was gone and I was alone with my little children. Would they not be merciful to me and the little ones? Some of the by-standers said: 'What a pity to destroy the children!'

"They put chains on my hands and feet as I sat on the ground and then ordered me to get up. I tried several times in vain, then told them it was impossible, and finally said my body was 'inconvenient,' and I could not rise without help. They then called two women who belonged to the jail to attend to women prisoners, and they led me to the prison, where I spent seventy-two days. They gave me coarse food and drink. After twenty days my baby was born. The official had ordered clothing for the child, and extra food for me, but these things did not reach me, being kept by the guards. The little one lived only three weeks. I did not know the fate of my poor children, from whom I had been separated, but I

[1] Pao Ting Fu.

prayed God every day to spare their lives and restore them to me.

"After a time two other Christians, a mother and a daughter who had given themselves up to the Boxers voluntarily, were put in with me, and we comforted each other. They were alone and knew they could not escape, so they went to the Boxer leaders and told them plainly that they were Christians, and would not give up Christ, and they could kill them at once. The Boxers did them no harm, but shut them up in the prison, and they came through safely with me.

"There was another woman prisoner there, one who had been very wicked, and who was awaiting her sentence at the law, expecting death. She was friendly and anxious to know about us, so we talked freely together. One day I asked her, 'If you must die have you any one to help you in the next world?' 'No, no one,' she said. I said, 'We have some one. We are not afraid to die.' So I told her about Jesus who died for us, and who takes away the fear of death. She was a very bright woman and learned quickly. We taught her to pray, and she learned to trust in Christ to forgive her many sins. I told her at last. 'If they come to deliver us, you may tell them you are a Christian too now, only you must never go back to your old life of sin.'

"Sure enough, when the foreign soldiers let us out she too was released. The interpreter for the troops was a missionary, and he asked her many questions to test her knowledge of the truth, and she answered them well. She has gone back to her father's home in a distant village, and I am going there to see her as soon as it is safe for me to walk there. The Lord saved me, body and soul, why shouldn't I try to save some one else, body and soul?

"After a time, before the soldiers came, we heard that some foreigners had been brought to the prison. 'Could it be Pastor Ewing, come to try and save us? Were they to be killed?' we asked. 'No,' the guard said, and then added, 'You need not worry, no one will kill them or you now,' I did not then know that they meant that the foreign armies were in Peking, and every one was afraid of their vengeance, but I felt sure we were safe and would in some way be delivered. In time I learned that the foreigners were Mr. and Mrs. Green and their party.

"At last the time came when they brought us out of prison and restored my four children to me. They had been taken to the city orphanage and cared for during my long stay in prison. They were sick and wasted from poor fare and lack of mother's care, but they had not been unkindly treated. After a time my husband came back, so we are all spared to each other. God has been very good to us. My children are His to do with just what He wants."

Dr. Ch'iu

Dr. Ch'iu was a former student with Dr. Atterbury at Peking, who was carrying on an independent practice, and had a medicine shop of his own.

As the Boxer altars multiplied in the city and danger to Christians increased, Dr. Ch'iu became alarmed for his own safety. He is very lame and this made it harder for him, rendering him conspicuous, and making it difficult for him to flee. This led him to go out of the city to relatives in a village a few li away, before the attack on the missions began. His relatives refused to allow him to remain, so after vainly trying to find a hiding-place, he returned to the city. Not long after that the great outbreak occurred. His shop of foreign medicines was looted, and his home also. He was seized by the Boxers and taken to their altar. In his fright he yielded to their demands and burned incense to their idols.

They were still bent on killing him, when some one suggested that he be kept alive to dress the wounds of those who had been wounded during the attack on the Legations. With this in view they took him to a temple, where were over thirty suffering from wounds, lying on the steps or in the court, or one of the rooms, while in another large room lay more than twenty bodies of those already killed. These bodies were to be kept, as the Boxer leaders promised that after a few days all would rise from the dead and again join them in exterminating Christians and foreigners.

For more than ten days Dr. Ch'iu was kept a close prisoner in this court, the decaying bodies of the dead, and the groans of the living, all about him, his own life depending on his success in healing those under his care. His guards never left him day or night. He knew it would be impossible for some of the wounded to recover, having no medicines or appliances to use for them, and he quietly waited the end, praying for forgiveness for yielding in the matter of burning incense.

Then came a sudden turn in affairs. A wealthy village had been pillaged by Boxers, although not related to the proscribed classes, foreigners or Christians. Their leading men came into the city and entered complaint, and the company at the temple where Dr. Ch'in was confined were summoned to appear. Some went to the official and the rest fled, leaving no guard. This was the opportunity for flight, but to flee into the streets was vain, as others would seize him. He succeeded in sending a message to his older brother, who came with a cart and took him to his home. This brother was a heathen, and not in danger for himself, and although during the days of attack he had refused shelter to his brother, he now took him in and hid him away, and for two months succeeded in keeping him from the Boxers. When the troops came in he was taken by the missionaries to a place of safety.

Wên Li

One of Miss Newton's school girls, Wên Li, was betrothed to a young doctor, Mr. Ma, of one of the leading families of the Presbyterian Mission.[1] Wên Li's own mother was not a Christian, and was out at service in a wealthy Chinese household. As Wên Li had no home when the school was disbanded, she was sent to her future mother-in-law.

The family desired to have a wedding in the usual manner,—to send the bride to a friend's house, and have her brought in a red bridal chair; but the streets were so disorderly, and the mobs so rude that they feared a wedding among Christians would attract notice and lead to trouble, so the matter was delayed from day to day. One day Mr. Ma received notice that they must give up their rented house to their landlord. They went to the Mission, where a few empty rooms were found, and there they made a temporary home. It then seemed best to have a quiet wedding which should place the young bride in better position to receive the protection of her husband.

That very night the mission houses were burned. A company of native Christians hid away in a court where there were trees and shrubs, but the light of the burning buildings betrayed their presence and they were pursued and struck with knives and axes. They made their escape but were soon separated. Wên Li, with her hus-

[1] Peking.

band's sister, hid in a ruined temple, the front of which was burning, so that the smoke of the fire gave them a veil as they crouched against the brick wall in the rear. By morning this hiding-place was searched, and those in hiding were taken to the Boxer altar to be tested. Wên Li was released, but the sister-in-law was killed.

The same day the young husband was also taken again and was put to death. Wên Li, the bride of a few hours was left alone, a widow. She carried two severe wounds on her neck from the Boxer knife, and in pain and terror made her way to her mother. But her mother could not keep her, and after going from place to place, she was taken into the home of a sister of Wên Yen a schoolmate, where she remained two months. The husband of the family was a Boxer, but he gave these girls his protection. They had to suffer from his reproaches, and constant efforts to make them recant.

One day he said to them, "I am bearing a bad name on your account. I am accused of making you my lower wives. I must give you up to the Boxers unless you recant." His wife then said, "We have protected them so long they must not die now." Wên Li was ill from her unhealed wounds and was discouraged, so when he lit a stick of incense and said, "You've only to kneel while this is burning and then you will be safe," she could hold out no longer. The wife took pity on her distress of mind and body and broke off the incense stick to only an inch or two, to make the time the shorter. As the poor girl told her story she broke down weeping, and asked me to pray for her forgiveness for yielding in the time of trial.

At the close of the siege she was taken to the place where the mission had established itself, and with care and kindness soon recovered. She was later again married to a young man whose fiancée had been killed during the Boxer reign of terror.

Mr. Chang and Mr. Wên

After the allied troops reached Peking, Mr. Tewksbury, with a company of helpers, went to T'ung Chou to learn the fate of the Christians who had not gone with them to Peking. They also went to the deserted yamens, gathering up documents which should give evidence as to Boxer leaders and their victories.

Among the papers of the city magistrate was one stating the trial of a Mr. Chang of the London mission. His home was in a village near T'ung Chou, but his business was in Peking. When the city became full of Boxers all business was broken up, and Mr. Chang went to his home and took his family and fled. Being recognized, he was seized by the Boxers, stripped of clothing, bound with ropes upon a cart and carried to T'ung Chou to the official yamen. The cords had worn off the flesh so that he was already covered with bleeding wounds when taken to his trial.

On being questioned he plainly stated his faith. He said that he had been several years in business when he was attracted to the street chapel of the London mission. The more he heard of the Jesus doctrine the more he considered it a good doctrine, and after attending church for a year he was baptized. He said, " This is my faith. I am ready to invite death. I am not afraid to die, and shall not give up my religion." The writer wrote out his statement and he affixed his mark, the impress of his second finger. He then knelt down and began to pray, when the official left the court and the Boxers fell upon him and hacked him in pieces.

Later his son gave a statement of his death, fully agreeing with the official record. Still later the magistrate when discussing with the missionary the terms of indemnity, also told of this man's trial, and then added, " How could I save his life when he said right out where all could hear him that he was a Christian? " That a man could die for his faith was beyond the heathen official's power to comprehend.

A Mr. Wên, with his wife and child, of the same mission, were taken to Prince Chuang's place by the Boxers, but through the influence of a friend were released. As they were leaving, Mr. Wên was again seized, his head was shaved, he was loaded with chains and taken to the country from village to village, the Boxers claiming that they were taking him to Peking for punishment but lacked funds. After levying money in one village they moved to another; in every place Mr. Wên was subjected to insult and indignity from the crowds. While being led about in this way the news reached his captors that the Allies had arrived, upon which they all took to their heels. Mr. Wên hastened to the capital which he reached safely, and later learned that his wife and child had found refuge in the country, so that they were soon reunited.

Mr. Chiang

Mr. Chiang, of the London Mission, was sixty-seven years old, a very saintly Christian, and a great Bible student. He was taken safely to the Methodist Mission, but was anxious about his youngest daughter who was still in the country, and wanted to leave his shelter to find her, At the first opportunity he slipped away and was not seen again.

On his way to the country home he was pointed out to

the Boxers. They seized him and told him they should kill him. He asked for a little time to pray, and falling on his knees he began—" Father forgive them— " but his prayer was not completed. The knives fell on him as he knelt and he was hacked to pieces.

One of the married school girls of this same Mission was saved by her husband in this way. In an unfrequented spot he built a stone hut leaning against a blank wall. It was about four feet square on the ground and six feet high with neither doors nor windows. When the wife and child were inside he bricked up the entrance, leaving only an opening for passing in food. Here the mother and child remained for six weeks, the husband going back and forth at the risk of his life to take them food. Sometimes he was unable to get to them for twenty-four hours together. The poor little child lived only a short time after they were able to leave the hiding place, being reduced about to starvation by the scanty supply of food.

Mr. and Mrs. Chang

One of the young preachers of the London Mission, Mr. Chang, whose wife was a former bright school girl, took his family to the Methodist Mission when the Christians were flocking there from all parts of the city. Later, not thinking that a safe place, he took them back to his adopted father's and left them for a short time. While he was gone the wife, little babe and blind old mother were turned upon the streets by the landlords.

As Mrs. Chang moved slowly along, guiding the steps of the blind mother—not knowing where to go, a Boxer came along, seized her by the sleeve and said "Follow me!" While they went along he had a Boxer trance.

Throwing himself on the ground, he foamed and raved a short time then rose and pointing a stiff finger at her, said " *You ersh mao tzu!* I will kill you!" He soon led her near a city gate where there was a soldier guard of about fifty men and not far away several bodies of those who had been killed.

Mrs. Chang thought she was to be killed and began praying for strength to bear witness for the Lord to the end. They began to question her. "Are you a Christian?" "I am." "Of what church?" "I am a Protestant." He then offered her a stick of incense and said "Burn this and your life will be spared." She replied firmly "Never!" The crowd which had gathered began to shout "Kill! Kill her and see if her body rises again and goes to Jesus Christ." She turned to them and said "My body cut into pieces will remain scattered on the ground like those others, but my spirit will escape you and rise to the Lord." The Boxer started off to get his knife. One of the soldiers called out "You hateful Christian! You ought to die, but what would become of your child? Quick! Run for your life!"

She trembled so she could scarcely step, but ran as fast as was in her power and with the soldiers helping her she escaped before the Boxer returned. Hidden away in a filthy corner she passed the night. Towards morning a man came along with a lantern as if looking for some one. As he drew near she saw it was her husband! He had been looking for her since noon of the day before. They got a cart and escaped to a village, where a friend bought safety by bribing the villagers not to report them. Later Mr. Chang went to the city to try to find his old mother, was arrested by the Boxers and murdered, and his head cut off and offered to the idol.

Christian Students

Wang Chih Shên was a student of the Methodist University, a senior. At the close of the school year he returned to his home at the east. He was well known as a Christian and was soon seized by the Boxers. They urged him to recant. He not only refused to do so but bore testimony before his persecutors to his faith. They tried to make him stop but he persisted in exhorting them and the crowd about him. They finally cut off his lips, then his tongue, and then cut him up limb from limb till he expired. Perhaps no case of greater bravery and greater suffering is known.

Another student when seized and asked "Are you a Christian?" first replied "What would you do with me if I were?" then said "Yes, I am a Christian." They killed him on the spot.

Wu Hsi K'ou was a member of the junior class. He was taken near Shan Hai Kuan where a heathen adopted him as a servant. He kept him safely through the stormy times and when the troops came, gave him clothing and money and sent him away.

At Tsun Hua the keeper of a tea-shop rescued one of the school boys, took him home as a son, cared for him through the time of danger and later when his uncle came searching for him gave him up safely.

Wên Lan was a former pupil of the girl's school and was employed as teacher at Tsun Hua. When the church and school were scattered, she with her grandmother and a few others fled to the hills. For two days they had no food. At last they thought they might as well run the risk of being found by Boxers as of starving to death, so they gathered sticks and lighted a fire. The smoke betrayed their hiding place. The Boxers came and seized them.

In their company was a former student of the University who had been employed on the railroad, and had grown cold in his faith. On the road Wên Lan began exhorting him in English to repent and make ready to die. He tried to stop her as the Boxers would recognize them as Christians, but she said, "We shall tell them plainly we are Christians." She encouraged the little band to be faithful to death. When they were about to be executed she asked to be allowed to speak to the people. It was permitted and she gave an earnest testimony of her faith, then said to her companions, "We shall soon be in heaven," then covered her head with a handkerchief and said "Kill me now." She died after two blows of the knife.

Wang Ching Lin had studied medicine, then entered the regular University course. He was put to death in the city, and it was reported that his body was cut in six pieces.

One student helper was seized and urged to recant. He refused repeatedly. At last they prepared a vessel to receive his blood, made him kneel over it, and began carving on his neck slowly. His courage failed him and he consented to burn the one stick of incense which saved his life.

Young P'u was a Christian servant who was with the missionaries, away from his family. His wife was seized by the Boxers and wounded with a knife. She was a fine appearing woman and they evidently wanted to spare her life. They tried to persuade her to become the wife of one of the Boxers. She refused to do so. They then shaved her head and put on the garments of a Buddhist nun, but she refused to act in this character. At last after vainly trying to make her recant, they decided that nothing was left to do but to kill her. She had two little children. As she was bound, the older child ran by her side carrying the younger, begging the Boxers to spare their mother. They killed the mother and the two children on the same spot.

Mrs. Ma

During the early days of the outbreak a native catechist of the Anglican Church was killed, leaving a wife and two children. Mrs. Ma disguised herself, took her two children and hid away in a temple. She was seen by a friend of her husband, a Mr. Wei, who was very sorry for her helpless condition. Although he was not a church member he was in danger from the Boxers because of friendly relations to foreigners. He had taken the precaution to obtain the good-will of one of the Boxer leaders as a measure of self-protection. He went to this man and told of the death of Mr. Ma, begging that if the wife and children were brought to him he would save their lives, as only Mr. Ma himself was a Christian.

In a short time Mrs. Ma and her children were taken to the altar and she was questioned. " Are you a Christian?" "Yes—I am!" The Boxer leader was perplexed, and finally had her put into a prison. He wrote a letter to Mr. Wei asking what it meant that he should have said she was not a Christian while she said she was. We do not know what further passed between them, but though Mrs. Ma remained true to her faith she was released in a few days and allowed to go unharmed.

Roman Catholic Christians

The refugee Christians of the Protestant Church bear witness to the faithful manner in which Catholics met death in many places.

Deacon Hêng said " In one place I saw the death of a Catholic family. A mother and two children were bound and led away. A neighbour begged for the younger child and took it to keep, but the mother and older child were led away and cut to death. I heard her cry ' O Lord! O Lord! receive my soul! ' That soul truly went to heaven."

Wên Ts'ui, the young girl saved in Shansi, said that the Catholics were very brave. The children when led to death said " You are bringing us great honour! This is our day of great joy! "

Deacon Li of T'ung Chou told of a Catholic hiding in disguise who when brought out and questioned confessed to being a Christian and died for his faith.

Notes of Persecutions of Christians in K'ai P'ing Circuit English Methodist Mission *

Li Fu, preacher at Ying Kê Chuang. Seized by Boxers in Lan Chou district; burned on the back and shoulders in several places; stabbed in the stomach, fortunately not deep enough to cause death; the back of both heels cut with knives so that he will be lame as long as he lives; then bound with ropes so tightly that the marks remain upon his breast to-day, and conveyed to the Yamen at Lan Chou. There his persecutors appealed to the magistrate to execute him, but whether from fear or kindness, he refused to do so, throwing Li Fu into prison, faint and

---

* Contributed at the request of the author by the Rev. John Hedley.

bleeding from his wounds. There he lay for about three months, cared for only by a fellow prisoner, who washed his wounds and shared his food with him. Li Fu was only released from prison when Mr. Hinds returned to Tientsin in September and wrote to the Lan Chou magistrate. The poor fellow suffered so much in the hands of his tormentors that he pleaded with them to put him out of his misery at once, or even to bury him alive. His wife and children were also very badly treated. Mrs. Li had her clothes torn off her back, and with her husband was bound with ropes on a cart. One child, four years old, was caught by the feet, and hurled across the courtyard like a log of wood. Another child received a bullet in her back, yet not a mortal wound. Li has since received a large sum of money as compensation for all his sufferings, but proposes to devote part of it to the building of a chapel, or the support of a preacher in the district where he suffered.

Li Shu Chih. Member at Yung P'ing Fu city chapel. He was caught by the rabble, headed by a wealthy Manchu, bound and carried to our own chapel where a mock trial was held. Here he boldly avowed his Christianity, and, although appealed to several times, absolutely refused to recant. He was beaten with 500 stripes, then thrown into city prison, where after about two months of awful sufferings, he passed away in the faith and hope of the Gospel.

Chang Shou Chên. Preacher at Hsiao Chi. With his wife and seven other members of his family, burned alive in their home.

Chang Yu Wen. A lad seventeen years old. Very earnest member. Resisted so bravely all temptation to recant that his body was chopped in pieces, nailed to wall, and offered for sale at 500 taels per piece—an only child.

At Hê Chuang, thirty li from Yung P'ing Fu, twenty-three members and probationers were killed, most of whom had opportunity to recant. Prominent among those who died were:—

Hê Ming Chang, one of the elders. His wife and little son also perished. Mr. Hê, with his wife and child, had escaped to the hills, but was pursued and recaptured. To all their offers he refused to listen and was burned alive. His wife and child were thrown from the precipice by the brother of Mrs. Hê, who afterward descended and kicked mother and infant to death.

Yang Lin and wife: Yang Yi Ch'ing, wife and daughter: Yang Shou: Yang Chung, one family of seven. Captured together and carried to a temple. Kept there for some hours, but unanimously refusing to recant they were murdered at midnight, their bodies being cut in pieces and flung apart.

Hsü Yang Hsi and daughter. Sister and niece of above Yang Yi Ch'ing. Neither of these had been baptised. Mrs. Hsü was a widow, thirty-two years of age. An uncle of her husband's had a grudge against her because she would not marry again, and himself led the Boxers to her home, where they wounded mother and daughter, and then drowned them in the River Lan. The uncle took possession of the property, but after the first visit of missionaries to Yung P'ing Fu, sent deeds, etc., to the preacher. The magistrate is dealing with this case, and making disposition of the land.

Chên Hsi Kung. Teacher at Pai Chia Tien Tze and a literary graduate. This man's courage and bearing so astonished his persecutors that after killing him they cut out his heart to see what had given him such fortitude. The heart was left for some days on a stone in the village.

Chên Jên Yi. This little fellow, only ten years old, had been baptised as an infant. The child was caught and

NATIVE CHRISTIAN REFUGEE

MANCHU FAMILY, SOME OF THEM CHRISTIANS

asked if he were a Christian, to which he replied that he was. Asked again if he would forsake Jesus, he refused most boldly and was cut down there and then. Two brothers and two nephews, although not baptised, died at the same time.

XXXVI

FIRE AND SWORD AMONG THE SHANSI CHRISTIANS

ON the 19th of September a native Chinese helper named Wang Lan P'u arrived in Peking, with a non-Christian acquaintance who had kindly come many hundred miles to see him safely through the disturbed districts. His story is of great interest, not only in itself, but for the incidental light which it sheds upon the modus in which the almost incredible fanaticism of the Boxers was introduced, took root, and bore its terrible fruits all within the space of a few days, and before any one could have supposed such results possible. Mr. Wang's story is very similar to another brought but two days before by Mr. Fei Ch'i Hao, a graduate in 1898 of the North China College of the American Board at T'ung Chou, who related with extreme circumstantiality the murder of most of the missionaries in the Tai Yuan Fu valley.

With this introduction we will let Mr. Wang tell his own story, which was heard in detail by the writer three different times, on the last occasion full notes being taken, and many details supplied. There was not only no attempt at embellishment, but his own sufferings and those of his family were dismissed in a very few sentences, as being too unimportant to be mentioned, or too terrible to be dwelt upon.

"In the fourth moon (in May) there is held here a large fair which lasts fifteen days, where many horses and mules are sold, and excellent theatrical exhibitions are given, thus attracting enormous crowds. At this fair the Boxer excitement was propagated, and an attack was planned upon the chapel of the China Inland Mission, which was only just completed.

"The local Magistrate, knowing what was going on, went out himself and drove away the crowds threatening the attack, using a whip on them till they were dispersed. This happened twice, but the third time the mob was uncontrollable and the Magistrate was himself beaten, his spectacles knocked off, and his sedan-chair broken in pieces. This was on Sunday, and the missionaries were at the chapel for a service. They escaped to the roof and then took refuge in the house of a church member named Chou, who was a carpenter. The rioters followed and pulled the shop down, the Magistrate losing his official hat in the scuffle. There was a military official there also, and between them they put the missionary (whose name was Larsson) and his companion (who had recently arrived and whose name I do not know) on a cart, the two Magistrates having whips in their hands, and riding outside the cart one on each side to protect the foreigners. The mob followed throwing clumps of dirt and the like, and the curtains of the cart were torn in pieces.

"It was now noon, and when the missionaries arrived their clothes had all been torn to bits, but the Magistrate gave them other clothes and took them into his yamen, saying that he would repay them for their losses. This official's surname was Juan (Rwan) from somewhere in the south of China. He had a kindness to Christianity because when he was a child he had been at a Mission school, and he used often to come into our chapel and look about.

"The missionaries remained in the yamen two or three days. At first nobody cared for the foreigners, they were so occupied in looting the chapel, which was torn down to the foundations, everything being carried away. Elsewhere the chapels were all burned. The Magistrate sent the missionaries on to Ying Chou in the night, as the mob kept coming to the yamen to try to get them. He lent them his own cart, with a Military Official for an escort, and two soldiers, or runners. For the church-members he hired a long cart, so that at Hun Yüan none were killed. At a later period, when they had returned, they were chased about the city and abused, being daubed with filth if they would not recant—but not one of them did so.

"Mr. Karlberg, with whom I worked, and myself remained at Ying Chou. On the 26th and 27th of the moon the people began to pray for rain, but the Magistrate thought there would be no trouble in consequence. He required those that were going through the rain-praying ceremonies to register their names—that is, the leaders—so as to know whom to hold responsible. He sent for the literati and enjoined them to prevent any trouble. Soon the leaders of the Boxers arrived at Ying Chou, inviting coöperation in killing foreigners. Even the children began to learn and practise the drill, and the whole thing was brought to a head within about three days. The Magistrate invited Mr. Karlberg and myself into the yamen, where we remained some days, but as we went in the night not many knew that we were there, and there was no external disturbance. Mr. Karlberg rode on horseback, and reached So P'ing in less than two days, escorted by men sent from the yamen, and there was no trouble anywhere.

"On the first day of the 6th moon things became so

bad that the Magistrate wanted me also to get away. He told me to put on the dress of a yamen courier, gave me one of the yamen horses, and wrote a dispatch to the prefect at So P'ing telling the conditions of things. As bearer of an official letter I should be much safer, though I was well known all along the road. I also took dispatches to the Magistrate at Tso Wei Hsien, the first county town, where I arrived at dark. I went at once to the yamen, just in time to see the chapel there set on fire by a mob. The church members saw me in the yamen, and none of them had then been injured. I only spent a part of the night there, as it was unsafe, and started very early the next morning getting twenty li before daylight, escorted by yamen men.

"By the middle of the forenoon I was in So P'ing Fu, where I went direct to the yamen with the horse and to deliver the dispatches, and then to the mission headquarters to tell the news. Everything was still quiet there. Four of us went to see the Magistrate. The Magistrate went over to see the Prefect when we applied to him, and the latter said, 'Do whatever you like about it,' meaning that he did not care. He is one of the Manchus, who all violently hated Christians, not for any particular reason, only they had a devil inside which made them do so. After this the Magistrate had no plan of his own. He was asked for an escort to Kalgan, and promised to furnish one to the boundaries of his own country. He ordered five or six carts, for which the price was agreed, and he paid it through the yamen men.

"We returned to the chapel much pleased that there appeared to be a way of escape, and were busy getting ready when a mob gathered. In a trice the door was forced, and looting began. We saw that things were hopeless, and again fled to the yamen, the Magistrate giving us one small room for all the missionaries, and another for the Christians, and they were outside not inside rooms. His treatment was very perfunctory, and boded us no good. At this time the crowd had not become savage; they were fully occupied in looting the premises. By noon we had reached the yamen, and the house was soon after burned.

"It was ingeniously proposed to represent to the people that I had come to the city with Imperial Orders just in from Peking, requiring all foreigners to be sent there in manacles. In this way the lives of the prisoners could be saved from the mob, and when we were clear of the city and of danger it would be easy to remove the fetters. To this the missionaries agreed as a shrewd device. A blacksmith was called who made six pairs of handcuffs, one for each of the men. As I had the yamen horse to take back, and my own family to look after, it was thought best that I should return to Ying Chou. I remained in the stable court of the yamen. During this whole day the missionaries were too excited to eat, and when they reached the yamen no one offered them anything, not even a drink. After I had been asleep some time, being very much exhausted, I was loudly called out by name, and everyone saw that mischief was meant. I could not escape, so I went out and found a great crowd of Boxers and Manchus, who began to beat me terribly and dragged me off to the still burning chapel to throw me into the fire.

"It was not long before I lost consciousness entirely, being half dead and supposed to be entirely so. I learned afterwards that the Boxers felt me to see if I was really dead and thinking that I was, they did not care to drag me the rest of the way simply for the trouble of throwing me into the fire. Besides, two men were standing by who befriended me by using a great deal of conciliatory language to the Boxers, begging them to let me die where I was. One of them was from a village near by, the other a sort of local bully in the city who had often seen me in the street chapel. He was fond of the doctrine, only he could never make up his mind to repent. They felt my heart and pulse, saw that I had no mortal wound, and waited by for me to revive, which the night-chill helped me do. The mob, meantime, had left me, to go back to the yamen and try to drag the missionaries out to kill them. There were ten or more Christians there, whom they beat severely; some of them probably were killed, but they did not get at the missionaries.

"My benefactors helped me up and took me back to the yamen, and wanted to lay me inside where I had been before, but the yamen men would not admit me on any terms. 'Suppose he should die here, who would be supposed to have killed him?' But they gave the two men my horse, clothes, bedding, cash-bag, and my dispatch, and while one of them led my horse the other one carried me on his back outside the city. Between them they helped me on the horse, though I was so weak and faint that unless supported by one while the other led the animal I could not have sat on him. They went with me all the way to an inn, where we happened to meet the cook of the missionary family. We dared not stay there, so they soon all helped me on the horse again.

"The cook returned to his home in Fên Chou Fu, and the man from the city went with me all the way to the end of the first day's journey. On the way, at a town forty li from the city, I met travellers who told me that that morning thirteen foreigners had been killed near So P'ing Fu. I heard this at two different times, and am sure it is true. They were probably manacled, and could make no resistance. I gave the men who escorted me some clothes for their kindness, as I had no money. In my feeble condition I was three days in getting to Ying Chou.

"When at a town forty li away from there I was told that it was useless to go back, as the place had been destroyed on the third of the sixth moon (June 29th). I heard also that my mother and others had been sent by the Magistrate in a cart to So P'ing Fu, but that she had been overtaken by the Boxers half a day's journey distant, brought back, and herself, with my brother, sister, my little child and an old lady named Wu (my wife had died in the second moon) buried alive. Not only this, but the head yamen-runner who had escorted them was also thrown into the fire, the cart burned, the mule killed and thrown into the flames, as well as the dog and chickens of the yard I lived in. People were not tied, but just thrown into the fire loose and driven back whenever they tried to get out. It was a slow and a bitter death, which I do not like to think of.

"All the church members were captured at the same time, except my brother who used to do a little trade and sell Christian books on his own account, and was away from home at the time. The Magistrate was informed of these events, and did his best to save the life of his own yamen servants, but was told that if he pressed the matter he himself would be thrown into the fire too.

"Notwithstanding these dreadful stories I could not give up the idea of returning to see for myself if this was true,—and there was the horse to be taken to the yamen. So I went on by myself. About ten li from the city a band of forty or more Boxers set on me, and recognizing me with glee, ordered me to get off the horse, tied me tightly and dragged me on to the city. They called their Head-master of Boxers, who happened to be a tinker, whose occupation was mending iron kettles. He could not even read, but now he was a 'Head-master.' The Magistrate soon had my arrival reported to him, and heard that the Head-master was trying the case. The Magistrate sent a polite invitation to the Head-master to come to him, which he did.

"Then the Magistrate said that he had all along felt grave doubts whether these were true Boxers, and whether they could, as pretended, keep out arrows and bullets. He now proposed to test this. 'Let your men go through their spells, make themselves invulnerable if they can, and I will attack them with guns. If you are not hurt, you may kill the courier Wang in any way you like; you are true Boxers and I will be one too; otherwise I shall know that you are not the true Boxers, and your claim is a fraud.' The Head-master had the Boxers from one village or region only with him, but he thought it over, and as it seemed a fair proposition he assented, but wished himself not to be in the ranks but to one side, so that he could tell when the Spirits had really arrived. He also insisted that the test should not begin until he announced that the Spirits had arrived. To this the Magistrate agreed.

"By this time it was late at night—nearly midnight—but, the story having got out, the whole city was there with torches and lanterns to see the spectacle. There was a Chên Wu Temple on the city wall, and in front of that the Boxers were drawn up making their passes in the air and otherwise practising for the trial.

"Most of the many onlookers were below the wall in a good position to see. The four yamen men that the Magistrate had appointed to guard me wanted to see and loosed me, so that we could all look on together. The

Magistrate had given careful directions and looked after the loading of the guns himself with balls as well as powder. Foreseeing that there was to be trouble he had engaged two hundred experts who could fight, wrestle and shoot, to be his guards, and it was these men that he set against the Boxers. They waited until the Head-master cried 'Shên lai la' (The spirits have come), when the Magistrate, who had a gun himself, gave the order 'K'ai ch'iang' (Open fire). Four or five of the Boxers were killed outright, six or seven were hurt so that they fell over the city wall, and not a single man among them was without a wound. Then they all scattered.

"The Magistrate now summoned me and told me how he had been unable to protect his own yamen headman, and that it was not safe for me to remain. He gave me twenty ounces of silver and some brass cash, together with an official letter which I was to take to T'ai Yuan Fu (where I expected to go), mainly as a protection to me in travelling. Although very unfit to ride a horse or even to move at all, I went away that night. We then knew nothing about the attitude of the Governor toward the missionaries, or I should never have thought of going in that direction.

"After about thirty li I got into serious trouble. There was a crowd at a large village who suspected me, and were sure that I was a follower of foreigners. They accused me of having little figures of men cut out of yellow paper, and foreign bewildering medicines about me, and searched me to see. In this way they found my silver, and also the official letter. It was nothing but the latter that saved my life. Then the crowd was divided, some crying: 'Kill him anyway and be done with him;' while the rest said: 'He is a courier, let him go on his official route; it is none of our business.' In this way they wrangled for a whole half day, and some well-intentioned people spoke a good word for me. In almost every mob there are some of this kind; not all are the very worst.

"I learned afterwards, what I did not then suspect, that there was a little party who privately agreed that it was best to let me go, and then they would pursue me on their own account, rob and kill me, and divide the silver among them. I went on as far as I could, and had got seven or eight li when some men came running after me, crying out that I must leave the big road and take a byway, for there was a band of men just behind intending to chase and kill me, who were armed with swords and guns. This perplexed me very much, and I was not sure but this was a plot to kill me. They were very urgent, so I yielded, and left the road where there was a pass in front and a mountain near. It was not a cart road, but for pack-mules only. I came to a village and begged them to let me rest there for a time, but they would have nothing to do with me.

"But at another small village an old man was kind to me, and advised me against going to T'ai Yuan Fu, which was 800 or 900 li, while it was only 600 or so to Pao Ting Fu, the capital of Chihli. Here I stayed for three days until the pursuers would have all gone back, and then I made a detour around the mountain and regained the main road. After this I went to Wu T'ai Hsien, where the famous mountain is, escorted by a man who was sent by my village friends, with whom I had to share my silver, so that I had very little left. Beyond this, at a place called Tai Ving, I met the Boxers again, and was once more examined. Here I told a different story from the former one, and said I was a trader returning home. I had torn up the official document which would now have implicated me. Not to have told different stories at different times would have been impossible; there was really no help for it. Finding that Boxers were worse and worse the further on I went, I resolved to turn back into the mountains again, 120 li to a city named Fu P'ing. I did not then know the characters, but as 'Fu' means happiness, and 'P'ing' peace, I thought the Lord was opening a way to both, and though the first character was wrong, I did get relief. I told my story to the inn-keeper, and he advised me to do a little trading with what small funds I had left.

" There was a neighbour of his who knew how to make twisted dough-nuts fried in oil, and I got to know him, gave all my things to him as security, and did a small business in this way with him for more than two months. There were no Boxers at all in that place. When it came to the 8th moon, I thought I might go on. In that time I had cleared a string and a half of cash, and bought a good many things besides. I had no adventures on the way to Pao Ting Fu, and there I heard that all the foreign buildings had been burned, and many church members killed. I did not hear of the murder of any foreigners there. On the way to Peking the Sikh soldiers took away the money of myself and the man who came down with me. It is a great joy to me to see so many Christians together again, and to tell and to hear of the Lord's mercies."

NOTE — The following are the names of the missionaries murdered at So P'ing Fu, so far as known —
Of the Swedish Union, Mr. and Mrs. S. A. Persson, Mr. N. Carleson, Mr. O. A. L. Larsson, Mr. G. E. Karlberg, Miss J. Lundell, Miss J. Engvall, Miss M. Hedlund, Miss A. Johannsson.
Of the Christian and Missionary Alliance, Mr. and Mrs. C. Blomberg and child.

XXXVII

A TWELVE-MONTH OF FOREIGN OCCUPATION

IMMEDIATELY after the siege was raised, Peking was divided among the armies of invasion for purposes of patrol and as a base for possible operations elsewhere. The Russians and the Japanese appeared to have the largest number of troops, but as the coming and going was incessant, no accurate statements were possible for more than a day at a time.

In about a month it was suddenly announced that the Russian forces were to be withdrawn, and, soon after, the Russian Legation actually departed for Tientsin, where it remained for a short time and then returned, its lead not being followed by any other Power. It was evident that the occupation of Manchuria was causing a great deal of trouble, and that if other armies could be persuaded to leave Peking at the suggestion of Russia, the latter would gain the credit for doing China a good turn, while at the same time serving her own interests.

For the remaining months, until the end of the year, there was an increasing series of military expeditions in every direction from Tientsin and from Peking, some of which were on a large scale and fully reported, while others attracted little attention. The one which was of the chief interest was that to Pao Ting Fu, starting both from Tientsin and Peking, the intention being to arrive simultaneously. The result illustrated the inherent weakness of a campaign in which eight distinct sets of armies bore a hand. The French from Tientsin arrived just a week before the British, the German, and the Italian contingent, and it was currently reported that they exacted a heavy "ransom" on their own account for sparing the city. Whether this is true it appears impossible to ascertain with certainty. Military operations anywhere are hard to follow and the facts difficult to verify. In this case they are at least eight times as obscure as usual, and some of them do not appear to be objects of knowledge at all.

It was soon perceived that if any one first-class Power had been dealing with China, progress would have been definite and steady. In the case of two Powers, the delays were twice as great and the progress twice as slow. With three Powers the friction was so much increased that the pace was diminished by a still larger percentage; and by the time that all eight armies had to be reckoned with, it becomes a complex and practically insoluble problem whether the decrease of efficiency has been inversely as the square of the number of Powers involved, or as the cube of the number of Major-Generals.

At Pao Ting Fu an investigation was held into the behaviour of the Provincial Treasurer, Ting Jung, who had been the patron of the Boxer movement for the whole year. As a result of that trial, he was condemned to be beheaded, together with the Tartar General of the City and the Lieutenant-Colonel of the camp, who had refused protection to foreigners, and whose soldiers had stood idly by while the burning of the Mission premises and the slaughter of missionaries was in progress. Of all the acts of the military since the capture of Peking, this is the one most righteous in itself and most salutary in its result, yet it has been perversely criticised as a bloodthirsty cry for "vengeance," unworthy of Western nations!

The German expedition to Kalgan, four days to the northwest of Peking, was widely known by reason of the accidental suffocation of one of the high military officers by the fumes of charcoal. What it amounted to it would be difficult to say with precision. There was a raid in the direction of the Imperial Tombs, for moral effect, with results hard to summarize beyond the exasperation of the Chinese and the demoralization of the troops. It is always a delicate matter to keep soldiers under control when in an enemy's country.

The circumstances of the Boxer uprising appear to have convinced the commanders of the armies of invasion that the rules of international law had no application to China at that time. There is, moreover, a contagious demoralization of fighting men when they perceive others acting in a lawless manner. War is itself a repeal of law; and of the extent to which it shall be abrogated the soldiers themselves must to a large extent be judges. If this, or anything like it, was true of the larger expeditions sent out incessantly, it was far more so of those minor raids of which the public knows little or nothing.

It would be a gross misrepresentation to affirm that all the commanders or all the soldiers of any section of the allied armies have been lawless and violent, for in that case the results would have been such as took place along the banks of the Amur River, where helpless, inoffensive villagers by the thousand were slaughtered and their bodies thrown into the broad stream until it was positively choked with them. But armies, like individuals, will be judged, not by the best but by the worst which they have done; and in this case the worst must be admitted to have been very bad indeed. There have been times when it has seemed as if the foreign troops had come to northern China for the express purpose of committing within the shortest time as many violations as possible of the sixth, the seventh, and the eighth Commandments. The combined result has been such a state of chaos in many districts as is at once incredible and indescribable. Of the promiscuous murder of non-combatants there is overwhelming evidence, which need not be cited. The only defence of this which is ordinarily made is to reply: " Oh yes, of course, war is always like that—what do you expect it to be?"

Of the looting and wholesale robbery with violence, both in expeditions and in districts which have been visited by small military parties, much has been written, but it will be long before the whole terrible catalogue of crimes is known. Long lists of the exactions made on Chinese officials and cities could be (and have been) made out, showing that the total sums extorted for alleged " protection " and " ransom " have been sufficient to impoverish the country for a long period. In some instances the same cities and towns have been visited repeatedly with reduplicated demands; and the fact that the expeditionary " spheres of influence " have been vaguely defined and imperfectly regarded, so that the same city might be raided by different sets of soldiers, has made the condition of large regions more or less anarchic.

Two expeditions should be mentioned which stand out especially as examples of what has been already mentioned, each under the conduct of the Germans. Of these the first was to Ts'ang Chou, a city about sixty miles south of Tientsin, on the Grand Canal. The Magistrate of the city had always been friendly to the foreigners, who had just removed the station of the London Mission to the vicinity and put up extensive buildings. The Chinese military officer in charge of the Chihli troops was General Mei, who was not only on the best of terms with the various foreigners living in that part of the province, but had made it his principal business for the greater part of the previous twelve months to fight the Boxers whenever and wherever they could be found, and had probably done more to defeat, disperse, and discourage them than any other man in China.

The Germans made a raid upon Ts'ang Chou, plundered the yamens of the Magistrate and that of General Mei, who prudently retired to a distance upon their approach. They released all the Boxer prisoners whom they found in the city jail, returning to Tientsin in triumph, whence a despatch was sent to Shanghai informing the world of " A Successful Attack," saying that " the Germans have routed General Mei's forces at Ts'ang Chou, looted his baggage, and killed forty-three men."

To those cognizant of the facts this inexcusable folly boded no good for the denizens of such territory as may hereafter come under German rule in Shantung or elsewhere. Is it any wonder that General Mei is said to have complained that " on all eight sides I have no face [self-respect and respect of others] left? "

In the district city of Yung Ch'ing Hsien, between Tientsin and Peking, where Messrs. Norman and Robinson were killed early in June, the Germans made a visit and killed nearly a hundred and fifty persons, with no loss to themselves, under circumstances so indefensible that the British remitted the monetary fines which had been imposed on the city, and employed the money in relieving the acute distress caused by the barbarity of the Germans! When attention was called to these and numerous similar acts of the Germans, their military authorities were greatly stirred up against Dr. Morrison, the correspondent of the London "Times," who had first formulated the feelings of those acquainted with the facts. The result is supposed to have been, not the threatened "court martial" of Dr. Morrison, who had purposely understated the facts, but the imposition of a certain amount of restraint upon German military action.

As the result of all that gloomy winter one of the lessons which have been impressed upon the Chinese in varied but convincing forms is the moral inferiority of foreigners to Chinese. This the Chinese had always known and believed, but had never been able to demonstrate.

Many years ago a son of Li Hung Chang, while under a foreign instructor in Tientsin told him that his father had once said that formerly he himself had supposed Westerners as a whole to be more honest and more truthful than Chinese, but his long and intimate experience of their ways had taught him the opposite. And, indeed, in the item of struggles for contracts with the Chinese Government, the Syndicates who had need to deal with the Viceroy, have not invariably illustrated the highest qualities of the civilization whence they sprung.

But with the occupation of China by foreign armies the veil—if there was one—has been torn away. The extent of the lawlessness committed by Western troops in China has probably been greatly exaggerated in the reports to the press, but the conditions at the beginning were horribly bad, though they steadily improved, partly no doubt in consequence of the "bright sunlight of publicity" which is nowhere without its deterrent force.

Making all abatements, however, the impression upon the Chinese, who only know or can know the facts through the repercussion of rumour and through distorted native journalistic media, is distinctly to lower the not too high estimate which the Chinese had previously placed upon Western character and morals. For them there is a simple and easy explanation—foreigners have never enjoyed the blessing of a thorough mastering of the contents of the Four Confucian Books, and the Five Confucian Classics. While they recognize with clearness that the worst that has happened in China is but a fraction of what the Chinese would have themselves perpetrated in any foreign country which they might have overrun, the fact that Western nations have always assumed the moral inferiority of the Chinese, and have posed as their instructors, not in abstract principles only but in their daily exemplification, has added to the sting of the disillusion.

The Chinese have also been enabled by these months of foreign occupation distinctly to perceive what all discerning persons predicted, that foreigners have no adequate talents for dealing with the Chinese on a large scale. The ancient and compact civilization of China has been in operation for millenniums, and there is a way and a rule for everything. The Westerner comes in with calm confidence that he will show them a thing (or perhaps two), and he does. The Chinese adapt themselves to the sinuosities of the Occidental temperament as the water fits the boat which rushes through it, or as the air closes about the flying projectile. But when the boat or the bullet has passed, the water and the air are *in situ,* ready for any number more of the same kind.

Despite the jaunty way in which even those of long experience in China and the Far East speak of the facility of governing China through foreign hands, and always cite "India" in evidence, it is plain to the discriminating observer that there is really no just analogy between the two. India is a museum of races and languages, while China is essentially a unit in its ideas and its ideals, as well as in its history, language, and institutions. It ought to be understood by this time that without the consent of the Chinese themselves no Power on earth can really rule them, though many Powers may overrun and endeavour to control them. If the Chinese, during this year of stress and strain have succeeded in finding out what "the Powers" want to do with the Chinese Empire when it is within their combined "sphere of influence," they have learned more than any one else knows or for some time to come is likely to know.

The inevitable division among foreign councils has been familiar to the Chinese ever since they have known foreigners at all, and the Chinese and the Turkish Governments have united (and competed) in their capacity and talent for making the most effective use of that fact against them all. But the phenomena of the past year, when all the Powers had the greatest possible motives for combination, which lasted until the Legations were relieved (and no longer), have taught the Chinese anew that in disunion is feebleness.

That China will escape from much that at first appeared inevitable as a punishment is as certain as that eleven different Nations have been worrying at her doors, awaiting the settlement of their claims and due "guarantees" for the future. The Chinese can and will give them all, for in that line they have seldom failed, and in this hour of their greatest distress are not likely to do so. An individual Chinese will and does make the most abundant promises, when he is in trouble, as to what he will do if only he is allowed another day of grace. The Chinese Government, which has been in a tighter place than any of its subjects ever imagined it could be, can do no other than adopt this policy, while the "experts" show in what way this can be accomplished—as very possibly it can be. Whether it will be, is another matter, for the future, even in the fixed and immobile Orient, is full of pleasant surprises. Still, like the cheerful Chinese, we shall hope for the best, and will await the result with what patience we may.

The Empress Dowager has recently been issuing the most admirable Imperial Edicts on the subject of the protection of missionaries and of converts. "The failure to do this last year was contrary to our wish often expressed, and hence many heads have fallen. Hereafter there must be no failure in this direction." How repentant this sounds, and how hollow as the supple bamboo, which yields to the strongest pressure in any given direction, and upon removal of the same instantly resumes its former position!

At Washington it is the fashion to look at the Chinese situation through the colored glasses furnished by the clever Mr. Wu, whose presence abroad at this crisis is to China the greatest stroke of good fortune. It is easy for him to represent that the Chinese Government is more than ready to take over the functions of office everywhere, and that it is quite capable of keeping order. But it cannot possibly be comprehended in Western lands how utterly the Government of China is dependent upon the temper of the officials and of the people to get its orders executed. The great storm which has swept over the face of China was raised by complex and long-continued causes, but it will not subside in a month nor in a year, and, unless all signs are deceptive, the tranquillity which will be everywhere reported after an interval will frequently be found to be only superficial.

During the period in January and February when the Court seemed to be hesitating to grant the irrevocable demands for the punishment of the more important guilty parties, the influence of that hesitation is known to have been felt immediately in the military camps in Shantung, under the command of Governor Yuan Shih K'ai. They were apparently ordered to be ready to march northward at an early day, and it was popularly supposed that a large body of southern troops had been somewhere gathered to support the advance, which was to be a death-struggle with the foreigner. Even if the army was beaten, it would at least make the whole country a waste, and so useless to the invader. While this was probably mere rumour, or at most a preparation for a possible contingency, and perhaps nothing but empty bluster, in either case it equally showed the determined bent of the Chinese mind.

The wild passions which have been raised are not to be spirited out of existence by a mere edict announcing that peace has been arranged for all within the Four Seas, for the facts which underlie the troubles have been at last ground into the Chinese national consciousness as never before. It is a significant circumstance that, simultaneously with this military programme, the Shantung Boxers have again begun to assert themselves, holding a formal gun-drill (such as last year announced actual hostilities) at a village within twenty miles of the home of the writer of these lines. That fact was accompanied by the open proclamation of an intention to resume the operations of last year, under the directions of the " Great Fairy," who superintended them. This dignitary has officially informed the Boxers that in the previous outbreaks they had squandered their opportunity by requiring ransom money, and by the spoliation of the houses of Christians, whereas this time all that was to be absolutely forbidden, and in the new attack every Christian was to

VICINITY OF LEGATION STREET, PEKING

be killed, as well as the chickens and the dogs, that there might be no root left alive when the grass should be cut up.

These renewed attempts, with the wide-spread brigandage that attends them, may be purely local. But they are not the less worthy of notice as an indication of what many of the Chinese would like to do were it within their power. There is no reasonable doubt of the intentions of Governor Yuan and other officers like-minded, but here again we must reckon with the "personal equation" on an enormous scale. No Chinese and no Manchu, whatever his rank, can conduct the work of his position against the united opposition of his subordinates. As the Chinese saying goes, "One can manage with Pluto, but it is with the small devils that the trouble comes." Yuan has issued the most stern proclamations, offering incentives and positive rewards for the total suppression of troubles with foreigners for a period of three years, but in many districts these proclamations remain unposted, and the people are left in ignorance of his utterances.

Another feature of the past twelve-month has been the manœuvring of China's great antagonist, Russia, to play, as at other times, the rôle of benevolent protector. The American public, especially, dislikes to entertain the smallest suspicion that it does not apprehend the basal facts of the Chinese situation to such an extent as to render the usual snap judgment safe. But it is not strange that the peculiar relations between the Chinese and the Russian Empires should not have been forced upon the notice of the Americans. To an unprejudiced spectator it is clear that no foe ever so gravely threatened the existence of the Chinese Government as Russia has done and is still doing, yet the Chinese, while shrewd observers and gifted with remarkable insight into motives and intentions, show little apparent perception of the real condition of their Empire as related to their colossal neighbour. Sometimes Chinese statesmen, when asked how it is that they have drifted into this condition, simply reply, "What could we do to prevent it?"—an inquiry to which it is not easy to formulate a satisfactory answer.

All the world was aroused during the early spring to the gravity of the situation in regard to Russian domination of Manchuria, although what the world proposes to do about it finally, other than to send Notes and to propose inquiries, is not apparent. Yet the situation is not inherently different from what it has been for some years, except that the folly of the Chinese, in their wanton attacks on Russian cities and settlements, put the handle of the sword into the hands of Russia, to use a Chinese phrase—an advantage which, whatever other Powers may say or do, she is not likely to surrender.

Ever since the conclusion of the war with Japan in the spring of 1895 such a state of things was distinctly foreshadowed, but nothing was then done about it. Lord Charles Beresford published in his literary weighty volume on "The Break-up of China," the protests handed to him by the representatives of the British Municipal Council of Tientsin, who informed him that at that time Manchuria was practically a Russian province. This was at least a brevet fact, if it had not then been promoted to the dignity of past history, but no attention seems to have been paid to it in our own country, except noting the statement.

Here is a door the closing of which will make a difference of unknown millions of dollars in American trade, and that door shows signs of being forcibly slammed shut. The State Department at Washington then secures written affirmations, from a great variety of sources, that each of the Powers approves in theory and will support in practice the plan of fastening the door open on equal terms to all. No one Power more cordially assents to this proposition than Russia. It is exactly in the line of her policy, her wishes, and her practice. We were all delighted to have American diplomacy score a decided and a unique triumph, impossible to other Powers with a less pronouncedly altruistic history; and essays on "The Open Door in China" filled the journals for many months. Meantime Russia goes on with her preparations, and when the heaven-sent fatuity of the Boxers gives the golden opportunity, she knocks out the chocks, slams the door, puts the key in her military chest, posts a strong guard in the province, warns off all others, draws up an agreement of a stringent character with China in the face of all the Powers, smiles blandly at the Anglo-German agreement, with which she is in full harmony, and cordially sympathizes with the dictum of Daniel Webster that "the past, at least, is secure."

The formal and merely nominal retirement of Russia from her claims for the signature of the Manchurian Convention may be laid to the partial agreement of some of the Powers most nearly concerned, as well as to the unexpected expression of Chinese sentiment all over the Empire, which it is certainly not to the interest of Russia to antagonize. That the disavowal of hostile intentions on the part of the great Empire of the North means anything more than the usual temporizing, until the times are more favourable, no one probably believes, whatever for diplomatic purposes he may say to the contrary. It is an ancient and a significant Chinese adage that "A monkey's hand drops no dates," and the same generalization applies to bears—especially to the species which has learned to be fond of Chinese dates. Every friend of

China and of Japan must sympathize with the difficult position of the latter (as well as the former), forced to choose a time for the inevitable conflict, the outcome of which no human intelligence can foresee.

The list of punishments demanded by the Powers upon guilty officials in consequence of their complicity in the atrocities of last year, is surprisingly small in the eyes of the Chinese themselves, the number of those to be executed embracing less than fifteen persons, although about 240 defenceless and innocent men, women and children, of several nationalities, were deliberately massacred by official orders, largely in yamens or by soldiers detailed for the purpose. The ostentatious leniency of the Russians is a strange exhibition from a nation which could tolerate the savage butchery of innocent Chinese on the banks of the Amur River.

When it is remembered what these men have done, and with what savage brutality many of them have plotted to exterminate every foreigner in their jurisdiction, it is evident to every one acquainted with the conditions that in the New China, that ought to ensue after peace negotiations have been completed, such officials ought not for a moment to be tolerated. The cry which appears to be so popular in the United States, that to demand the capital punishment of less than two score Chinese officials as a partial expiation of the deliberate crime of the Chinese Government is an exhibition of " bloodthirstiness," betrays a hopeless incapacity to comprehend the real conditions in China, and, what is of more importance, to grasp the aspects in which the matter must present itself to the Chinese mind.

If Western Powers, whether moved by sentimentality or by a desire to trade upon the supposed good will of the Chinese, to be gained by minimizing the guilt of the guilty, are to slur over the past and deal weakly with those who are not only criminals in our eyes but in those of the Chinese themselves, the inevitable result must be to reawaken in all Chinese officials and people alike a thorough contempt for Westerners who are so easily hoodwinked. The Chinese will attribute the result to every motive but the real one, and will certainly think and feel that Powers who have held the sword in hand so long, and yet have failed to employ it as Chinese know that it ought to be employed, are not to be dreaded in the future; and it is a moral certainty that the Chinese will act in accordance with this view.

There was a special incongruity in this false sympathy for Chinese wrong-doers when the Powers were governing the cities of Tientsin, Pao Ting Fu, and Peking, and were inflicting punishments upon Chinese miscreants in accordance with Chinese law, without reference to Western codes. The Germans particularly are reported to have cut off the heads of many hundred Chinese within their jurisdiction, many of them for absolutely trivial offenses. This is regarded as simply a question of military administration, and no notice whatever seems to be taken of it, while the settlement of the penalties for the great international crime of 1900 is hindered from sources the most opposite, through selfishness and sentimentality.

In this connection it is well to mention that renewed attention has just been called in the foreign press of China to the terrible nature of the sufferings to which the martyred missionaries were in many cases subjected. The matter is a painful and a delicate one, especially in the case of the ladies, but the suspicion that there is an effort to suppress the facts, lest the knowledge of them should lead to restrictions upon missionary work in the interior, has only led to the publication of the most terribly shocking details, said to have been obtained from the lips of eye-witnesses. It is undoubtedly better that the whole truth should be known, for it must sooner or later come to the surface, and it is only by a calm contemplation of all the facts that a wise conclusion can be reached as to what ought to be done to prevent a recurrence of similar atrocities.

The prospect for such prevention is by no means as hopeful as it should be. For ten months this part of China has practically been embarked upon a foreign fleet, tossing about in a stormy sea. Now the time has arrived when the passengers and crew must be transferred back to the old unseaworthy Chinese junks in which they were before. The gangways are all down, the water is full of small sampans waiting to take men and cargo, but there is so much of a swell that the exchange is not an easy one to effect, and some will probably get drowned.

The very first step toward the safe transfer is the return of the court to Peking. But that the Emperor should return alone, though much desired by foreigners and by the most patriotic Chinese, seems not to have been suggested. This means, the Occidental reader will do well to bear in mind, that the relation of the Empress Dowager to the Chinese Government—a relation of essential identity—is exactly what it was when one year ago she gave the order to fire upon the Legations. It is not known that the question of her right to rule the Empire which she has brought to the verge of ruin and disruption has been so much as seriously considered.

The most melancholy feature of a situation full of varying shades of colour, with a predominance of the darker ones, is that the Powers have taken no notice whatever of the deposition of the rightful Emperor, of the fact that his present anomalous relations to the Government of his Empire are unsatisfactory and fraught with peril, that the recognized Heir Apparent is a youth destitute of character, whose assumption of power would probably complete the ruin of the country within a year, and that the Empress Dowager, who has brought this condition of things upon China and the World, still holds the scepter undisputed and irresistible.

It is vain to cherish the fiction that these circumstances have no relation to anything which the Powers can do. It is these conditions which have brought the present crisis, and to ignore them is to invite future disaster, as is clearly foreseen and constantly predicted by the discerning. Yet as a year ago at this time, nothing is done about the perils visibly imminent, and the hopeless disagreement of the Powers probably renders action of real unity impossible.

The Rev. Timothy Richard has visited Peking at the request of the Governor of Shansi and the Chinese Peace Commissioners, and has drawn up a scheme for the settlement of the Protestant cases in that province which is so conspicuously fair and just (and so utterly in contrast to the Roman Catholic demands) that the Chinese press comments upon it with uniform approbation. In consideration of the fact that the people were acting under orders in their riots of last year, he suggests that one Boxer leader in each district be punished as a warning; that the losses of converts be provided for and provision made for widows and orphans; that the province raise half a million taels, one-tenth to be paid each year, for the establishment of schools to enlighten the people of Shansi, thus avoiding delusions in the future—one educated foreigner and one educated Chinese to manage the business; monumental stones to be erected wherever converts were killed; the officials, gentry, scholars, and people to receive courteously missionaries whenever again sent, and apologize for the past; equal treatment to be granted converts and non-converts in everything; and lists to be kept of the names of rioters, that they may be punished if they again offend. These principles have been agreed to by the representatives of the Protestant societies working in Shansi—the China Inland Mission, the American Board, the English Baptist, the Gospel Mission, and an independent organization.

These suggestions were submitted to Li Hung Chang, who is said to have been exceedingly pleased with the moderation of the demands, exclaiming that never yet had there been in China such an enlightened and moderate gentleman as Dr. Richard had shown himself to be, and that if these suggestions were put into effect there would be no more missionary troubles in the Empire. Dr. Richard's long residence in Shansi—from 1876 to 1886—his devotion and tact in distributing famine relief at the beginning of that period, his cordial relations with officials from the Governor down, and his wide reputation as the best known and most representative Protestant missionary in China, combine to give his recommendations great weight.

Representatives of nine of the important missionary societies in China have recently issued, both in English and in Chinese, a "Statement" in regard to the connection between missionaries and the present crisis. It is of the nature of an explanation, and incidentally a defence, and has attracted favourable comment from the leading foreign journals of Shanghai for its conspicuous fairness and moderation of language. A paragraph from an article in the "North China Daily News" dealing with it should be quoted: "The charge that missionaries have manifested an improper desire to see vengeance done on

DR. AMENT RECEIVING VILLAGE DEPUTATION

FOREIGN OCCUPATION

the perpetrators of last year's outrages is, except in possible isolated cases, as unfounded as Mark Twain's ignorant charges against Dr. Ament and his colleagues in Peking and its vicinity. Men who have examined the whole question with an honest desire to arrive at the truth without prejudice or partiality allow that the behaviour of the missionaries as a body has not only been above reproach, but worthy of praise and gratitude. They have been anxious, as we have all been anxious, to see outrages such as those of last year made impossible in the future, and as long as human nature is what it is, men must be deterred from crime by the conviction that it will be followed by punishment; and not to have punished, and punished severely, the culprits of last year, would have been to invite a repetition of their crimes."

It is a hopeful circumstance that Minister Conger will soon be on his way out again. It is simply a fact that at the present time there is no other man who can take his place, or who ought to take it. Like all the other Ministers, he did not foresee the coming cyclone in China, but when it came he proved a tower of strength, not to Americans only, but to the common defence—a service ill requited by the theory prevalent at Washington that because his insight was so much greater and more accurate than that of any one in Washington, his "mind was affected!" As President Lincoln desired more Generals who drank the "whisky" to which General Grant was alleged to be addicted, so the United States Legations abroad would do well to lay in a stock of Ministers who have the common sense and the manliness of Mr. Conger.

It is incidentally a gratification to many whose sense of justice has been outraged by the captious criticisms of those with neither knowledge nor candour to comprehend existing conditions, to see that Mr. Conger has not hesitated to take the responsibility for his own advice consistently given to American citizens acting in times of storm and stress. He has comprehensively replied to all the current criticism by the remark: " I am prepared to justify the conduct of the missionaries before the siege, during the siege, and after the siege."

It is well for the friends of those moral reforms without which the regeneration of this Empire is utterly impossible, to bear in mind that existing conditions do not alter our duty to China, but only modify present action. If anything is certain it is that there is to be in some form a new China. For that we should watch, and perhaps wait, but not idly nor as those without hope. All mission methods should be re-examined, as ships are overhauled in the dry-docks, but always with reference to a new and a longer voyage than the last.

XXXVIII

THE OUTLOOK

THE questions arising in consequence of the Convulsion in China are too numerous and too comprehensive to be recapitulated in a closing chapter, even if from a single point of view they could all be understood. In the preceding pages an effort has been made to point out some of the remoter underlying and predisposing causes of this great movement, which in the peculiar condition existing was an inevitable part of the evolution of the international relations of mankind. Other nations were driven toward intercourse with China by an impulse which they could no more resist than the waters of the ocean can withstand the pull of the moon, clearly recognizing that no nation has either the right or the power to refuse such intercourse. As a result China was forced into relations with the West, unwillingly accepting treaties which she intended to keep only while they could not be evaded or broken.

Had the Occidental Powers invariably observed the far-reaching rule of Lord Elgin never to make an unjust demand and never to retreat from a just demand once made, China would have been peacefully coerced into right relations with the rest of the World, to her own unspeakable benefit and ours. As it was, the impact of Western Nations on China was met by unvarying evasion, duplicity, falsehood, arrogance, and an intolerable insolence which from time to time brought on conflicts, and always with the same ultimate results.

The occurrences of the year 1900 displayed upon a great scale the emptiness of those Chinese pretensions which have never been and are not yet abandoned. They have also exhibited, notwithstanding the universal prevalence of a lofty system of theoretical morality, a " dauntless mendacity," a barbaric cruelty, and a colossal pride, unexampled in modern history. The result of the humiliation of China before the Powers is to leave them confronted with the gravest problem which Occidental civilization has ever faced. Great issues hang upon the outcome, both for China and for the World. That the wishes and the supposed interests of the Powers are not only not identical but apparently hopelessly irreconcilable, has long been plain, from which arises the ominous and significant fact that the only progress possible has been by the composition of counteracting forces.

The outline of the terms of settlement with China involved a mission of apology to Germany for the murder of her minister; monuments in desecrated cemeteries; a prohibition of the importation of arms and munitions of war; the destruction of the Taku and other forts; a Legation area in Peking, defended by foreign guards, with provision for other forces elsewhere; a financial indemnity of perhaps 450,000,000 taels of silver, the payment of which is to be distributed through the coming thirty or fifty years; the punishment of specified persons who were most guilty in the late uprising; the suspension for five years of examinations in cities where foreigners were murdered; the universal publication of the fact of these punishments, a strict prohibition under penalty of death of all anti-foreign societies, and an Imperial Edict distinctly recognizing the future responsibility of officials for outrages occurring within their districts.

There are undoubtedly some items in this list to which exception may be taken as injudicious, but those most familiar with the circumstances are most likely to agree that they are not in themselves unjust. Yet they are altogether inadequate, being mainly punitive, privitive, and destructive in character, and containing no seed of future promise. A unique opportunity for aiding in the rehabilitation of the most populous and most ancient of Empires seems to have been lost. For this, the simple and adequate explanation is that the numerous Powers involved in the settlement do not desire for China the same things. A more impressive object-lesson of the failure of diplomacy to achieve constructive results, when unhampered by external conditions and operating on a large scale, has seldom been seen. Unless China is in some way essentially changed, past conditions may gradually recur, but for these changes we shall look in vain to Prime Ministers of Western Powers, or to Ministers resident in China.

The long cherished and confident expectation that China was to be gradually regenerated by her contact with Western Civilization, by commerce, by steamships, railways, telegraphs, and mines, has been demonstrated to be utterly insubstantial. It is these very appliances of " funded civilization " which more than anything else have helped to bring about the Convulsion in China. They are in themselves disturbing forces destitute of moral qualities, not only not remedying the evils which they inevitably occasion in an Empire like China, and among a people like the Chinese, but having no tendency to do so.

There remains the method of education, so earnestly

advocated by Chang Chih Tung in his work already quoted. By this means light is to be gradually introduced into China, making in future such a crusade as that of 1900 impossible.

Education is indeed a valuable and an indispensable agency, which to some extent has already been employed, and which must be used upon a scale ten thousand fold greater before the darkness of the masses of China can be expelled and replaced by light. But there are many kinds of education. That which deals only with co-ordinated physical or mental facts, conducted with whatever degree of thoroughness, has never yet proved adequate for the regulation of the conduct of mankind. It is intellectual only, leaving the highest parts of man's nature unsatisfied and untouched. It is a two-edged sword certain to cut in both directions.

The Chinese themselves have already perceived that the rigid prohibition of the importation of arms and munitions of war will eventually compel them to become the producers of implements of destruction, perhaps upon a scale never before seen in any land. The mere bulk of the Chinese people, unmilitary as they have always been, might conceivably make them, when once aroused, a menace to mankind. Will a knowledge of chemistry, and an ability to calculate the curves of falling bodies, and the velocity of projectiles in itself suffice to keep the Chinese under due restraint, with countless Lamps of Aladdin always in their hands, always waiting to be rubbed?

It is true of China more than of any other non-Christian people, that they have never been profoundly moved by other than moral forces. The rapid and irresistible progress destined to be made by Western science in the Chinese Empire will speedily and surely undermine

Chinese faith in the "Book of Changes," which underlies the pyramid of Chinese philosophy. Whatever is permanently true will remain in imperishable blocks, but the structure as a whole will be left in ruins, with Chinese ideals pitilessly and irrevocably shattered. At this critical period of the disintegration of outworn forces, what new moral ideas are to replace the old?

Christianity has been in China a disturber, as it always is and always has been everywhere. It had the fortune (or misfortune) to be formally introduced to the Chinese in connection with treaties imposed by force for ends which the Chinese detested,—in this respect, however, standing on a level with the rights of trade. It has also had the additional disadvantage of being in one of its forms indissolubly associated in the minds of the Chinese with political agencies, which they dread with reason and instinctively antagonize. There has been much in the method of its propagation in China which is open to just criticism, and which at this crucial juncture ought to be fearlessly exposed, frankly admitted, and honestly abandoned, new and better methods replacing those which have proved faulty and unworthy.

But Christianity is itself an integral part of modern civilization, from which it can no more be dissociated than the rays of light and of heat can be untwisted from the sunbeam. The attempt on the part of the Chinese to expel from their Empire spiritual forces, is an uprising of the Middle Ages against the Twentieth Century. The effort on the part of some who have been cradled in Christian lands, in an unspiritual and a materialistic age, to pinion and hand-cuff the disintegrating yet constructive forces of Christianity in their operation in China, is a futile struggle to reverse the tide of human development, and to arrest the slow but irresistible progress of a law of man's spiritual nature. Let it be distinctly recognized that the development of Christianity in China will be and must be marked by conflict, perhaps not more so than elsewhere, but surely not less. It will undermine idolatry as it did in the Roman Empire, and upon the wreck of the old will build a structure as much fairer than the Roman as the moral ideals of the Chinese race are higher and purer than those of that ancient state.

When adopted, and even imperfectly put in practice, it may be expected to alter the life of the court, as it has done in Western lands, inadequately Christianized though these be. It will make the dry bones of Chinese scholarship live by unifying, and for the first time completing, their knowledge of " Heaven, Earth, and Man." By the introduction of new standards and new sanctions it will begin to purify the Augean stable of Chinese officialdom, a task, under right conditions, by no means impossible of performance. For the mass of the Chinese people it would at least make life worth living, joining the present and the future by golden links in a manner at present wholly inconceivable, yet the inevitable outcome of spiritual enlightenment.

The wide diffusion of Christianity in its best form will not suddenly introduce into China the Millennium, for no goal can be reached without passing through all the intermediate stages. But it will, for the first time in Chinese history, realize the motto of the ancient T'ang, quoted at the opening of the Great Learning, " Renovate, renovate the people." Thus alone can the Empire be adapted to the altered conditions brought about by the impact of Western civilization, with its Pandora Box of evil and of good.

The immediate future of China will depend on the one hand upon her relations with the Powers, and on the other upon the temper of the court, the temper of the officials, the temper of the literati, and the temper of the people. There is no possible way of reaching these various classes so well and so directly as through the native Chinese Church, which has already suffered so much and borne such witness to its faith by its life, and by the heroic death of many of its number. This truth has found expression in the notable magazine article in which Sir Robert Hart frankly declares that if, in spite of official opposition and popular irritation, " Christianity were to make a mighty advance," it might " so spread through the land as to convert China into the friendliest of friendly Powers, and the foremost patron of all that makes for peace and goodwill." This, he thinks, " would prick the Boxer balloon and disperse the noxious gas which threatens to swell the race-hatred programme, and poison and imperil the world's future."

It is well that the dilemma should be recognized and squarely faced. Unless China is essentially altered she will continue to " imperil the world's future." Other forces have been to some extent experimented with, and have been shown to be hopelessly inadequate. Christianity has been tried upon a small scale only, and has already brought forth fruits after its kind. When it shall have been thoroughly tested, and have had opportunity to develop its potentialities, it will give to China intellectually, morally, and spiritually, the Elixir of a New Life.

APPENDIX

APPENDIX

THE GREATEST CYCLOPÆDIA IN THE WORLD.

A brief summary of what is known of this great work may be of interest.

In the annals of bibliography, remarks a great Chinese scholar (the late Alexander Wylie), there are few incidents comparable to the gigantic effort made by Yung Lê, the second Emperor of the Ming Dynasty, who reigned from 1403-1425.

Desiring to compile an all-comprehensive cyclopædia, he issued in A. D. 1403, a commission to a native scholar to undertake the work, assisted by a hundred and forty-seven literary men. These having completed their labours in a year and a half, the result was presented to the Emperor. As the work, however, fell far short of His Majesty's idea, a much more extensive committee of scholars was appointed, with a commission to collect in one body the substance of all the classical, historical, philosophical, and literary works hitherto published, embracing astronomy, geography, the occult sciences, medicine, Buddhism, Taoism, and the arts. Three scholars were now designated as presidents of the commission, and under them were five chief directors and twenty sub-directors, beside two thousand one hundred and sixty-nine subordinates. The work was brought to a conclusion near the close of the year 1407, containing in all 22,877 books, besides the table of contents, which occupied sixty books. There is some irregularity in the principle of quotation; sometimes single clauses are given containing the head character; sometimes whole sections of books; and sometimes works are given entire if pertaining to the subject.

When the first draft was laid before the throne, orders were given to have it transcribed for printing, and the copy was finished in 1409; but in consideration of the great outlay that would be necessary for the workmanship, the blocks for printing were never cut; and on the removal of the court to Peking the copy was deposited in an Imperial apartment. What became of this copy is not known, but it probably perished in a fire which occurred in the palace in 1557, for in 1562 we find a hundred transcribers appointed by the Board of Rites to make two new copies. Three leaves a day was considered each man's work, at which rate they completed their task in 1567. During the disturbances that occurred at the overthrow of the Ming Dynasty and the coming of the Manchus (1644), one of the copies, and also the original draft which had been kept at Nanking, were both destroyed by fire; and on the restoration of peace, one copy was found to be deficient 2,422 books.

This great work has proved of service to Chinese literature in a way not probably anticipated by its originators. The wholesale selections were at one time considered as a defect, but have now become the most important feature of the whole; for by this means three hundred and eighty-five rare and ancient works have been preserved, which would otherwise have been irrevocably lost; and many of them have since been reprinted and extensively circulated. Such is the history of the most elaborate and most comprehensive work perhaps in any literature, never published, yet always destroyed only to come forth from its ashes. It is not

APPENDIX 745

a little remarkable that it now owes its preservation—so far as it has been saved—to the hated foreign devil, but the separate volumes have been dispersed all over the world, and a few have found their way into American libraries as unique curiosities.

DIRECTORY OF THE SIEGE IN PEKING.

This Register of the Siege is of varied interest, apart from the personality of any of the participants, as a species of index to the mode by which a handful of Occidentals, confronted by unnumbered Asiatics, so disposed of their limited forces as to make the most of them, and, in the end, to win success from the very jaws of defeat and extinction.

MILITARY.

Major Sir Claude MacDonald, in charge of Defence Operations.

Officers belonging to Foreign Detachments.

Austro-Hungarian, Capt. Winterhalder; Capt. Kollar, Sub. Lt. Tom Meyer; Baron Boynberg.

British, Capt. Halliday (wounded, hospital); Capt. Wray.

French, Lt. Darcy; Sub. Lt. Darcy (Pei T'ang).

German, Lt. Graf von Soden.

Italian, Lt. Paolini; Lt. Olivieri (Pei T'ang).

Japanese, Lt. Hara.

Russian, Lt. Baron von Raden; Lt. Dehn.

United States, Capt. Myers (wounded, hospital); Capt. Hall.

Officer in command at the Su Wang Fu, Col. Shiba (Jap.).

In charge Italian post, Su Wang Fu, Lt. Paolini; Mr. Caetani.

Personal Staff of Sir Claude MacDonald, Mr. Herbert G. Squiers (former Lt. U. S. A.), Chief of Staff; Capt. Poole, Adjutant: Orderlies, Messrs. Fliche, Hewlitt, Squiers, Jr., Barr.

Officers doing regular duty in charge of post on south city wall, Capt. Hall, Capt. Labrouse, Capt. Percy Smith, Capt. Wronbleffesky, Lt. von Loesch.

Fortification Staff, Chief of Staff, Mr. F. D. Gamewell; Aides,

Messrs. Chapin, Ewing, Killie, Norris, Howard Smith, Stonehouse, and others.

In charge fortifications on south city wall, Mr. Squiers; Aides, Messrs. Pethick, Cheshire, Moore, Splingard, and others.

Volunteers, general charge, Capt. Poole. In charge Customs Volunteers, Lt. von Strauch. In charge of Russians, Mr. Wassilieff. In charge of French, M. Bureau.

Customs Volunteers. Lt. von Strauch, Messrs. Piry, Brazier, Brewitt-Taylor, Reutenfeld, Macown, Richardson, Wintour, Simpson, Konovaloff, Sandercock, Smyth, Bismarck, Bethell, Ferguson, Lanon, De Courcey, Le Luca, Destallan, Diehr, Encarnascao, De Pinna, Dupree, Mears (Attached), Fliche, Barbier, Hageman.

British Legation Volunteers. Messrs. Dering, Ker, Tours, Russell (in charge), Hancock, Flaherty, Bristow, Giles, Porter, Kirke, Hewlitt, Drury, Townsend, Barr.

Board of Works, Mr. Cowan. Attached to British Legation, Mr. Thornhill. Peking Syndicate, Messrs. Bristow, Sabbione. Imperial Chinese Bank, Messrs. Houston, Oliphant. Hongkong and Shanghai Bank, Messrs. Tweed, Brent.

Russian Volunteers. Messrs. Wassilieff (in charge), Alexandroff, Koehler, Brackmann, Osipoff, Posdneyeff, Mirny, Wihlfahrt, Piskinoff, Polujanoff, Orlovsky.

French Volunteers. Messrs. Parrot, Bertaux, Philippine, Demeyer, Chibant, La France, Berthe, Saussine, Bureau, Cuillierde, Gieter.

Belgian Volunteers. Messrs. Yoostens, Goffinet, Roland, DeMelotte.

Miscellaneous Volunteers. Messrs. Ament, Turner, Norris, Allen, Peel, Allardyce, Peachey, Backhouse, Coltman, Jr., Dr. Coltman.

MEDICAL DEPARTMENT.

Doctors in charge. American Detachment, **Surgeon Lippett** (wounded), Dr. Lowry, *vice*.

French and Austrian Detachments, Dr. Matignon.

Japanese Detachment, Capt. Nakagawa.

International Hospital, Dr. Poole, Dr. Velde.

Medical Assistants. Messrs. Amati (Italian), Döse (German), Fuller (British), Yamagata (Jap.), Stanley (Am.).

International Hospital Nursing Staff. Miss Lambert, Matron. Drs. Anna Gloss, Eliza Leonard, Maud Mackie, Emma Martin,

APPENDIX 747

Lillie Saville; Miss McKillican, Miss Newton, Miss Shilston, Mrs. Woodward, Deaconess Jessie Ransome, Sisters Marie and Stephanie.

Honorary Stewards to Hospital. Messrs. R. Allen, Richardson.

In charge of hospital kitchen, Misses Chapin, Gowans, Russell.

Occasional Helpers at Hospital, Mme. de Giers and Russian ladies, Mrs. Houston, Miss Sheffield.

CIVILIAN.

General Committee of Public Comfort. Messrs. Tewksbury (Chairman), Bredon, Cockburn, Hobart, Kruger, Morisse, Popoff. Secretaries, Messrs. Stelle and Galt.

Sub-Committees, bakery, Mr. Tewksbury; carpentry and blacksmithing, Messrs. Galt, Gamewell.

Confiscated Chinese Goods. Mr. Ament.

Fire Department. Messrs. Tours, Tweed.

Food Supply. Messrs. King, Berteaux, Clarke, Thornhill, Fenn, Kolossoff, Oliver, Russell; mutton, Mr. Brazier; horsemeat, Mr. Allardyce.

Fuel Supply. Messrs. Bailie, Wherry, Kanahami, Barbier.

Gate Day Watchmen. North Gate, Messrs. Martin, Smith; South Gate, French Brothers; Tunnel, Russian Volunteers.

Kitchen for Chinese Workmen. Messrs. Hobart, Goodrich, Whiting, Walker.

Labour, Chinese Christians. Messrs. Hobart, Verity; Chinese servants, Messrs. Stelle, Galt; foreign, Mr. Cockburn.

Laundry. Mr. Brazier.

Markets, eggs, vegetables. Messrs. Brent, Allardyce.

Messenger Service. Chinese (English speaking), Mr. Hobart; To Tientsin, etc., Mr. Tewksbury.

Milling. Mr. Fenn.

Registration. Messrs. Stelle, Galt, Cockburn.

Sanitation. British Legation, Messrs. Poole, Dudgeon, Inglis, Herring; Su Wang Fu, Fathers Banteynie, Bafcop, Drs. Ingram and Ts'ao.

Shoe-repairing. Mr. Hobart.

Stabling, with care and selection of animals. Messrs. Deering, Dupree, Ker, Brazier.

Watch Repairing. Mr. Stelle.

Water Inspection. Mr. Davis.

Index

ABBÉ HUC, the, 35
Adaptability of Chinese, illustration of, 581
Admiral Courbet, naval battle of, 25
Admirals, council of, 436
Advertisements in Peking, 528
Allen, Y. J.; publisher "Review of the Times," Shanghai, 129
Allied Forces in China, arrival of, 432; composition of, 439; difficulties, 446; inactivity, 448; inadequate equipment, 453; start for Peking, 454; raising the siege, 461; conduct of troops, 715, 716, 718
Allied generals, conference of, 453
Ament, Dr., goods placed in charge of, 281; charges against, 731
American Bible Society, gives Bible to Emperor, 129
American Board Mission, annual meeting of, at T'ung Chou, 230; T'ung Chou compound, 557; destruction, 564; massacre of missionaries, 610, 613, 616
American Legation, foreigners take refuge in, 258; attacks on, 335, 425, 428
American Methodist Episcopal Compound in Peking, Americans gather in, 215
American Methodist Episcopal Mission, annual meeting of, at Peking, 230
American Missionaries in Methodist Compound, letter from Mr. Conger to, 249

American railroads, 118
American sailor, executed, 15
American text books, funds for, 142
American troops, Temple of Agriculture headquarters of, 546; composition of, 454
Americanising Chinese, effect of, 23
Americans in China, ill treated, 21; plan defence, 233; organization among, 273, 509; adopt resolutions, 494
Amur, massacre at the, 607
An Ching Fu, riot at, 82
Ancestral tablets of Manchu dynasty, British seizure of, 548
Ancestral Worship, question of, 34; decision of Pope against, 47
Anglo-Chinese College, President of, on French treachery, 25
Anglo-German railroad, 119
Anglo-Saxon, and Chinese, 5
Anhui, troubles in, 156
Annam, Roman Catholic Bishop in, influence of, 48
Anti-foreign governor of Peking, appointment of, 224; literature, issue of, 79; movements, 87, 185, 223; pamphlet, 77; picture gallery, 81; proclamation, 73; propaganda and its results, 77-87; riots, 65-76
Antipathy, remoter sources of, 3-13
Antiquity of Chinese, 4
Argent, Mr., murder of, 83
Armistice, the 340-364; arranging terms, 355

Arms, discoveries of, 451
Army, the Chinese, disappearance of, 501
Army of Avengers, nucleus of, 223
Arsenal, the siege, 333
Arsenals at Tientsin, Provisional Government takes, 581, 586
Ashmore, William, on "Outrages," 55
Astronomical Observatory, dismantling of, 545
Athletic sects not Boxers, 171
Attacks on Legations, 253-271; renewed, 402-418
Atwater family, murder of, 616
Austrian Legation, troops fire on, 266; abandoned, 394
Audience question, the, 27
Australia, suffering of Chinese in, 21

BAGNALL, Mr. and Mrs., and daughter, murder of, 610
Bakery, starting a, 307
"Barbarians," Chinese view of, 10; their desires, 122; dealing with the, 15
Barbarities of Boxers, 616
Barricades, the, 468
Battles, summary of, 393
Belgian engineers, flight of, 212; from Pao Ting Fu, 575
Beresford, Lord Charles, on "Break-up of China," 115, 724; on duties collected at Tientsin, 573
Besieged, condition of the, 485
Beynon, Mr., murder of, 614
Bible, Emperor asks for, 129
Bible and Tract Societies, work of, 41
Big Knife Societies approved by Throne, 188; their suppression demanded by foreign ministers, 190
Bird, Miss, murder of, 613
Bishop, Mrs. Isabella Bird, on native Christians, 663
Bishop of Colon, the, 35

Bishop of Northern Cathedral, the, 504, 507
Blagovestchensk, massacre at, 607
Blomberg family, murder of, 712
Board of Punishment, the, 540
Board of Rites, punishment of officers of, 146
Bomb proof, strengthening the, 305
Bombs, refuges from, 293
Book depots, establishment of, 137
"Book of Changes," Chinese faith in, 737
Books, Western, bureau for translation of, 141
"Boxer altar," explanation of, 661
Boxer banners, capture of, 334; characters on, 566
Boxer chiefs, authorities seek, 539
Boxer Militia, the, 377: exhorted to patriotic service, 379
Boxer uprising and treaty of Tientsin, events between, 22
Boxer movement, its purpose 150; patronized by Empress Dowager, 150; its genesis, 152-174; basis, 197; arrives in T'ung Chou, 563; in Tientsin, 574, 576; planned for the eighth month, 606
Boxer Society, proclamation against, 229
Boxer tiger, fierceness of, 240
Boxers, the, 154; defeated, 167; superstitions of, 169, 172, 659; invulnerability of, 170, 245, 576, 709; children among, 172, 661, 662; persecute Christians, 175, 177, 654-657; their power, 187; approved by Throne, 188, 224, 225; suppression demanded, 190; their incantations, 197; exercises, 198; charms, 199; posters, 200, 201; Buddhist Patriotic

INDEX

League of, 200; relation to Chinese troops, 214; to Chinese government, 218-231; auxiliary to army of avengers, 223; practice openly, 230; arrive in Peking, 518; leader in T'ung Chou, 565; ordered to kill Christians, 657; resume drill in Shantung, 722; superintended by the Great Fairy, 722
Boys, Christian, massacre of, 673, 699
Boys in Boxer Movement, 661
"Break-up of China," Lord Charles Beresford on, 724
British and French allies, 19
British, attacks upon, 112
British engineers, Kansu troops attack, 163
British claim, justice of, 18
British fleet, loss of, 19
British government, fluctuating policy of, 68; its demands, 111; recognition of services, 481; loan to Chinese Viceroy, 603
British Legation: attack on students of, 229; visited by Yamen ministers, 236; made general headquarters, 261; Americans ordered to, 263; its defence, 272; sanitation, 295; attacks on, 420, 422, 425, 427, 428; fortifications, 468, 477
British railroads, the, 118, 119
British students, bravery of, 309
British troops in allied forces, 272, 454
British White Book, siege dispatches in, 479
Brooks, Mr., murdered by Boxers, 182
Buddhist Patriotic League of Boxers, 200
Buddhist priests, Chinese employment of, 7; attitude toward Christianity, 39
Buildings, Imperial, foreign occupation of, 541

Bully, Chinese, 50, 86
Burlingame Mission, the, 22

CANADIAN PRESBYTERIAN MISSION, notable experiences of, 621-632
Canal, the Grand, 56; the Imperial, 260
Canton, causes of troubles in, 13; diplomatic representatives, 14; right of entering granted, 17; riots at, 71; patriotic defence, 112
Capital in transformation, the, 535-554
Carles, Mr., British Consul at Tientsin, 205
Carleson, Mr., murder of, 712
Cassini Convention, the, 104, 107, 117
Casualties, table of siege, 488, 489
Cathedral at Canton, hatred of, 57
Cathedral, Tientsin, destruction of, 56, 69
Cathedral, Northern, siege of, 503-507
Catholic (see Roman Catholic)
Celestial Empire, the, 6
Cemetery, foreign, wreck of, 238
Cemetery, the Protestant, desecration of, 498
Censor, memorial of a, 130
Censor Wang, Imperial interview with, 224
Censors, reforms advocated by, 144
Census of the siege, 298, 411
Central Asia, nomads of, 5
Central Empire, division of inhabitants, 9
Chaffee, General, 455
Chamot, M., brave rescue by, 209
Chang, Mr., personal narrative of, 691
Chang, Mr. and Mrs., personal narrative of, 693

INDEX

Chang Chih Tung, issues proclamation, 73; receives loan from British, 602; aids foreigners, 631
Chang Ch'ing Hsiang, personal narrative of, 682
Ch'ang Hsin Tien, siege of foreigners at, 209
Chao Shu Ch'iao, 227
Chapin, Miss, Red Cross given, 494
Charms, the Boxer, 199
Chefoo, growth of, 12; helpfulness of American consul at, 604
Chêkiang, Roman Catholics in, 56; murder of foreigners at, 605
Ch'en Pao Chên, reform efforts of, 141
Chêng Ting Fu, safety of foreigners at, 610
Chiang, Mr., personal narrative of, 692
Chiang Pei, riot in, 86
Chien Ning Fu, riot at, 86
Chihli, mission affairs in, 51; riots in, 165; foreigners escape from, 609
Children in the Boxer bands, 172
Children, massacre of, 299, 605, 610, 614, 616, 665, 670, 673, 697, 698, 700, 701
Children, siege play of, 486
China, complex population of, 3; isolation of, compared with Egypt, 4; foreign commerce of, 12; causes of outbreaks in, 13; Irishmen of, 13; Merchants Company, the, 139; Merchants' Steam Navigation Company, 212; relation with foreign Powers, 268; Christianity in, 637; peculiar relations with Russia, 723; attitude toward Western nations, 8, 733; terms of settlement with, 734; regeneration of, 735; educational problem, 736; " China and Christianity," Michie, 45

China Inland Mission, the, 65; massacre of missionaries, 605, 610, 613, 616; notable experiences of, 635-643
Chinese, the, moral code of, 6; golden age of, 7; relation to the Three Religions, 7; relation to sages, 7; to trade, 9; a century ago. 10; in treaty ports, 12; use of opium, 15; and exterritorial rights, 17; in foreign lands, 21; relation to other nations, 22; Americanised, persecution of, 24; foreigners' view of, 218, 719
Chinese army, co-operates with Boxers, 5, 77
Chinese bubble, the, 26
bully, the, 50
Church, faithfulness of, 657
courts, no justice in, 50
empire, size of, 10, 14
fans, pictures on, 10
history, puzzle of, 5
institutions an evolution, 5
junk, the, 10
law, punishments inflicted according to, 727
laws and foreigners, 16
labor strike, 13
ministers abroad; policy of government criticised by, 599, 600
point of view, 20
race, origin of, 3
resistance of foreign force, 18
sages, the, 6
scholar and foreign ideals, 77
servants, courage of, 307
ships destroyed by French, 25
soldiers, 8
Chinese, characteristics of: pride of race, 5; ideals of, 6; aversion to war, 7; timidity on sea, 10; antipathy to foreigners, 12; saying vs. doing, 12; untruthfulness of, 12; pride, 15; treachery, 19; attitude toward treaties, 29; love

# INDEX

of revenge, 37; forbearance, 37; animosity, 30; adaptability, 520; fatalism, 652; clannishness, 657; timidity, 657
Chinese government and foreign trade, 9; its conceit, 15; ignores treaty, 18; relation to world, 20; indemnity demanded from, 25; loans to, 121; seclusion of, 127; encourages Boxer rising, 205; its treachery, 229; asks assistance from Powers, 361; present relation of Empress Dowager to, 728; of Emperor, 728
Chinese officials and trading class, 9; knowledge of geography, 11; bitterness toward domineering Occidentals, 24; their duplicity, 179, 188; their punishment, 550; flight from Tientsin, 579; their exactions, 716; opposition of people to, 723
"Chinese Progress," official organ, 139
"Chinese Recorder," the, article in, 54, 55
Ch'ing Tao, Germans in, 106, 160
Chinkiang, foreign settlement in, 13
Ch'iu, Dr., personal narrative of, 687
Chou Han, placards of, 79
Christian Alliance Missionaries, murder of, 712
Christian Church and ancestral worship, 35; and non-Christian Chinese, 43
Christian literature in Imperial palace and Hunan, 43
Christian students, personal narratives of, 695
Christianity and heathen priests, 39
Christianity proposed as State religion, 145
Christianity in China, effect of, 737

Christians, nonconformity to Chinese custom, 33
Christians, the Chinese; missionaries refuse to abandon, 232
Ch'un, Prince, influence of, 128
Church, the attitude of, toward non-Christian Chinese, 43 (see also Christian)
Church members, unworthy, 38
Cipher telegrams, sending of, 412, 414
Clapp, Mr. and Mrs., murder of, 613
Classics, study of, 136
Clothing, supply of, 511
Coal Hill, the, 532
Code, moral; of Chinese, 6
Colquhoun, A. R., 52
Commerce and Chinese, 10
Commercial intrusion, the, 88-101
Commercial diplomacy, tangle of, 121
Commercial prosperity of Peking, 521
Commemoration Day for the Six Martyrs, 150
Commissariat, appointment of a, 374
Commission, American, appointment of, 75
Committee, General; members of, 274
Committees, organization of, 273
Comprador, functions of the, 89
Confiscated goods, method of dealing with, 372; work of committee on, 411
Confucian Analects, study of, 136
Confucian colleges, foreigners asked to visit the, 137
Confucianism, tenets of, accepted by Chinese, 6, 7
Confucius, service of, to China, 33; on reciprocity, 62
Conger, Minister, 179, 188, 190; thanks the American missionaries, 494; his services, 731

INDEX

Conservative Party, resist reforms, 139; joint memorial of, to Empress Dowager, 147
Consuls, helpfulness of, 67
Continental troops, vandalism of, 546
Converts, decree on, 379
Coolie traffic, the, 21
Cooper, Mr., murder of, 610
Copyright and Patent Laws, establishment of, 139
Cotton goods, trade of, 90
Courts, Chinese, no justice in, 50
Cousins, Edmund; Missionaries aided by, 445
Customs Staff, quarters of, abandoned, 230, 257
Customs mess, the siege, 463
Cyclopædia, the greatest in the world, 743

D'Addosio, Père, saving of, 237
"Daily News," Shanghai, letter of Griffith John to, 79
Dark Days, 318-339
Davis, F. W., murder of, 613
Davis, John W., first U. S. Minister to China, 14
Days of waiting, 382-401
"Death to the devil's religion," circulation of, 79
Decrees, Imperial, on foreigners, 375; praising Boxers, 377; native Christians, 379; safeguarding Empire, 380; on cause of disturbances, 381; despatching troops, 407; departure of ministers, 414 (see also Edicts)
Defence, Americans organise for, 233; materials for, 511
De Giers, Madame, 486
Demon possession, instance of, 661
Denby, Minister, despatch of, 75
Departments, proposed new, 135
Dering, Mr., assists in defences, 479

Despatches from Tientsin, sending, 437
Despatches, siege, 479
Devastation, scenes of, 496
Diedrichs, Admiral; commands German fleet, 108
Diplomatic corps telegraph for guards, 210
Director of China Inland Mission; list of Protestant missionary martyrs prepared by, 647, 648, 649
Directory of the Siege, 745
Disease, freedom from, during siege, 514
Dixon, Mr. and Mrs., murder of, 634
Dorward, Gen., leader of British forces, 449
Drought, effect of, 219
Duplicity of Chinese officials, 178, 179, 188

Eastern Empress, death of, 125
East India Company, relation of, to Chinese, 15
Eastern Arsenal in Tientsin, taking of, 446
Edicts, Imperial, anti-foreign, 225; on Christianity in China, 226; character of, 435; on protection of missionaries, 721 (see also Decrees)
Edicts, the Vermilion Pencil; despatch of, 553
Education in China, problem of, 736
Egyptians, ancient; contemporary with Chinese, 4
"Eight Diagram" sects, 42
Eighth moon, disturbances expected in the, 219; Boxer rising planned for, 606
Eldred, Miss, murder of, 616
Elgin, Lord; rule of, 733
Emperor K'ang Hsi, see K'ang Hsi
Emperor Kuang Hsü; plans reforms, 43, his history, 124;

INDEX 755

begins reign, 126; learns English, 129; obtains Bible, 129; issues reform decrees, 131; threatens to abdicate, 146; imprisoned in palace, 148; forced to abdicate, 149; opposes Manchu policy, 246, 269; anomalous relation to government, 728
Emperor Tao Kuang, 14
Empress Dowager; issues war edicts, 28; receives legation ladies, 28; sketch of, 125; given New Testament, 128; reviews troops, 142; opposes Emperor, 147; repeals reforms, 149; heads Boxer movement, 150; nominates heir apparent, 186; favors Boxers, 223; believes in divine mission of Boxers, 226; anti-foreign attitude, 230, 244; issues edict to exterminate foreigners, 270; intends to escape, 393; her flight, 501; confiscates palace, 535; second enforced flight, 55; sanctions anti-foreign decrees, 596, 597; issues edicts to protect missionaries, 721; present relation to government, 728
Encyclopædia, the greatest, 743
English Baptist Mission, notable experiences of, 632-635; massacre of missionaries, 613
English Methodist Christians, personal narrative of, 698
Engvall, Miss, murder of, 712
Envoys, received by Emperor, 28; treatment of, 343
Escapes, narrow, 297
Escort to Tientsin, Yamen offers, 412, 413
Examination Grounds, destruction of, 546
Exercises, the Boxer, 198
Expatriated subjects: Chinese attitude toward, 21
Explosions, effect of, 337
Extermination Edict issued, 270

Exterritorial rights and the Japanese, 17
Eunuchs, baleful influence of, 221

FAMINE in Kiangsu, 157
Far East; Shanghai the commercial capital of, 12
Farthing family; murder of, 614
Fashoda incident, the, 110
Fathers, the Catholic, Chinese suspicions of, 60
Favier, Mgr., appeals from Peking to French Minister, 206; his courage, 507
Fengshui, the, 57, 96, 324
Feng Tai, opposition to innovations at, 99; attack on railway, 207
Fenn, Mr., milling in charge of, 275
Financial methods of Roman Catholic Church, 58
Fire and Sword among Shansi Christians, 702-712
Fire, danger from, 280, 281, 287
Fire Brigade, captains of, 480
First overt act of pillage, 166
First Week of the siege, the, 272-296
" Fists of United Harmony," the, see also " Boxers," 168
" Five Storms of Wrath," 57
Flag, legation, hauled down, 22
Flags, Chinese use of, after siege, 520
Fleet, Allied; Chinese fire upon, 437
Fleming, Mr., murder of, 87
Fleury, Father, capture of, 86
Fliche, M., heads rescue party, 237
Flight from Peking, preparations for, 249
Food supply, inventory of, 276; horse-meat, 291; work of Committee on, 402; scarcity of, 420, 421, 424, 425; at Northern Cathedral, 505; amount of, 510

INDEX

Foreign buildings, destruction of, 237
Foreign commerce and China, 12
"Foreign devils," ban upon the term, 225
Foreigners in China, Chinese opinion of, 11, 12, 218, 518, 573, 718; classification of, 88; expulsion desired by Empress Dowager, 187; extermination planned by Boxers, 206; imprisonment in Peking, 231; census of in Peking, 298; immunity from attack, 509; experiences in the Interior, 594-620, 659; Manchu hostility toward, 599
Foreign journals, Empress Dowager influenced by, 598
Legations, pressure of, 180
Ministers demand Imperial decree suppressing Boxer and Big Knife Societies, 190
Ministers, meeting of, 248
missionaries, edict on, 49
occupation, a twelve-month of, 713-732
Powers, Empress Dowager urges destruction of, 244
relations of Chinese empire, 14
settlements; jurisdiction of Chinese over, 17; location in Tientsin, 444; attack on, 445, 448; military occupation of, 590
stores, looting of, 313
teachers, education by, 135
teachers and Chinese language, 36
trade and Chinese government, 9, 10
troops, arrival of, 432
Formosa, blockade of, by French, 25; Japanese possession of, 103
Fortifications, work of, 274
Fortifications, the, 462-484; in charge of F. D. Gamewell, 468; military opinion of, 476

Fowler, John, U. S. Consul, 604
France, war with, cause of, 24; demands indemnity, 25; protects Jesuits, 48; uses missionaries, 53
Frazer, E. H., Hankow, 603
French Minister, the, and Roman Catholic outrages, 55; appeal from Mgr. Favier to, 206
French, The: animosity against, 69; at Shanghai, opposition to, 70; further encroachments, 113, 121; massacre in Tientsin, 572
"French beef," 291
French Legation, assistance asked for, 301; attack on, 304, 319, 337, 429; British marines sent to assistance of, 331; condition of, 360
French missionaries, rescue of, 237
French railroads, the, 119
French troops in allied forces, the, 455
Freedom of speech, Emperor insists on, 146
Fu Chou, blockade of, by French, 25; turbulence of people in, 13
Fuel supply, the, 511
Fukushima, Gen., leads Japanese forces, 449

GAMEWELL, F. D., plans fortifications, 274, 468
Garrigues, Père, murder of, 237
Gaselee, General, 454
Gates of Peking, the, 522
Gathering of the Storm, 175-195
Genähr, Immanuel, of Rhenish Mission, 54
Genghis Khan, 4
General Committee, members of, 274; letter to chairman, 495
German expedition, a punitive, 160
aggression at Kiaochou, effect of, 161
barricade, attack on, 304

INDEX   757

expedition to Kalgan, 715; to Ts'ang Chou, 716; to Yung Ch'ing Hsien, 717
mines and railway, hostility to, 182
railroads, the, 119
Legation, attack on, 338, 358, 424, 428
possessions in China, 106, 108
Girls in Boxer Movement, use of, 662
"Glorified Tigers," the, 223
Golden age of Chinese, 7
Gould, Miss, murder of, 610
Government bureaus, Chinese; military occupation of, 539
Granaries, Imperial; Japan seizes the, 540
Grand Council of Manchus and Chinese, a, 244
Great Britain in China, 16; prestige of, 23, 219; policy of, 104, 110; in Yangtze Valley, 121
"Great Fairy," Boxers superintended by the, 722
"Great Sword Society," the, 135; hatred of Catholics, 106 (see Boxers)
Green, Mr., murder of, 83
Greig, Dr., attack on, 84
Guinness, G. W., and party; notable experiences of, 635-638
Gun, manufacturing a, 325
Gun-platforms, the Chinese, 502
Guns, location of, 308

HALL OF FASTING, British army occupy, 548
Hamer, Bishop, murder of, 619
Hand of God in the siege, the, 508-516
Hanlin University, burning of, 281; destruction of, 542; defences in the, 471
Hanlins, reform advocated by the, 144
Harahara, Mr., death of, 384
Hart, Sir Robert, 109, 286, 596, 597, 739

Hedlund, Miss, murder of, 712
Heir Apparent, nomination of, 186
Heng Chou Fu, foreign priests in, 60
Hêng, Deacon; personal narrative of, 673
History, Chinese; loss of materials for, 545
Hoddle, Mr., murder of, 614
Hodge, Dr. and Mrs., murder of, 610
Honan, beginning of trouble in, 621
Hongkong coolie regiment, 19
Hospital, patients in, 299, 308, 313; work in kitchen, 467; the International, 490; number of cases, 493
Hostilities, cessation of, 356
Hotel de Pékin, retreat upon, 307; condition of, 359
"House and Opium Tax," the, 130
Hung Hsin Ch'üan, founder of Taiping rebellion, 31
House-keeping, siege, 646
Hsi An Fu, 14; purchase of books in, 137; Imperial refugees arrive in, 554
Hsi Ku, Arsenal, 582
Hsiao Chang, riot in, 165
Hu Yü Fên, Governor, 164
Huo, Mrs.; personal narrative of, 685
Hunan, anti-foreign literature issues from, 79; reform measures in, 141
Hunan pamphlets, the, 41

I CH'ANG FU, riots at, 13, 83, 160, 162
Ideals, the Chinese, 6
I Ho Ch'üan, the Boxer Society, 154; second stage in development, 209; appointment of leaders, 225 (see Boxers)
Imperial buildings, foreign occupation of, 541
Chinese Armory, relief expedition takes, 442

INDEX

Imperial Court, culpable, 549; favours Boxers, 574
 edicts, insincerity of, 188, 243; favourable to Boxers, 189; against them, 191; ordering punishments, 550; authorises destruction of legations, 566; anti-foreign, 594
 family, flight of, 551
 Maritime Customs, 120, 264
 Palace instigates riots, 76
 Palaces, fate of the, 529, 534
 Pavilion, burning of the, 545
 resorts, destruction of, 20
 troops instigating riots, 13; relation to Boxers, 228; attacked by allied forces, 441
 tutors, appointment of, 186
 University, decree on, 138
Improvements, allies introduce, the, 525
Incantations, the Boxer, 197
Indemnity, demand for, 67; refused, 68; German demand, 106; payment of, 161; claims for, 276; question of, 567; Protestant scheme for, 729
Institutions, Chinese; an evolution, 5
Intercalary eighth moon, Chinese superstition about, 219
Interior, foreigners in, 594-620
"International," the new gun, 328, 373, 429, 470, 511
International club, an, 543
 complications, 14-29; danger of, 187
 Hospital, the, 490; cases in, 493
 law, effect of, on Chinese, 21; questions of, 436
 prison, an, 541
 trade, study of, 142
Inundation of country round Tientsin, the effect of, 572
"Irishmen of China," 13
Italian Government, demands of, 114

JAMES, PROF., murder of, 267
Jameson, C. D., helpfulness of, 628
Japan, war with, 26, 129; usurpation of Chinese territory by, 76; military readiness of, 452
Japanese, the: and exterritorial rights, 17; their courage, 301; courtesy, 322; Dr. Sheffield asked to make terms with, 558
Japanese Decoration Day, 417
Japanese indemnity, automatic payment of, 540
Japanese Legation, murder of chancellor of, 235; death of secretary of, 384
Japanese Minister, letter received by, 354
Japanese Soldier—Information-Bureau, the 387
Japanese troops in allied forces, the, 455; good work of, 457
Jesuits protected by France, 48
Johannsson, Miss, murder of, 712
John, Griffith, 79
Julien, Roman Catholic priest, attacks Rhenish missionaries, 54
Jung Lu, 148
Junk, the Chinese, 10; discontinuance of, 95
Junk masters, influence of, against railways, 98

KALGAN, peril of missionaries in, 231; escape of foreigners, 610; German expedition to, 715
Kalgan to Kiakhta, notable experiences in flight from, 643-647
K'ang Hsi, Emperor, 35; on ancestral worship, 47; precedent of, 135
K'ang Yü Wei, "The Modern Sage and Reformer," 133; suggests reforms, 134; audience with Emperor, 135; escape of, 148

INDEX

Kao Hsin, personal narrative of, 665
Karlburg, Mr., murder of, 712
Kempff, Admiral, on taking Taku forts, 436
Ketteler, Baron von, 191; Boxer beaten by, 236; sketch of, 254; murder of, 255; memorial service for, 499
Kiangsu, troubles in, 155
Kiaochou, German possession of, 106, 108
Kotow, omitting the, 27
Ku Chëng, riot at, 85
K'ü Chou Fu, massacre, 605
Kuang Hsü, Emperor, 125 (see Emperor Kuang Hsü)
Kuang provinces, governor general of, 15
Kueichou, murder of missionary in, 87
Kung, Prince, position of, 127, 134

LABOUR STRIKE in China, 13
Labour system, the coolie; charges against, 21
Labour, work of Superintendent of, 365; demand for, 366
"Laffan" News Telegraph Agency, despatches from, 256
Lambert, Miss, Red Cross given, 493
Lands, granting of, 17
Lang Tang, 439
Language, the Chinese, missionary use of, 36
Lansdowne, commendatory despatches from, 481, 483
Larsson, Mr., murder of, 712
Legation guards, arrival of, 211, 508
Legation ladies, Empress Dowager receives, 28; kindness of, 262
Legations in Peking, the, 187; attack planned on, 206; their protection, 210, 288; guarding Legation Street, 241; Marquis Tsêng urges they be respected, 245; attacks on, 253, 271, 420, 422, 424, 425, 428, 429; topography of district, 259; burning of Italian and Dutch compounds, 279; foreigners asked to leave, 341, 362, 386; condition of German, 358; of French, 360; Tsung Li Yamen sends supplies, 362; arrival of allied forces, 461; extent of fortifications, 468; attempted betrayal, 475; extent of area, 548
"Lest we forget," 527
Letters, commendatory, 494, 495
Li, Deacon; personal narrative of, 671
"Light of the Red Lamp," the, 202
Li Hung Chang, on relation of America to Chinese, 21; as peace maker, 23; cancels railway plans, 98; dismissed from Tsung Li Yamen, 146; appointed Viceroy of Chihli, 380; appointed Peace Commissioner, 420; reinstates antiforeign official, 566; appoints native officials, 585; Chinese appeal to, 588; his opinion of foreigners, 718; approves Protestant indemnity plans, 730
Li Lien Ying, Eunuch, influence of, 221
Li Pen Yuan, Mrs.; personal narrative of, 676
Li Ping Hêng. 550
Likin taxes, proposed abolition of, 135
Literary class, antipathy of, 32
Literary essay, edict abolishing the, 135
Literati, reforms advocated by, 144
Literature of Protestant missions; inadequate, 40; in Imperial palace and Hunan, 43 on Roman Catholics in China, 45; anti-foreign issue of,

79; circulation of, 137; practical Chinese schools for, 139
Liu K'un Yi, 602
Loan, national, plan for, 130
Loans, Chinese government needs, 121
London Mission refugees, experiences of, 537; destruction of station, 609
Loot, soldiers forbidden to, 321; permission given to, 374
Looting in Tientsin, the, 583, 584
Lord Elgin, Diary of, 18; his motto, 69
"Lord of Heaven" religion, Chinese familiar with, 31
Lottery in Canton, the 139
Lovitt family, murder of, 614
Lu-Han railroad, Belgian management of, 99; work on, 117; decree on, 138; wreck of, 211
Lundell, Miss, murder of, 712
Lundgren, Mr. and Mrs., murder of, 616

MACAO, centre of coolie traffic, 21
McCalla, Capt., 242, 439
McCarthy, Justin, declaration of, 18
MacDonald, Lady, 261
MacDonald, Sir Claude, 187, 195, 206; asked by Powers to take charge of defences, 278; official report of, 475
McKinley (see President)
Machinery, introduction of, proposed 142
Magistrates, hostility of, 38; to Catholics, 52; inactivity of, 178; reproved, for repressing Boxers, 205
Ma, Mrs.; personal narrative of, 697
Manchu Clan, election of emperor by, 125
Dynasty, and the Boxer Movement, 187

policy, the 245, 600
rulers, purpose of, 30
soldiers, murder of missionary by, 85
Manchuria, Roman Catholics in, 55; insurrection in, 84; Russian work in, 99; extent of, 102; railroads in, 104; affected by Russo-Chinese agreement, 105; anti-foreign movement in, 606; friction with Russians in, 607; number of Protestants in, 650; Russian occupation of, 713, 724
Manchurian Convention, attitude of Russia toward, 725
Manchus and Chinese, governmental relation of, 220
Manchus, superstition of, 226; complicity in Peking, 501; hostile to foreigners, 599
March to Peking, the, 453-461
Margary, murder of, 22
Marines, courage of, 315; recognition of services, 494
Mark Twain, charges of, 731
Martin, W. A. P., 140
Martyrs, missionary, list of, 647-649; the unknown, 672; memorial service at Pao Ting Fu, 682
Massacre, the Tientsin, 13, 22, 572; ferocity, 69
Meadows, T. T., 64
Medal, designs for a siege, 422, 430
Medhurst, Consul, Shanghai, 66
Medicine, Chinese practice of, 41; handmaid of Christianity, 41
Memorials, presentation of, to throne, 144; in the "Peking Gazette," 193; character of, 396, 397; Governor of Shansi issues, 406
Memorial service for Baron von Ketteler, 499; for martyrs, 682
Mencius, service of, to China, 33

INDEX

Mêng Chi Hsien, pastor; personal narrative of, 680
Menus, planning the, 467
Messengers, 329, 331, 340, 347, 353; reports of, 383, 386, 388, 391, 395, 396, 398 400, 404, 405, 406, 409, 411, 420, 422, 423, 453
Methodist Mission, foreigners take refuge in, 232; flight from, 257; condition, after siege, 496
Mikado, proposal that Emperor and Empress Dowager visit the, 745
Military Commanders, Tientsin Provisional government organized by, 451
Commission, Chinese officials executed by, 611
examinations, changes proposed in, 138
expeditions, a series of 713
force in China, 16
life, attitude of Chinese toward, 8
Militia, anti-foreign, voluntary enrollment of, 81
Minister Wu; influence at Washington of, 721
Ministers, Chinese; selection of, for foreign lands, 131
Ministers, foreign, appeals to Yamen of, 203, 204, 207; letter from Tsung Li Yamen, 267; reply to, 268
Miner, Miss Luella, 551
Ming Dynasty, the preceding, cause of fall of, 221
Mings, attitude of, to Roman Catholic Church, 47
Mining, antipathy to, 101; possible concessions for, 121
Mining, danger from, in Legations, 338; threat of, 512
Mission affairs in Chihli and Shantung, 51
property, amount destroyed, 498
records, Boxers, seek, 658
work, effect of, 161

Missionaries, preaching of, 33; Foreign Ministers endeavour to protect, 204; their peril, 231; American, letter from Minister Conger to, 494; fearful experiences, 616, 727; their character, 618; their work, 660; edicts on protection of, 721; in the present crisis; a statement, 730; justified by Minister Conger, 732
Missionaries, Massacre of: American Board, 610, 613, 616; American Presbyterian, 610, China Inland, 605, 610, 613, 616; English Baptist, 613; Roman Catholic, 614, 619
Missionary conference at Shanghai, 78
Missionary Societies in China, statement of, 730
Missions, annual meetings of, 230
Missions, located in Chinese dwellings, 537
Mitchie, Alex., on " China and Christianity," 45
" Mixed courts" undesirability of, 17
Mongol dynasty, the, 4
Mongol Market, attack at, 337
Mongolia, spread of foreign rising in, 611
Monroe Doctrine, a Chinese, necessary, 121
Moral Code of Chinese, 6
Morrill, Miss, murder of, 610
Morrison, Dr., 480
Mother Superior of Northern Cathedral, the, 504
Moule, Bishop, brings charges against Roman Catholics in China, 56
Mountain of Ten Thousand Ages, the, 532
Mukden, 606

NANKING, riot at, 82
Narratives, personal, 665-701

Native Christians: attitude toward idolatrous ceremonies, 36; persecution of, 37, 175; rescue of, 238; protection of, 250; exemplary conduct of, 259; a refuge for, 265; clothing of the, 2°1; identification of, 312, 321; helpfulness of, 371; Prince Ch'ing suggests sending out, 390; decree on, 399; in Tientsin, 445; their safety, 509; murder of, 615; character, 651; asked to recant, 653; Boxers persecute, 654-657; faithfulness of, 657, 658; funds entrusted to, 658; courage of, 659; testimony of Mrs. Isabella Bird Bishop on, 663; wild rumours of, 668
Native Church; catastrophe to the, 650-664; its faithfulness, 657; possible power of, 739
Native preachers; missionaries intrust money to, 658
Naval Brigade, the, 454
Naval demonstration, need of, 193
Naval officers, consultation of, 438
Newchwang, treaty port of; dispute over, 111
New Testament, gift of, to Empress Dowager, 128
New Year, Chinese forbidden to celebrate, 580
Newspapers, native; influence of, 22
Newspapers, on Boxer Movements, 183, 185, 193
Ningpo men in Shanghai, 13
Non-Christian families, removal of, 233
Non-Christians, what to do with, 324
Nordenfelt gun, 308
Norman, Mr., murder of, 717
Norris, Chaplain; services of, 479
North China College, flight from, 214; destruction of buildings, 236, 564; location of, 557
"North China Daily News," 183, 222; on Empress Dowager, 598
Northern Roman Catholic Cathedral, foreigners take refuge in, 232; siege of, 503-507
Notable experiences, 621-649; Canadian Presbyterian Mission, 621-632; English Baptist Mission, 632-635; China Inland Mission, 635-643; Kalgan to Kiakhta, 643-647
Noyes, Mr., on "Five Storms of Wrath," 57

OCCIDENTAL, Chinese incomprehensible to, 5
Occidental civilization, grave problem of, 734
Occidentals, domineering; bitterness of Chinese officials toward, 24; extermination of, discussed, 508
Offices, abrogation of, 143
Officials, Chinese, and trading class, 9
Officials, liberal; execution of 408; punishment demanded by Powers, 726
Ogren, Mr. and Mrs.; story of, 638-643
"Open Door," the 724-725
Open Ports, prosperity of, 573
Opium, British trade in, 15; sale of, 91; Chinese opinion of, 92, 93
Opium war, purpose of, 16
Opium Commission, report of, 92
Orphanages, Roman Catholic, Tsung Li Yamen on, 58
Outbreaks in China, causes of, 13
Outlook, the, 733-739
"Overland to China," 52

PALACE, IMPERIAL; foreigners visit the, 529

INDEX

Palace examinations, abolition of, 142
Palace where Emperor was imprisoned, 530
Palaces, sale of abandoned, 501
Pamphlets, the Hunan, 41
P'ang Chuang missionaries, protest of, 180
P'ang Chuang, riot at, 609; Boxers, checked at, 610
Pao Ting Fu, disturbance at, 206, 207; Belgian engineers escape from, 212; massacre at, 610; memorial service held at, 682; military expedition to, 713; punishment of native officials at, 714
Parkes, Mr., seized by Chinese, 20
Parliament, English, on war with China, 15
Partition of China, 115, 184
Partridge, Miss, murder of, 613
Patriotic Harmony Society of Boxers, the, 227
Pavilion, British Legation, 263
Peace conditions, defence of Legations included in, 548
Pearl River, capture of forts, 18
Peiho, the, railway connection with, 26
Pei T'ang Cathedral, 264, 304, 456, 503
Peking, Manchu government in, 21; city gates, 26; Roman Catholic mission in, 206; arrival of allied forces, 261; anarchy in, 270; condition during siege, 329; anti-foreign, 517; its punishment, 517-534; first occupied by European troops, 517; devastation, 519; street lighting, 526; military expeditions from, 713
"Peking and Tientsin Times," 185
"Peking Gazette," ministers request publication of Edict in, 191
Persecution of native Christians, 37
Personal narratives, 665-701; Kao Hsin, 665; Deacon Li, 671; Deacon Hêng, 673; Mrs. Li Pên Yuan, 676; the T'sai family, 679; pastor Mêng Chi Hsien, 680; Chang Ch'ing Hsiang, 682; Mrs. Huo, 685; Dr. Ch'iu, 687; Wên Li, 689; Messrs. Chang and Wên, 691; Mr. Chiang, 692; Mr. and Mrs. Chang, 693; Christian students, 695; Mrs. Ma, 697; Roman Catholic Christians, 698; English Methodist Christians, 698
Persson, Mr. and Mrs., murder of, 712
Pethick, W. N., heads rescue party, 238
Philological studies, opportunities for, 527
Physicians, the siege, 515
Pigott family, murder of, 615
Pitkin, Mr., murder of, 610
Placards, anti-foreign, circulation of, 80
Placard, Boxer; range of complaint in, 201
Polk, President, letter of, 14
Population of China, complex problem of, 3
Port Arthur, Russian occupation of, 110
Ports, opening of new, 16
Posters, Boxer, 200
Powers, The; relation to Japan, 452; appropriation of Tientsin lands by 587, 589; friction among the, 714, 720; "spheres of influence," 716, 720
"Practice of Virtue," Chinese respect for, 152
Preaching of Occidentals, prejudice aroused by, 40
Preparatory Schools, establishment of, ordered, 140

764 INDEX

Presbyterian Missionaries, massacre of, 610
Prescription, a Divine, 200
President McKinley, appeal to, 216; congratulations telegraphed by, 495
Press, the foreign, on break up of China, 116
Price family, murder of, 616
Priests, Buddhist and Taoist, 7; leaders in disturbances, 40
Prince Ch'ing, interview of British Minister with, 228
Prince Ch'ing and Others, correspondence with, 340, 343, 348, 362, 364, 386, 389, 390, 399, 403
Proclamation, anti-foreign, 73
Progress, Chinese idea of, 89
Promoter, the typical. 100
Property, claim of Roman Catholics to, 56, 58; purchase by foreigners, 57; foreigners hand to Chinese Government, 230; wholesale destruction, 238, 498
Prophecy of Boxer troubles, remarkable, 222
Protestant missions, literature of, 40
organizations, diversity of, 42
societies, agreement of, in indemnity scheme, 730
martyrs, number of, 613, 647, 648
Christians in China, number of, 650
Protestants in China, 30-44; Chinese view of, 31
Providential care, evidences of, 512, 513
Provincial guilds, the, 152
Provisional Government, Tientsin, 451
Public buildings, losses in, 264
Pu Chün, Heir Apparent, 185
Public Harmony Volunteers, the, 174
Punishment of Peking, the, 517-534

Punishments demanded by Powers, small list of, 726
Puzzle of Chinese history, 5

QUEEN VICTORIA, congratulations telegraphed by, 496
Queue, proposed abolition of, 145

RAILWAYS, Imperial sanction of, 25; development, 26, 524; arouse opposition, 96, 120, 182, 559, 560; the Peking road, 97; the trans-Siberian, 104, 117; list of concessions, 117; defence of 228, 609; trains stopped, 235; a new terminus, 523
Rank, official; repeal of purchase and sale of, 140
Ransome, Miss, Red Cross given to, 493
Rations, issuing, 276
Reaction against reform, 124-151
Reactionary Imperial Decrees, effect of, 162
Recant, native Christians given opportunity to, 653
Reciprocity, Confucius on, 62; Chinese thought of, 101
Records, Chinese Yamens; fate of, 544
Red Cross, siege ladies receive order of, 493
"Red Lantern Light" Society; the, 662
Reform Translating Bureau, 141
Reforms, desire for, 11, 130; planned by Emperor, 43: edict on, 131; plan for, 134; books on, presented to Emperor, 135; effect of, 136; conservatives resist, 139; governors censured for slowness in, 143; repealed by Empress Dowager, 149
Refuge pits, digging of, 293
Refugees, experiences of, 537; condition of T'ung Chou described by, 565

INDEX 765

Regeneration of China, problem of, 735
Regiment, the Hongkong coolie, 19
Register of siege, publication of, 418; directory, 745
Registrar, work of, 365
Regulations, eight, of Tsung Li Yamen, 58
"Regulations for the Maintenance of Order in Peking," 228
Reid, Gilbert, 45, 88, 505
Relief, the, 419, 434
Relief expedition, the Seymour-McCalla, expected in Peking, 235; word from 236, 299; effort to send word to 242; futile effort to stop, 246; its trials, 440; takes Imperial armory, 442; its character, 443; plan of, 599
Relief expedition, The final; word from, 354, 385, 392, 409, 422; anxiety about, 320; efforts to communicate with, 415, 418; approaches Peking, 430; enters city, 432
Remoter sources of antipathy, 3-13
Renewal of the attack, the, 402-418
Restitution to Christians, Boxers offer to make, 538
Revenue, raising of, 135
Revolt of conservatives, 147
Rice, the tribute; method of carrying to Peking, 99
Rice junks; boatmen on, 13
Richard, Timothy, 78, 150; scheme for Protestant indemnities, 729
Riots in Yangtze Valley, 26
Riots, cause of, 59; anti-foreign, 65-76; season of, 86; at Yang Chou, 65; Chên Chiâng, 65; Shanghai, 70; Canton, 71; Szechuan, 75; instigated by Imperial palace, 76; at Wu Hu, Nanking. An Ching Fu, Tan Yang, 82; Wu Hsüeh,

I Ch'ang Fu, 83; Sungpu, Ku Chêng, 85; Chien Ning Fu, Chiang Pei, Szechuan, 86; spread of, 155, 156, 158; investigation ordered, 203
Rising, the popular; prediction of, 62; primary sources of, 63
Ritualists, the, 172
Roberts, James H.; flight from Kalgan, 643-647
Robinson and Norman, Messrs.; murder of, 227
Rock Springs, treatment of Chinese in, 21
Roman Catholic Church, Unity of contrasted with Protestants, 31
Roman Catholic Church, believed a political agent, 47; believed a shelter of bad men, 52; its property, 56; its financial methods, 58; its secrecy, 60; its good work, 61; hostility to rites of, 61; its semi-political administration, 61
Roman Catholics in China, the, 45-64; bishops, rank adopted by, 48; missionaries, power of, 49; outrages of, 55; rising against, 157; successful defence of, 179; fortifications of, 207; rescue of, 251; massacre of missionaries, 614, 619; list of martyrs, 649; number in China, 650; personal narrative of converts, 698
Ruin of T'ung Chou, the, 555, 570
Russia, a menace to China, 723; dominates Manchuria, 724
Russian Cemetery, desecration of, 499
railroads, the, 118
soldiers, barbarities of, 670
troops in allied forces, the, 455
Russians in Manchuria, friction with, 607
leniency of, 726

relation of, Chinese, 357
Russo-Chinese agreement, the, 104
Russo-French alliance, the, 103

SAGES, the Chinese, 6
Salisbury, Lord, unwilling to resort to naval action, 193 telegram to, 195
Sand bags, demand for, 279; manufacture of, 289; materials for, 511
Sanitary care of British Legation during siege, 295; improvements, 820
Scholars, classification of, 9
Schools and colleges, establishment of, 139
Searchlight, sight of, 304, 312
Secret societies, number of, 153; forbidden by government, 173
Segers, Father, murder of, 620
Semi-siege, in Peking, the, 232-252
Servants, Chinese, faithfulness of Christian, 657, 658
Settlement with China, terms of, 734
Seville, Miss, Red Cross given, 494
Seymour-McCalla expedition, the, 235, 236, 299, 242, 246, 438, 440, 442, 443, 599 (see Relief Expeditions)
Seymour, Mr., U. S. Consul at Canton, 55
Shanghai, commercial capital of the Far East, 12; Ningpo men in, 13; foreign settlement in, 17; agreement of Powers over, 24; conference at, 55, 78; riot at, 70
Shanghai journals, Ningpo correspondents of, 71
Shanghai Agricultural Association, the, 138
Shanghai Cathedral, supposed foundation of on infants, 97
Shansi, foreigners escape from, 616; Boxers authorized to kill all Christians in, 657

Shansi Christians, fire and sword among, 702-712
Shantung, mission affairs in, 50; German work in, 99; murder of priests in, 106; policy of governor of, 603; foreigners protected, 604; drill resumed by Boxers, 722
Sheffield, D. Z., asked to mediate with Japanese, 558
Shen Taotai of T'ung Chou, help of, 215
Shensi, travelling in, 14; policy of governor of, 603; spread of anti-foreign rising in, 611
Shimonoseki, treaty of, 29
Shots fired at Legations, number of, 514
Siege, the; first week of, 272-296
Siege life, 365-382
Siege, raising the, 433
Siege, after the, 485-507
Siege child, a, 298
Simcox, Mr. and Mrs., murder of, 610
Slimmon, James A., notable experience of, 621-632
Simpson, Mr., murder of, 614
Smith, Miss Georgiana, distinguished services of, 537
Smyth, G. B., on French treachery, 25
So P'ing Fu, massacre of missionaries at, 613, 707, 712
" Society for the Diffusion of Christian and General Knowledge," 43, 150
Society to Protect the Heavenly Dynasty, tenet of, 224
Soldiers, Chinese, 8
Soldiers, Continental, conduct of, 500
" Sources of Anti-Foreign Disturbances in China," 88
South African War, effect of, on China, 220
" Spheres of influence," expeditionary, 716, 720
" Spirits," Boxers aided by, 172
Spread of the Rising, 196-217

INDEX 767

Squiers, Herbert G., 346
Squiers, Mrs., 262
Stampede, an international, 277
State Department code, telegram received in, 346
Steam navigation, opposition to, 96
Stevenson, J. W., list of Protestant missionary martyrs prepared by, 647, 648, 649
Stewart family, murder of, 85
Strategy, Chinese, illustrated, 397
Streets in Peking, care of, 526; renaming of, 527
Strike, labour, in China, 13
Strouts, Capt., death of, 345
Struggle for the wall, The, 297-317
Student interpreters, praise of, 480
Students, Christian, personal narrative of, 695
Su, Prince, 265
Su Wang Fu, 265, 273; Japanese ordered to abandon the, 277
Sugiyama, Japanese chancellor, murdered, 235
Summer Palace, the, 532
Sun Chia Nai, approval of regulations of, 140
Sung and Ming Dynasties, methods of government of, 132
Sungpu, riot in, 85
Supplies, difficulties in purchasing, 241
Supplies, the siege, 509
Swedish Union missionaries, murder of, 712
Syndicates, agents of, 88; mining lands sought by, 121
Szechuan, riots in, 73, 86

TA TAO HUI, the, 106
Tablets, ancestral, of the Manchu dynasty, British seize the, 548
Tablets of pre-Imperial Ancestors, removal of, 549

T'ai Ku Hsien, massacre of missionaries at, 613
Taiping rebellion, the, 22, 30
T'ai Yuan Fu, massacre of missionaries at, 613
Taku forts, capture of, 18, 19, 336; surrender demanded, 247; effect of capture, 436
Taku Forts to relief of Peking, From, 435-461
Tan Yang, riot at, 82
T'ang dynasty, emperor of, quoted, on Confucianism, 7
T'ang, motto of, 738
"T'ang-tzu," the, 335
Taoist priests, employment of, by Chinese, 7
Taoist priests and Christianity, 39
Taotai of Shanghai, riot planned by, 67
Taotai of T'ung Chou, appeal to, 212; Boxers intimidate the, 566
Tartar dynasty, presage of fall of, 239
Taxation, protest against, 120
Taxes, remission of, 553
Taylor, Dr. Geo. Yardley, murder of, 610
Taylor, J. Hudson, beginning of China Inland Mission by, 65
Telegram in State Department Code, Mr. Conger receives, 346
Telegram from Paris, 361
Telegrams to governments, question of, 386, 389
Telegrams, receipt of, 404, 405, 412, 414, 423
Telegraph, opposition to, 96; sending of edicts by, 143; sending appeals by, 216; communication, stopped, 235
Telescope, Chinese fear of, 214
Temple of Agriculture, American troops occupy the, 546
Temple of Heaven, foreigners enter the, 547
Temples in T'ung Chou, destruction of, 546

INDEX

Temples, proposed use of, for schools, 139
Territorial Aggression, 101-123
Tewksbury, Mr., 274, 495
Thunder shower, effect on Chinese of, 303
Tientsin, metropolis of four provinces, 12; supplies furnished by, 19; cathedral at, 56; riots in, 58; effect of capture of, 342; serious situation at, 437; relief of, 438; location of foreign settlement, 444; attack, 445; Eastern Arsenal taken, 446; foreigners leaving, 447; taking city, 451; story of siege, 444; after the siege, 571-593; location of, 571; character of men of, 571; massacre, the, 572; population of, 572; prosperity of, 573; antipathy to foreigners in, 573; devastation of, 577, 582; provisional government of, 578; taken by foreign troops, 579; British municipal council of, 586; wall removed, 588; new roads in, 588, 589; business conditions in, 591; military expeditions from, 713
Tientsin Road, the, destruction of, 591
Tientsin, treaty of, 18, 20, 21
Tientsin Massacre, the, 13, 22, 46, 69
Tiger, the Chinese, 122
Tombs, Imperial; raid in direction of, 715
Topography of Legation district, 259
Tower of city gate, burning of, 239
Territory, cession of, to foreigners, 16
Tract and Bible Societies, work of, 41
Trade, foreign, effect on China of, 90
Trade in Tientsin, 591
Traders and Chinese, 9

Tragedies, a chapter of, 617, 618
Trans-Asian railway, terminus of, 110
Trans-Siberian railway, the, 104, 117
Transformation of Tientsin, 588-593
Translators in Great Britain and France, Chinese Ministers ordered to engage, 142
Transportation, Western modes of, 525
Treaties, present, a growth, 14
 attitude of China toward, 29
 of Nanking, causes of, 16
 of 1842 ignored by Emperor, 17
 of Shimonoski, 29
 of Tientsin, 18, 20, 21, 22
 ratification of, at Peking, 19
Treaty ports in China, 12
"Triad" Society, 153
Tribute grain, arrival of, at T'ung Chou, 556; effect of railway on, 561
Tribute Rice transport by Grand Canal, abolition of, 144
Truce, a flag of, 292, 346
T'sai family; personal narrative of, 679
Tsai Li, or the Ritualists, 172
Ts'ang Chou, German raid of, 716
Tsêng, Marquis, 245
Tsung Li Yamen, the, 46; memorandum of, 52, 56, 59, 61; French influence over, 55; American Minister sends protests to, 192; protection promised by, 210; Prince Tuan appointed president of, 230; request withdrawal of foreign troops, 242; request foreign ministers to leave, 247; ministers reply, 248, 268; letter to Legation ministers, 267; messenger from, 346; provisions sent from, 362, 390; despatch from, 420, 426, 427; fate of, 544; alleged

INDEX

cause for execution of its ministers, 595
Tuan Fang, Gov. of Shensi, helpfulness of, 603
Tuan, Prince, bribed by Empress Dowager, 147; appointed President of Tsung Li Yamen, 230, 269
T'ung Chou; capitulates, 19, 558; arrival of Boxers, 204, 563; troubles, 212; foreigners flee, 214, 564; wreck of Post Office and mission, 235; meaning of name, 555; ruin of, 555-570; composite structure of city, 556; population, 556, 568; people friendly to foreigners, 558; affected by railway, 561; magistrate hostile to foreigners, 564; Boxer leader in, 565; destruction of, 564, 567-570
T'ung Chou Christians in Peking, location of, 535
Tung Fu Hsiang, 163
Tung Kun, resentment of Chinese at, 113
"Turbid-Stars," at Tientsin, 12

UNITED STATES, educational mission to, 23; first minister to China, 14; suffering of Chinese in, 21
United Village Associations, 174
Unity during siege, the remarkable, 515
University in Peking, importance of, 133; condition of after the siege, 497

VEGETARIAN SOCIETY, murder of missionaries by, 85
Vermilion Pencil Edicts, despatch of, 553
Viceroys, uprising checked by, 603, 605
Victory, an important, 316
Victoria, see Queen, 496
Vileness of Hunan pamphlets, 81

Village, Christian, Boxer attack on, 177, 207, 214
Volunteers, the, 174

WADE, SIR THOMAS, experiences of, in China, 23
Waldersee, Count von, 611
Wall of Tientsin, removal of, 588
Wall, the struggle for, 297-317; defences on, 403
Wang Lan P'u, story of, 702
War of 1840-41, 15
War with Japan, China at close of, 102
War edicts of Empress Dowager, 28
Warren, P. L., British Consul, Shanghai, 602
Washington, Chinese situation viewed from, 721
Water, supply of, 280, 511
Watson, Joseph, on "China and the Present Crisis," 117
Watt, James, despatches taken by, 437
Watts Jones, Capt., murder of, 612

Weather, the siege, 332
Wei Hei Wei, British demand for, 111; occupied by Japan, 103
Wên Hsiang, character of, 46
Wên, Mr., personal narrative of, 691
Wên Li, personal narrative of, 689
Wêng T'ung Ho, Emperor's tutor, 134
Western Empress, death of, 125
Western innovations, introducers of, 26; their effect, 94
Learning Schools, graduates of, 138
nations and China, 8
powers, opportunity of, 87
science in China, power of, 736
troops in China, lawlessness of, 718

Whitehouse, Mr., murder of, 614
"White Lily" Society, 153
Williams, Dr., on Treaty of Nanking, 16
Williams, Fred'k, "History of China," 46, 70
Williams, G. L., murder of, 613
Wilson, Dr., murder of, 614
Women, bravery of, 485
given Red Cross, 493
Women, massacre of, 338, 605, 610, 614, 615, 616, 617, 670, 680, 696, 697, 698, 700
Workmen, classification of, 9
Wu Ting Fang, telegram from, 350; influence at Washington of, 721
Wu Hu, riot at, 82
Wu Hsieh, riot at, 83
Wu Hsüeh, riot at, 83
Wylie, J. A., murder of, 85

YAMEN, Ministers, British Legation visited by, 236

Yamaguchi, Gen., leads Japanese forces, 455
Yang Chou, riot in, 65
Yang Ts'un, 440, 456
Yangtze Valley, riots in, 26, 58; Great Britain in, 121
Yeh, Gov.-Gen., British capture of, 57
Yellow River, rising of, 162
Yuan Shih K'ai, 148, 155, 180, 602; proclamations of, 723
Yü Hsien, career of, 168; removal of, 180; collusion with Boxers, 192; condemned, 550; influence in Shansi, 611
Yü Lu, Gov. of Chihli, 574
Yung Ch'ing Hsien, 228; German raid on, 717; British remit taxes on, 717
Yung Wing, influence of, 23
Yunnan, struggle of French for, 121

ZAHN, FRANZ, attacked by Catholics, 54